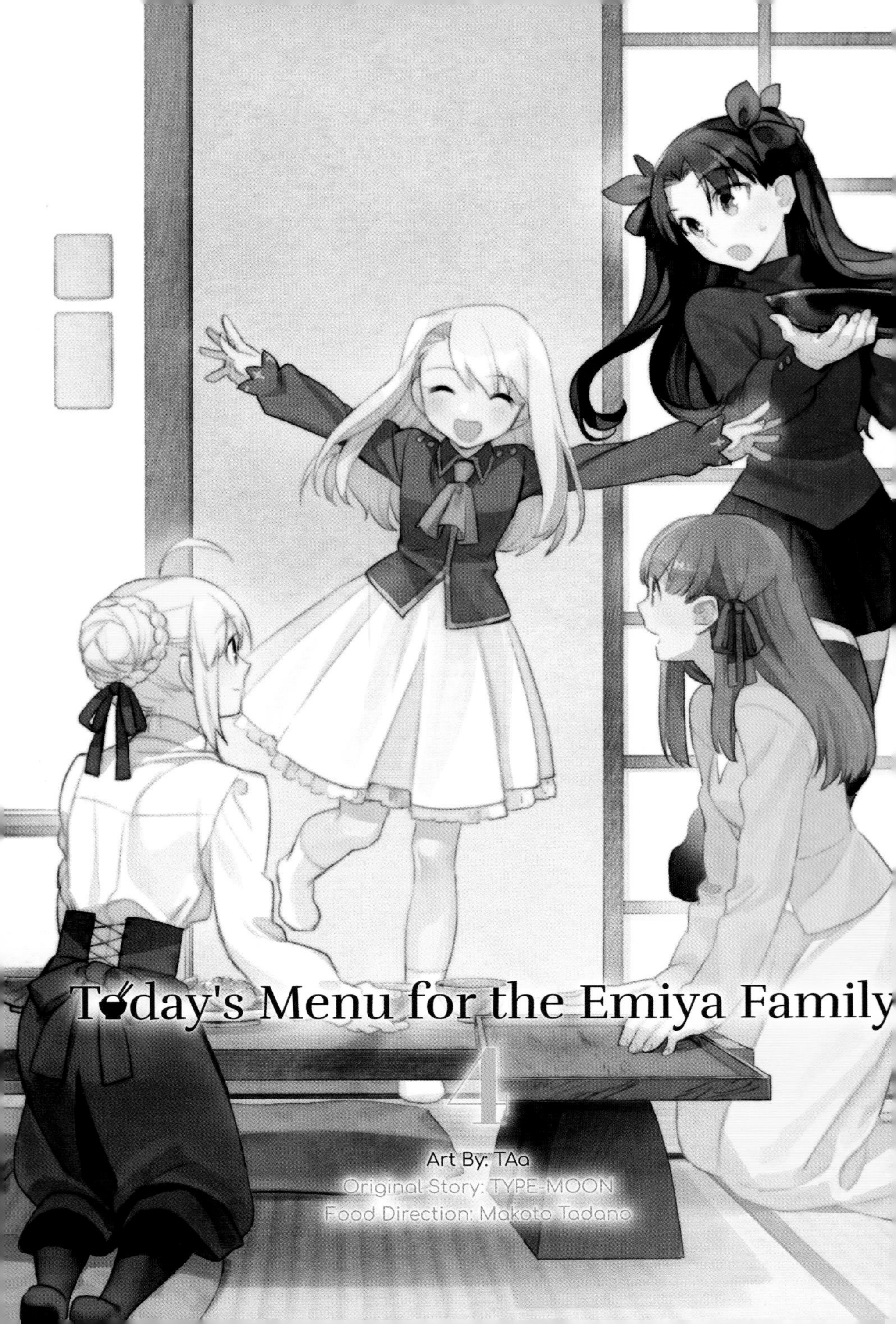

Today's Menu for the Emiya Family
4
Art By: TAa
Original Story: TYPE-MOON
Food Direction: Makoto Tadano

Today's Menu for the Emiya Family

Art By: TAa
Original Story: TYPE-MOON
Food Direction: Makoto Tadano

4

Table of Contents

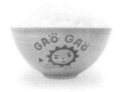

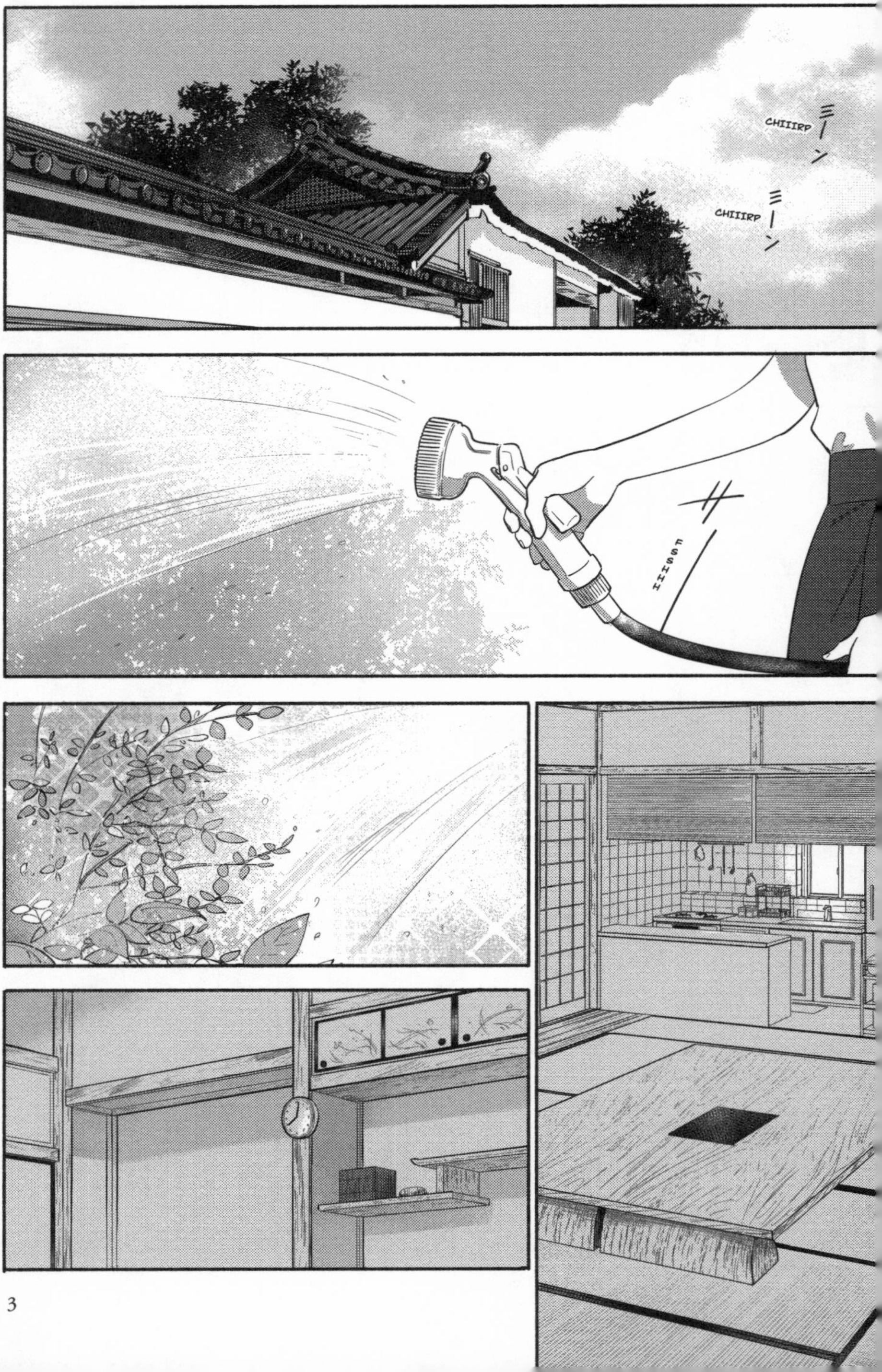
CHIIIRP
CHIIIRP
FSSHHH

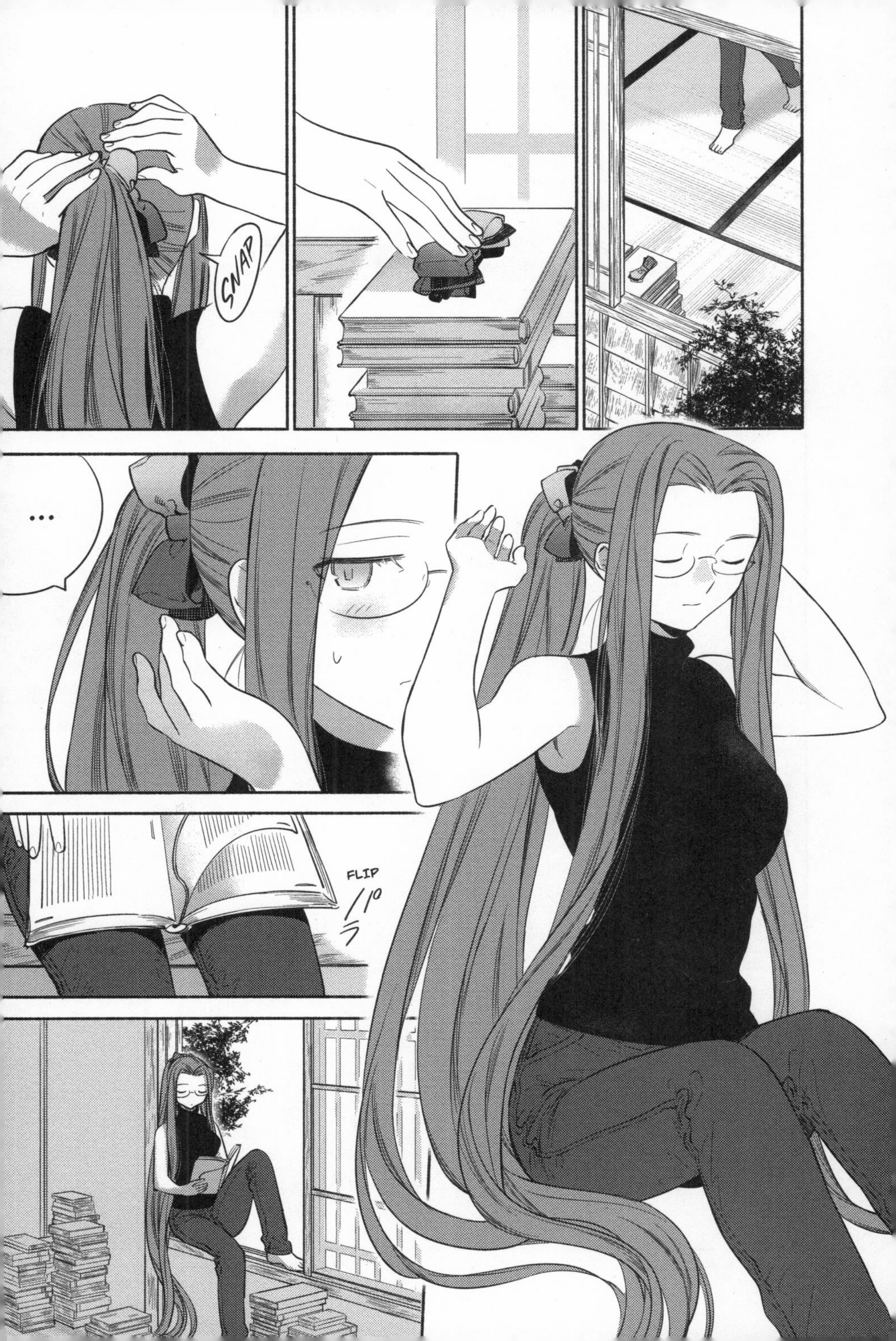
SNAP
...
FLIP
パラ

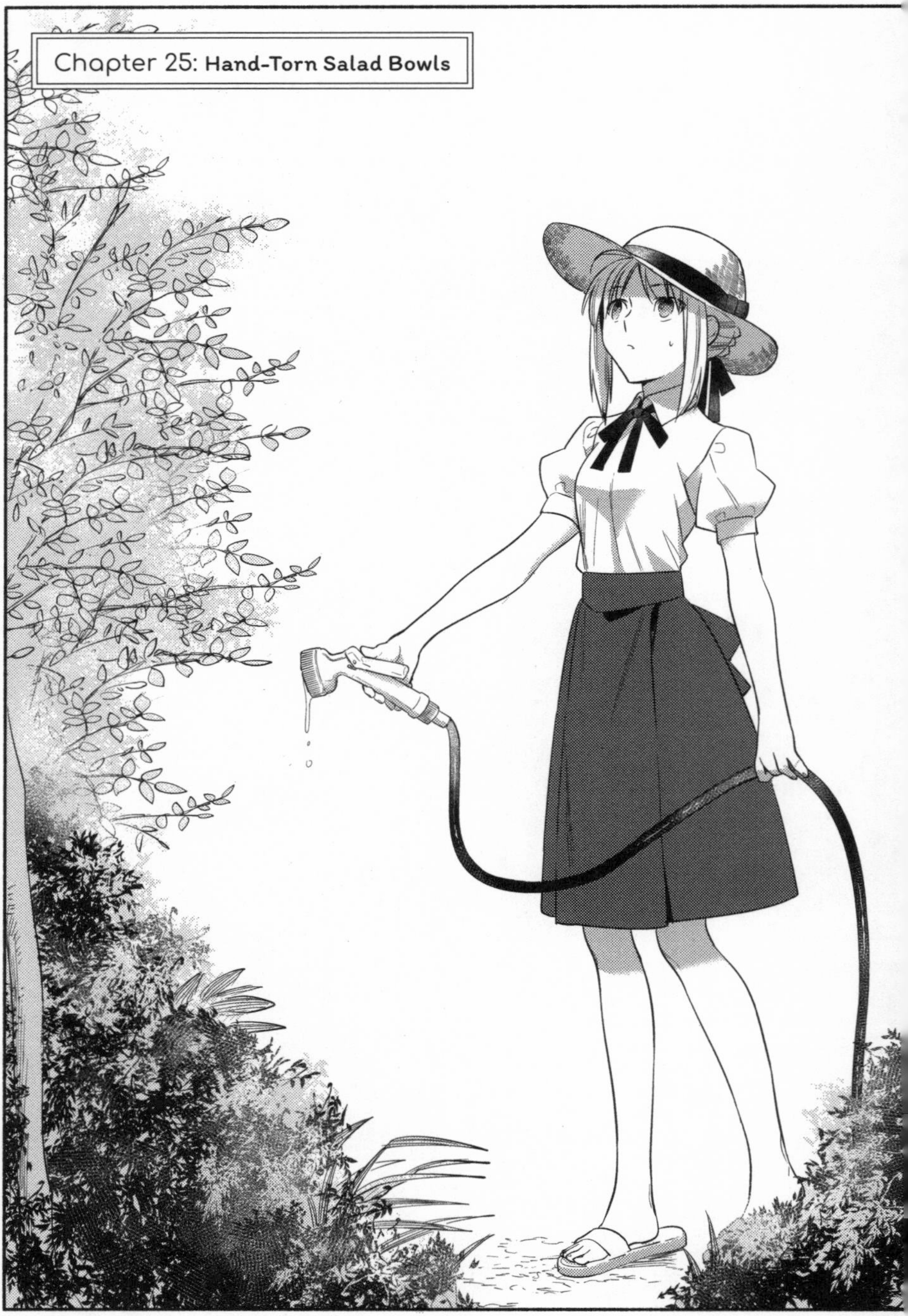
Chapter 25: Hand-Torn Salad Bowls

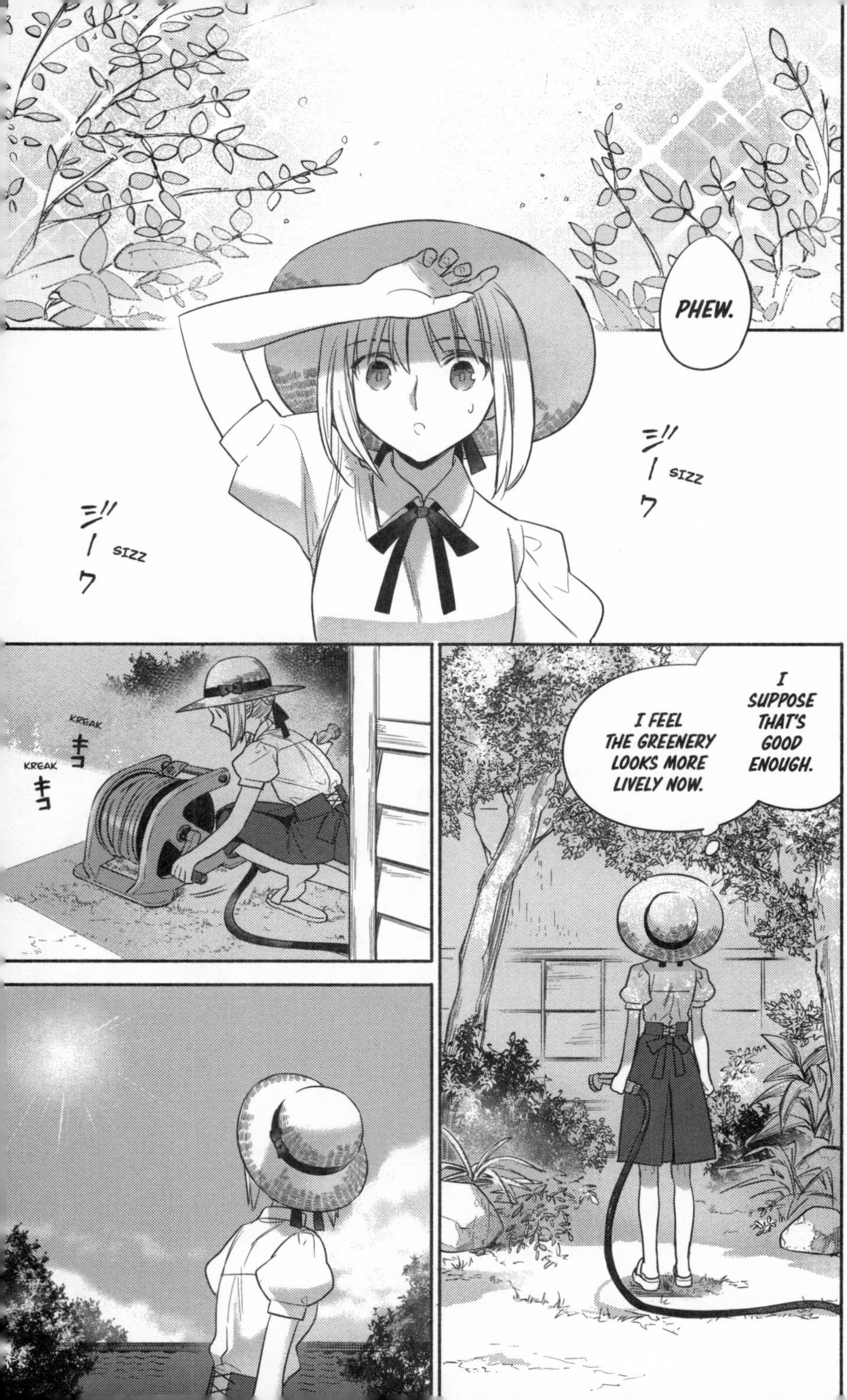
PHEW.
ジーワ
SIZZ
ジーワ
SIZZ
I SUPPOSE THAT'S GOOD ENOUGH.
I FEEL THE GREENERY LOOKS MORE LIVELY NOW.
キコ
KREAK
キコ
KREAK

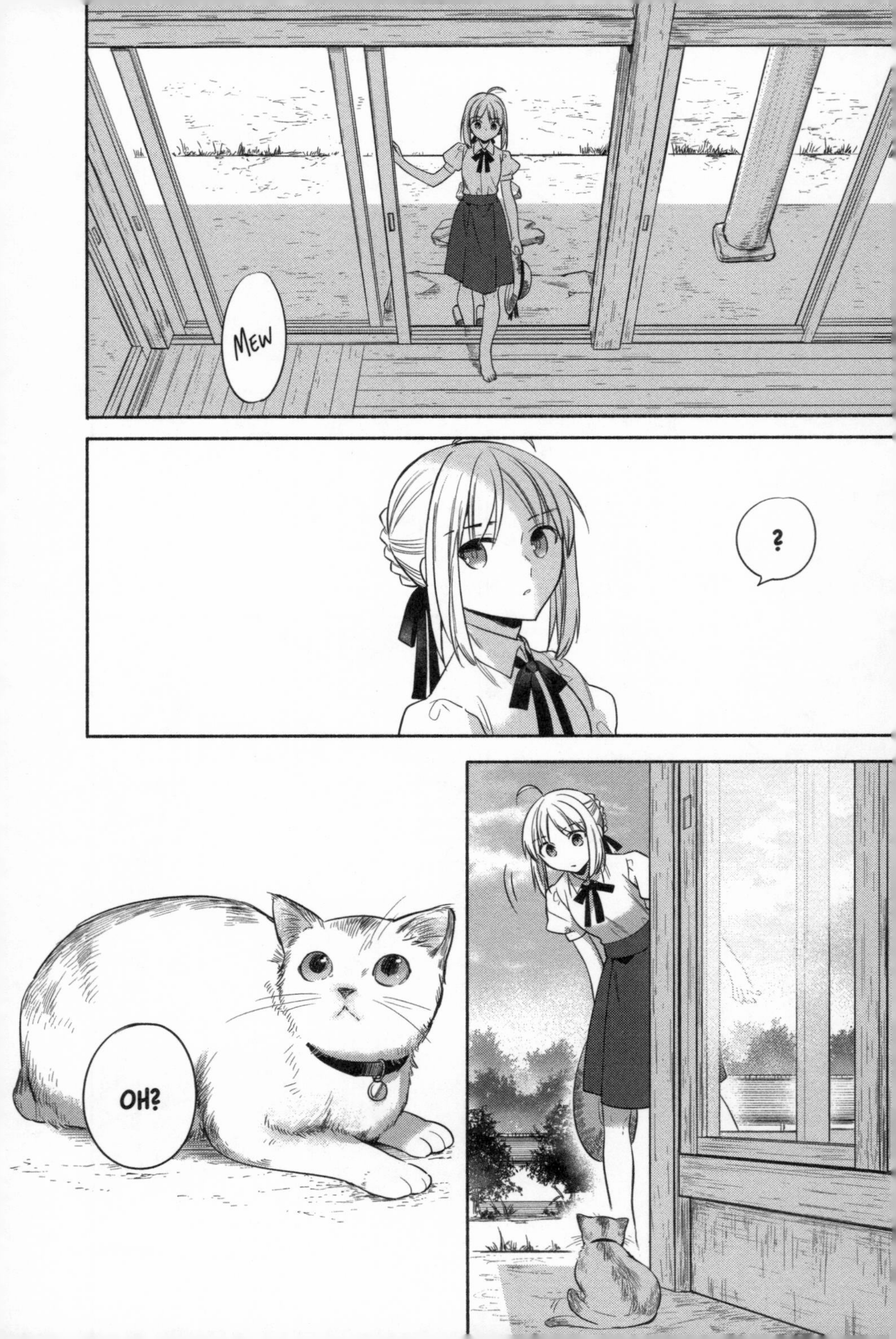
MEW
?
OH?

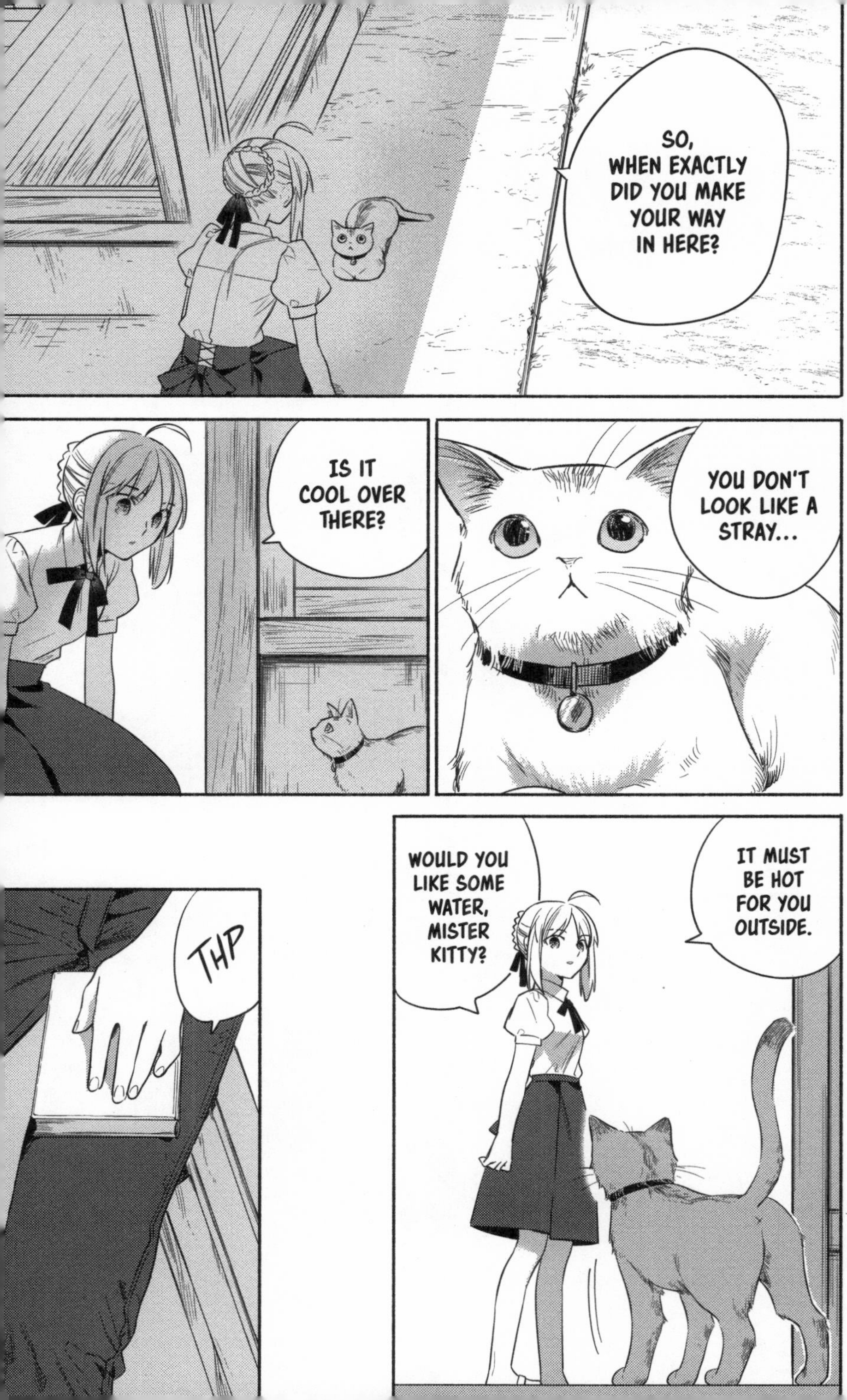
SO, WHEN EXACTLY DID YOU MAKE YOUR WAY IN HERE?
YOU DON'T LOOK LIKE A STRAY...
IS IT COOL OVER THERE?
IT MUST BE HOT FOR YOU OUTSIDE.
WOULD YOU LIKE SOME WATER, MISTER KITTY?
THP

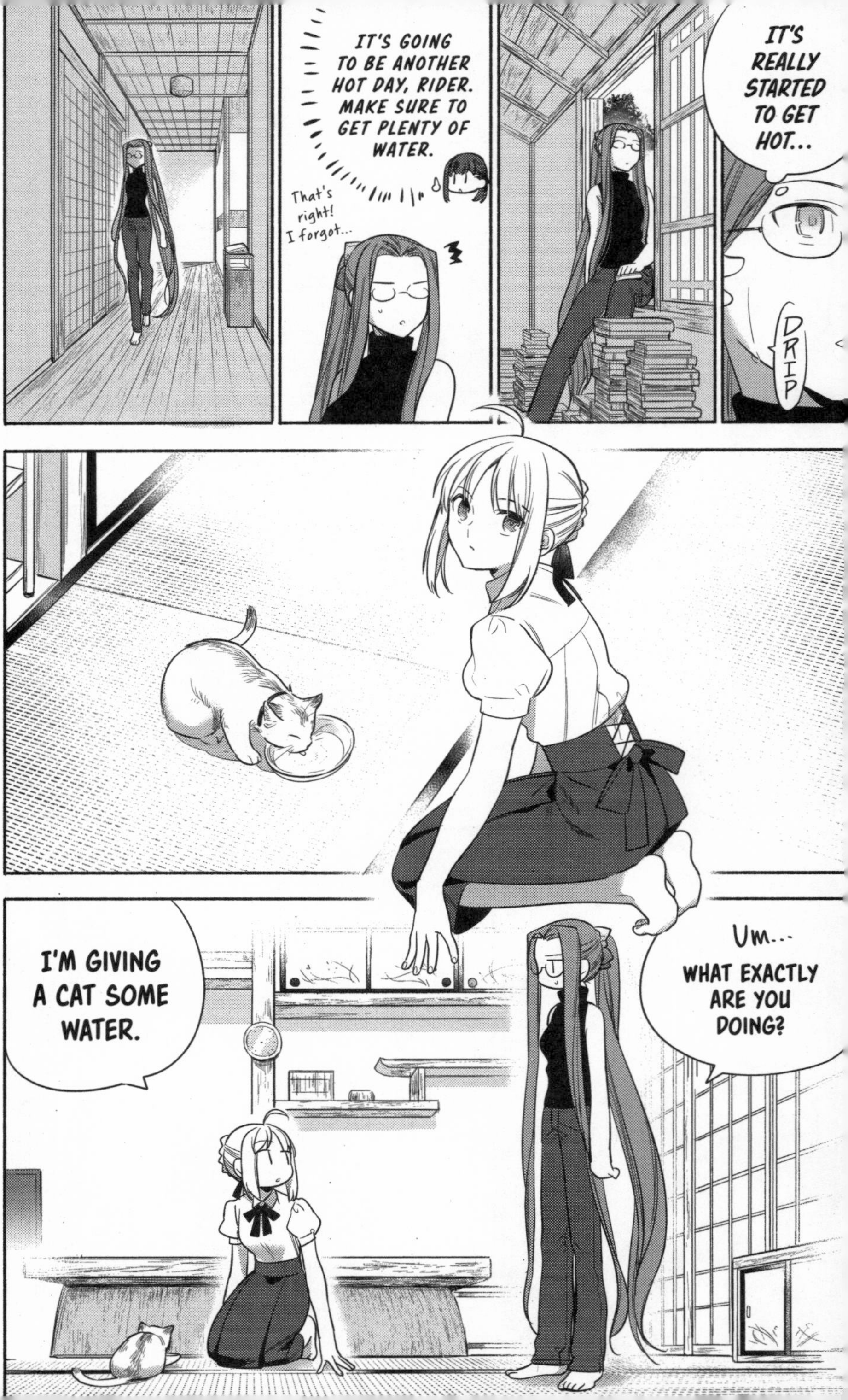
IT'S REALLY STARTED TO GET HOT...
DRIP
IT'S GOING TO BE ANOTHER HOT DAY, RIDER. MAKE SURE TO GET PLENTY OF WATER.
That's right! I forgot...
Um... WHAT EXACTLY ARE YOU DOING?
I'M GIVING A CAT SOME WATER.

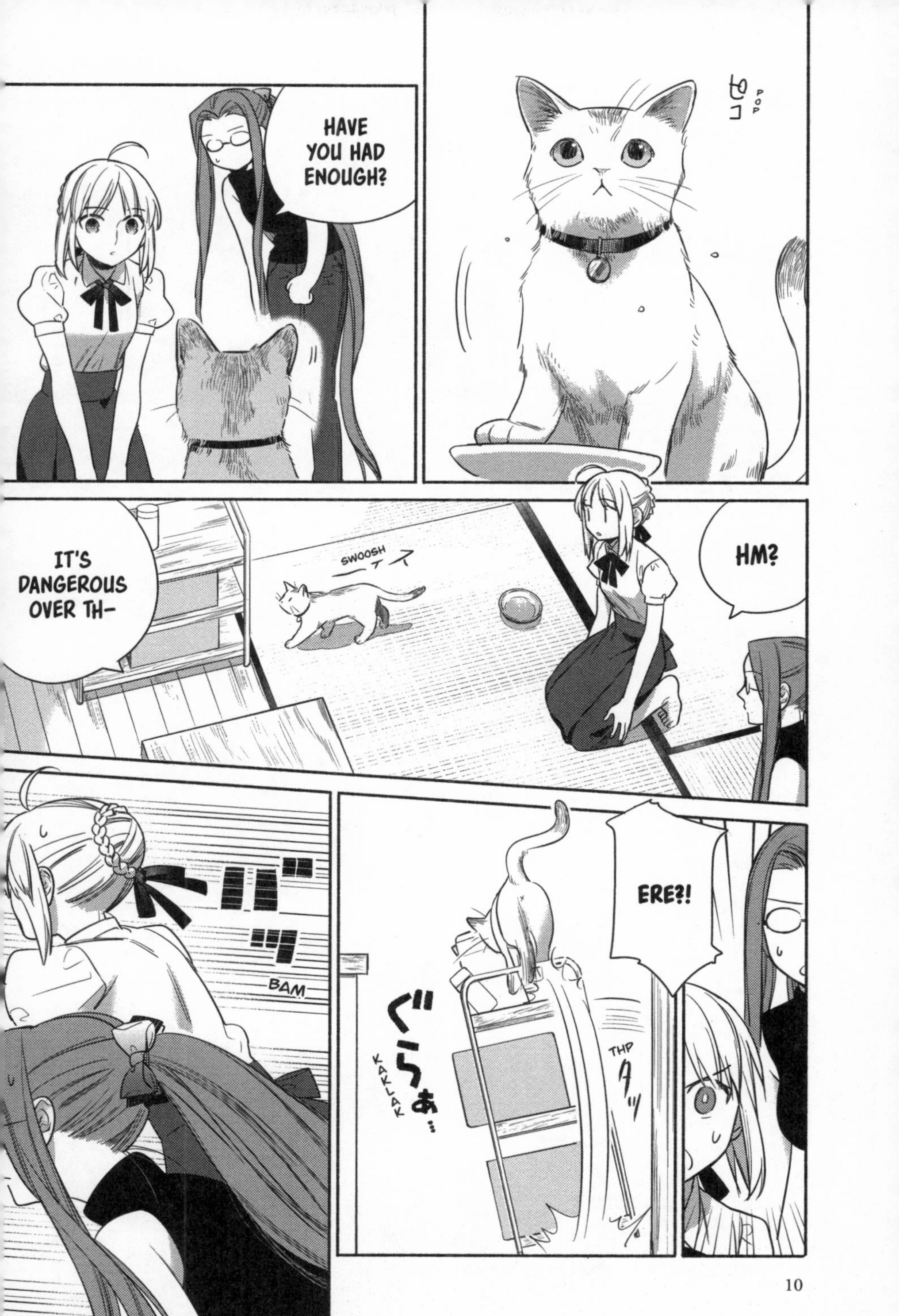
POP
HAVE YOU HAD ENOUGH?
HM?
SWOOSH
IT'S DANGEROUS OVER TH-
ERE?!
THP
KAKLAK
BAM

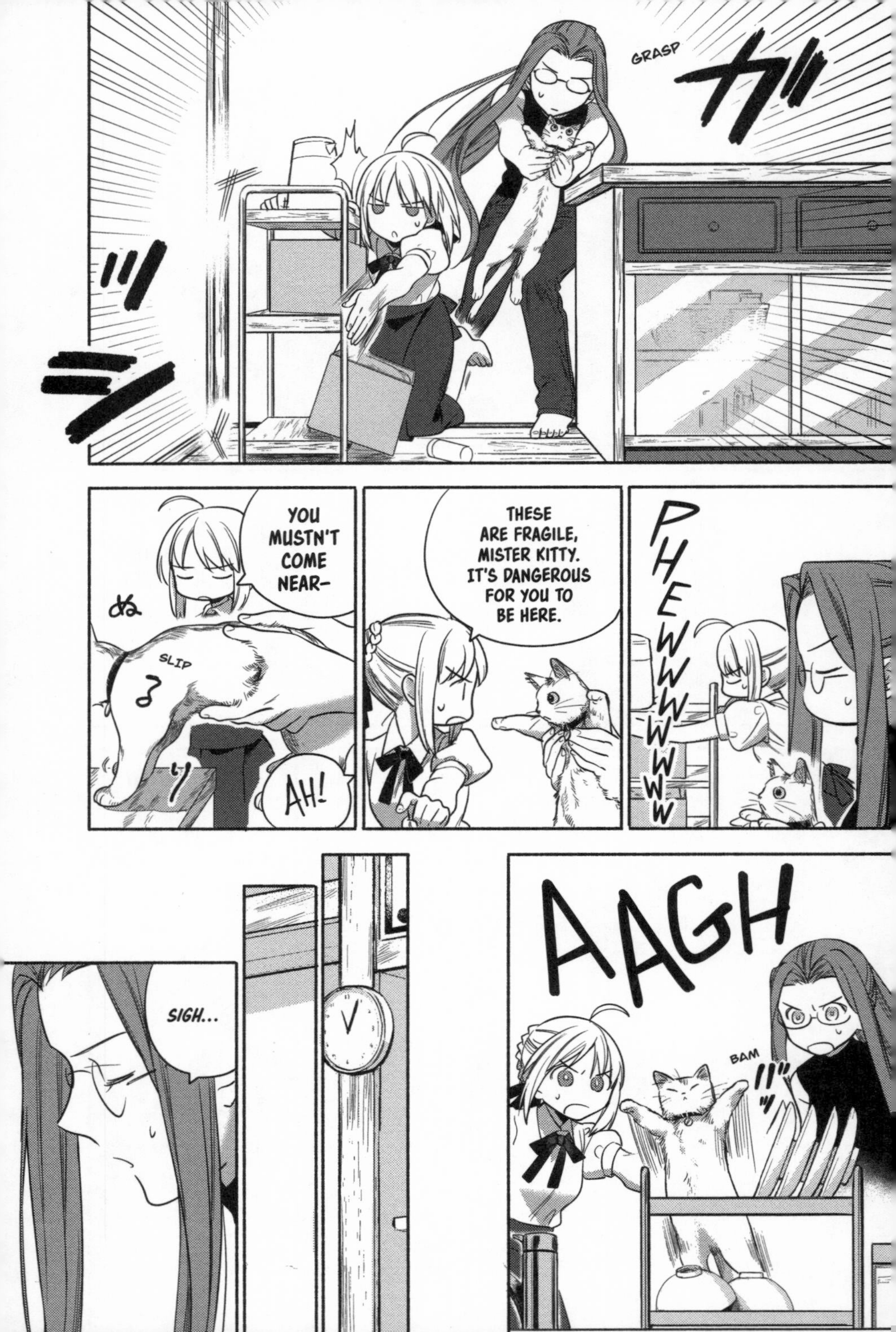
GRASP
ガッ
ツン
PHEWWWWWWWW
THESE ARE FRAGILE, MISTER KITTY. IT'S DANGEROUS FOR YOU TO BE HERE.
YOU MUSTN'T COME NEAR–
ぬ
SLIP
る
り
AH!
AAGH
BAM
SIGH...

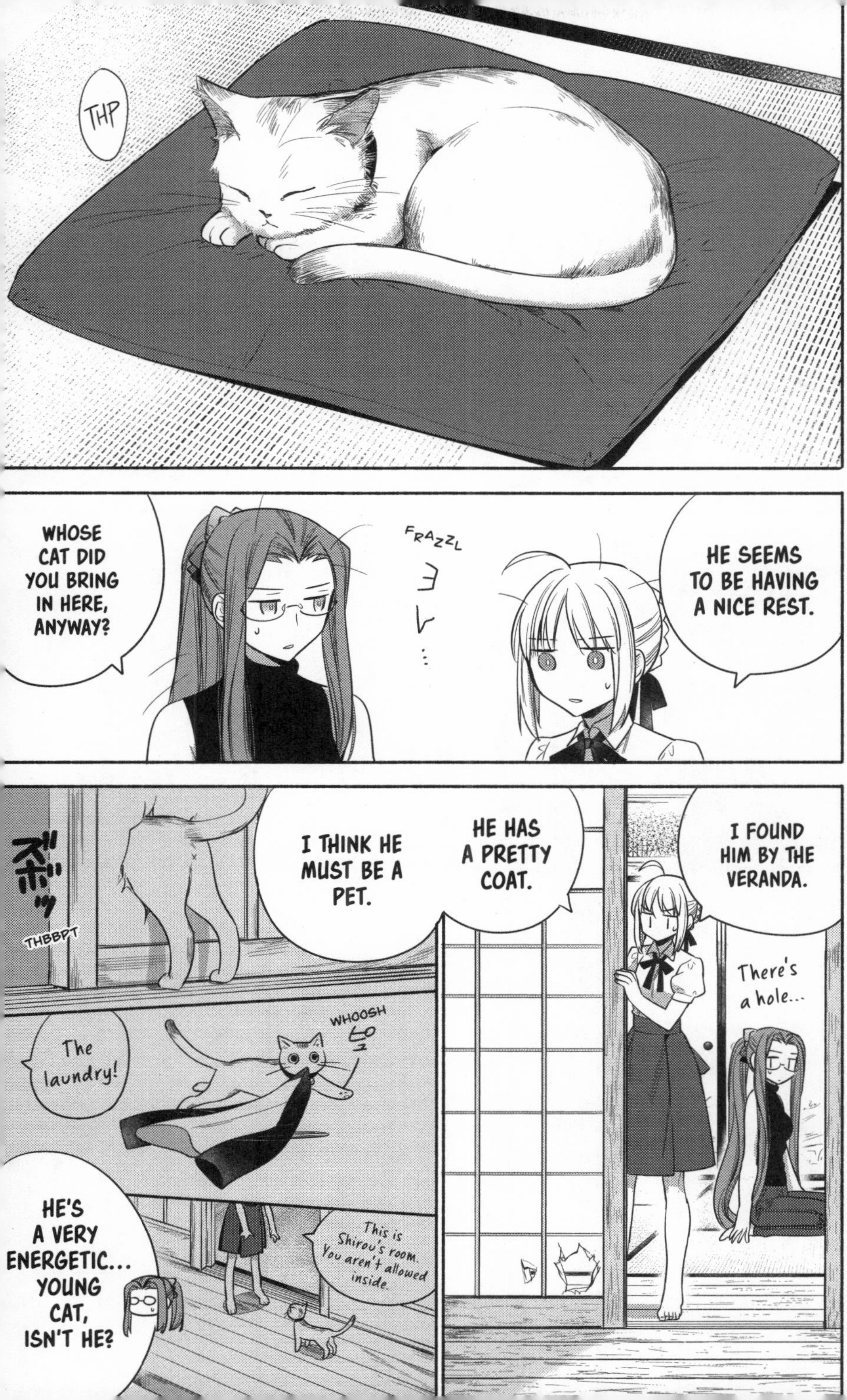
THP
HE SEEMS TO BE HAVING A NICE REST.
FRAZZL
ヨレ…
WHOSE CAT DID YOU BRING IN HERE, ANYWAY?
I FOUND HIM BY THE VERANDA.
There's a hole...
HE HAS A PRETTY COAT.
I THINK HE MUST BE A PET.
ズボッ
THBBPT
WHOOSH
The laundry!
This is Shirou's room. You aren't allowed inside.
HE'S A VERY ENERGETIC... YOUNG CAT, ISN'T HE?

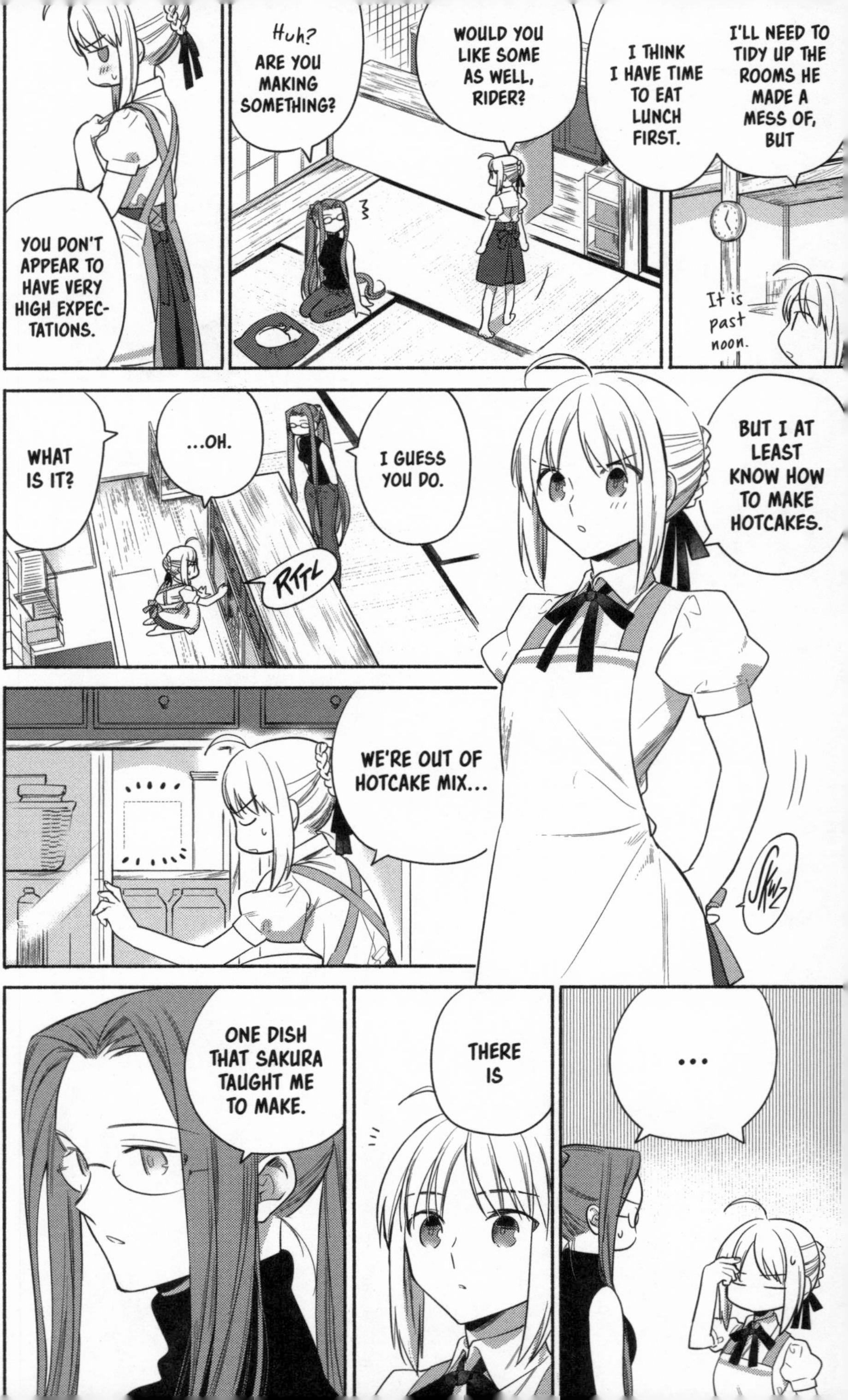
I'LL NEED TO TIDY UP THE ROOMS HE MADE A MESS OF, BUT
I THINK I HAVE TIME TO EAT LUNCH FIRST.
It is past noon.
WOULD YOU LIKE SOME AS WELL, RIDER?
Huh? ARE YOU MAKING SOMETHING?
YOU DON'T APPEAR TO HAVE VERY HIGH EXPEC-TATIONS.
BUT I AT LEAST KNOW HOW TO MAKE HOTCAKES.
SKWZ
I GUESS YOU DO.
...OH.
WHAT IS IT?
RTTL
WE'RE OUT OF HOTCAKE MIX...
...
THERE IS
ONE DISH THAT SAKURA TAUGHT ME TO MAKE.

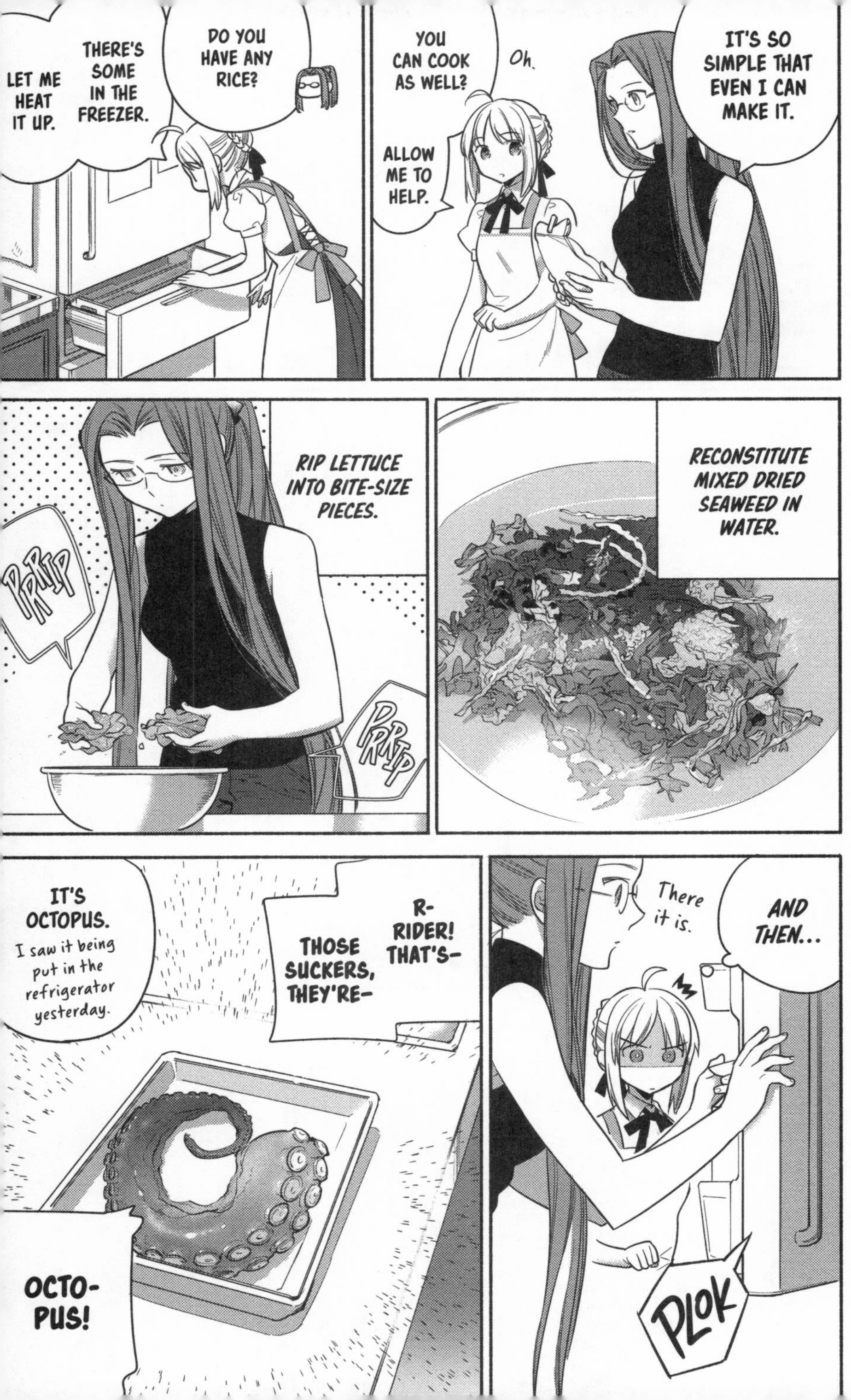
IT'S SO SIMPLE THAT EVEN I CAN MAKE IT.
Oh.
YOU CAN COOK AS WELL?
ALLOW ME TO HELP.
DO YOU HAVE ANY RICE?
THERE'S SOME IN THE FREEZER.
LET ME HEAT IT UP.
RECONSTITUTE MIXED DRIED SEAWEED IN WATER.
RIP LETTUCE INTO BITE-SIZE PIECES.
PRRIP
PRRIP
AND THEN...
There it is.
PLOK
R-RIDER! THAT'S-
THOSE SUCKERS, THEY'RE-
IT'S OCTOPUS.
I saw it being put in the refrigerator yesterday.
OCTO-PUS!

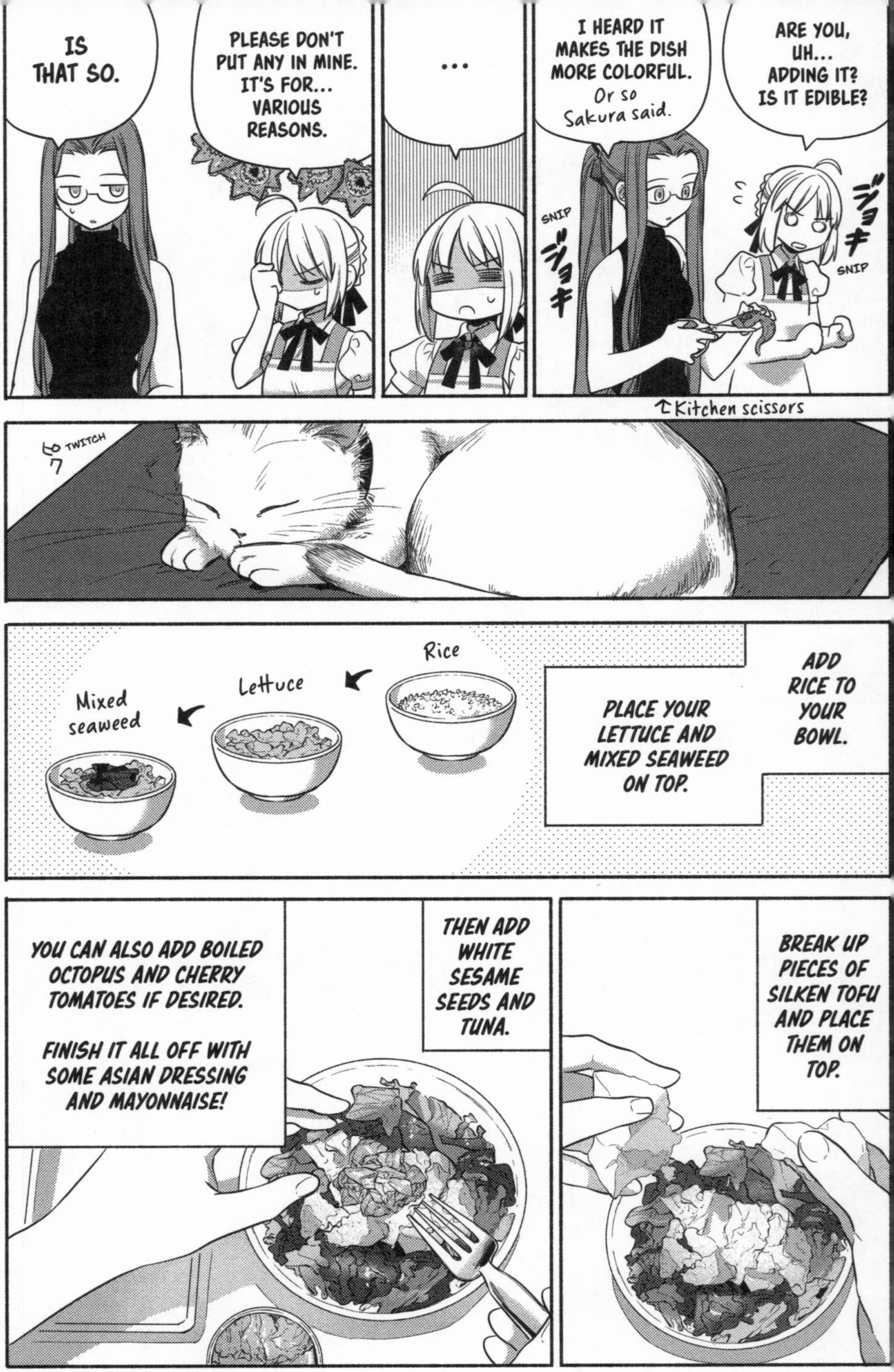
ARE YOU, UH... ADDING IT? IS IT EDIBLE?
ジョキ
SNIP
I HEARD IT MAKES THE DISH MORE COLORFUL.
Or so Sakura said.
ジョキ
SNIP
Kitchen scissors
...
PLEASE DON'T PUT ANY IN MINE. IT'S FOR... VARIOUS REASONS.
IS THAT SO.
TWITCH
ADD RICE TO YOUR BOWL.
PLACE YOUR LETTUCE AND MIXED SEAWEED ON TOP.
Rice
Lettuce
Mixed seaweed
BREAK UP PIECES OF SILKEN TOFU AND PLACE THEM ON TOP.
THEN ADD WHITE SESAME SEEDS AND TUNA.
YOU CAN ALSO ADD BOILED OCTOPUS AND CHERRY TOMATOES IF DESIRED.
FINISH IT ALL OFF WITH SOME ASIAN DRESSING AND MAYONNAISE!

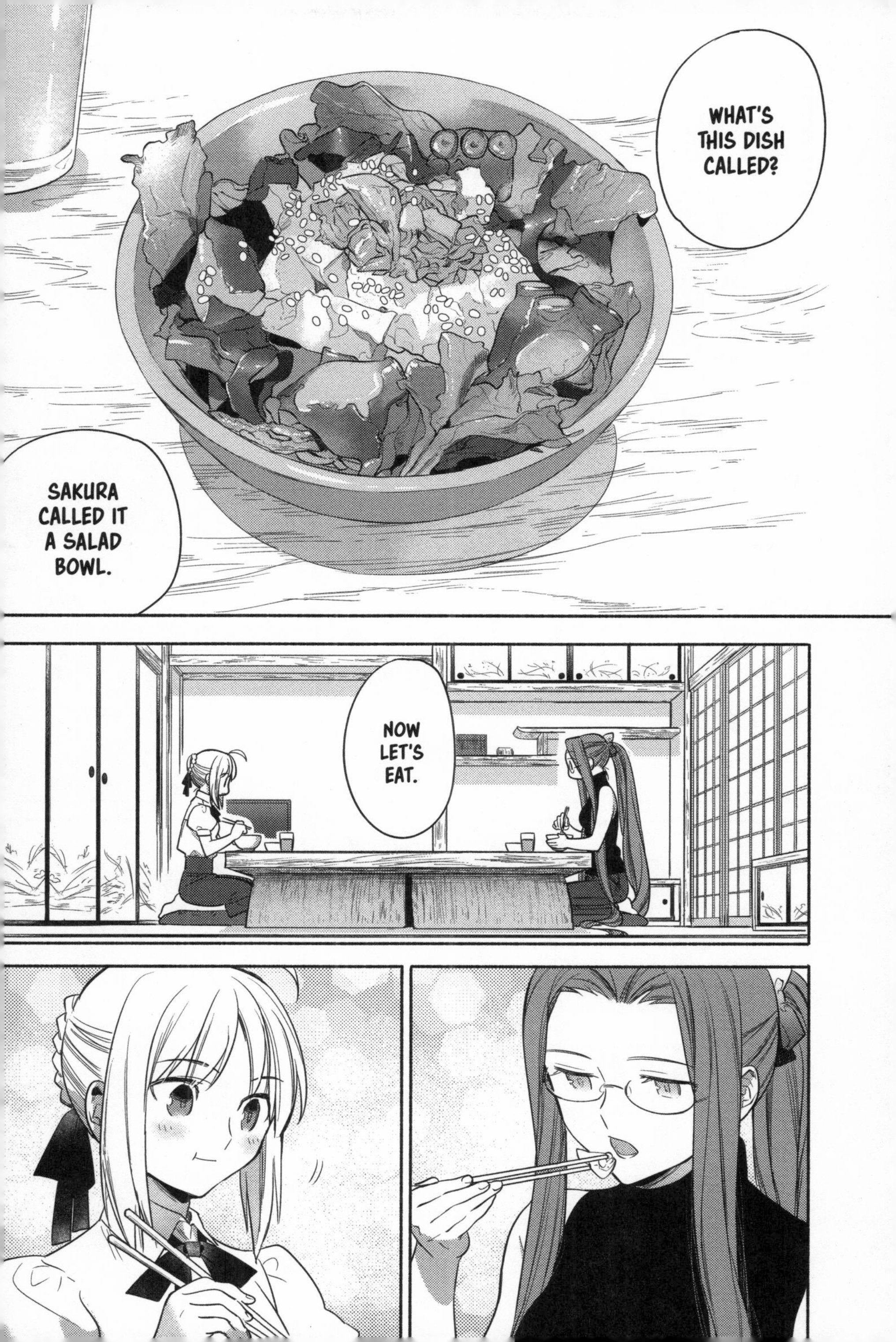
WHAT'S THIS DISH CALLED?
SAKURA CALLED IT A SALAD BOWL.
NOW LET'S EAT.

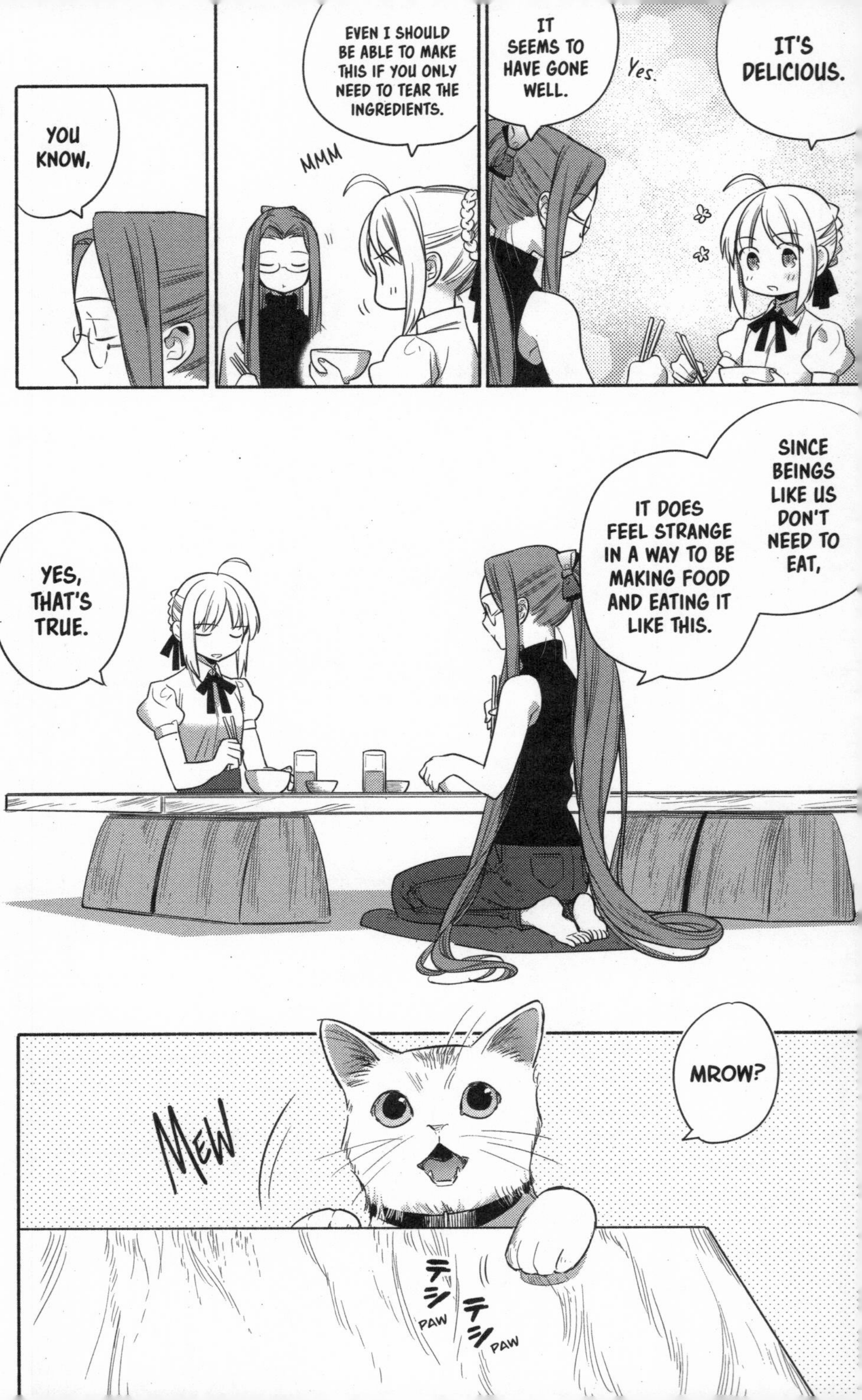
IT'S DELICIOUS.
Yes.
IT SEEMS TO HAVE GONE WELL.
EVEN I SHOULD BE ABLE TO MAKE THIS IF YOU ONLY NEED TO TEAR THE INGREDIENTS.
MMM
YOU KNOW,
SINCE BEINGS LIKE US DON'T NEED TO EAT,
IT DOES FEEL STRANGE IN A WAY TO BE MAKING FOOD AND EATING IT LIKE THIS.
YES, THAT'S TRUE.
MROW?
MEW
テシ PAW
テシ PAW

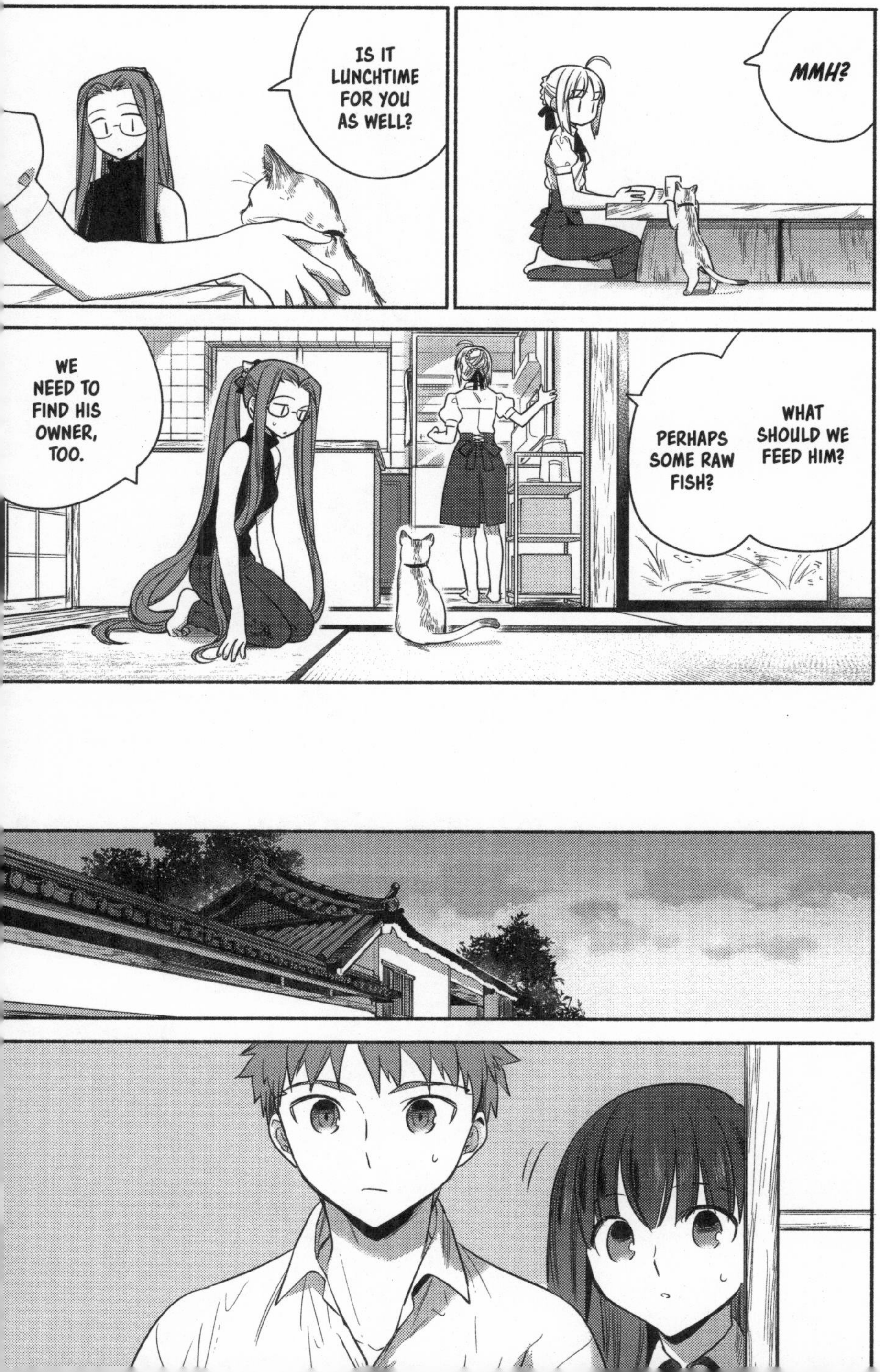
MMH?
IS IT LUNCHTIME FOR YOU AS WELL?
WHAT SHOULD WE FEED HIM?
PERHAPS SOME RAW FISH?
WE NEED TO FIND HIS OWNER, TOO.

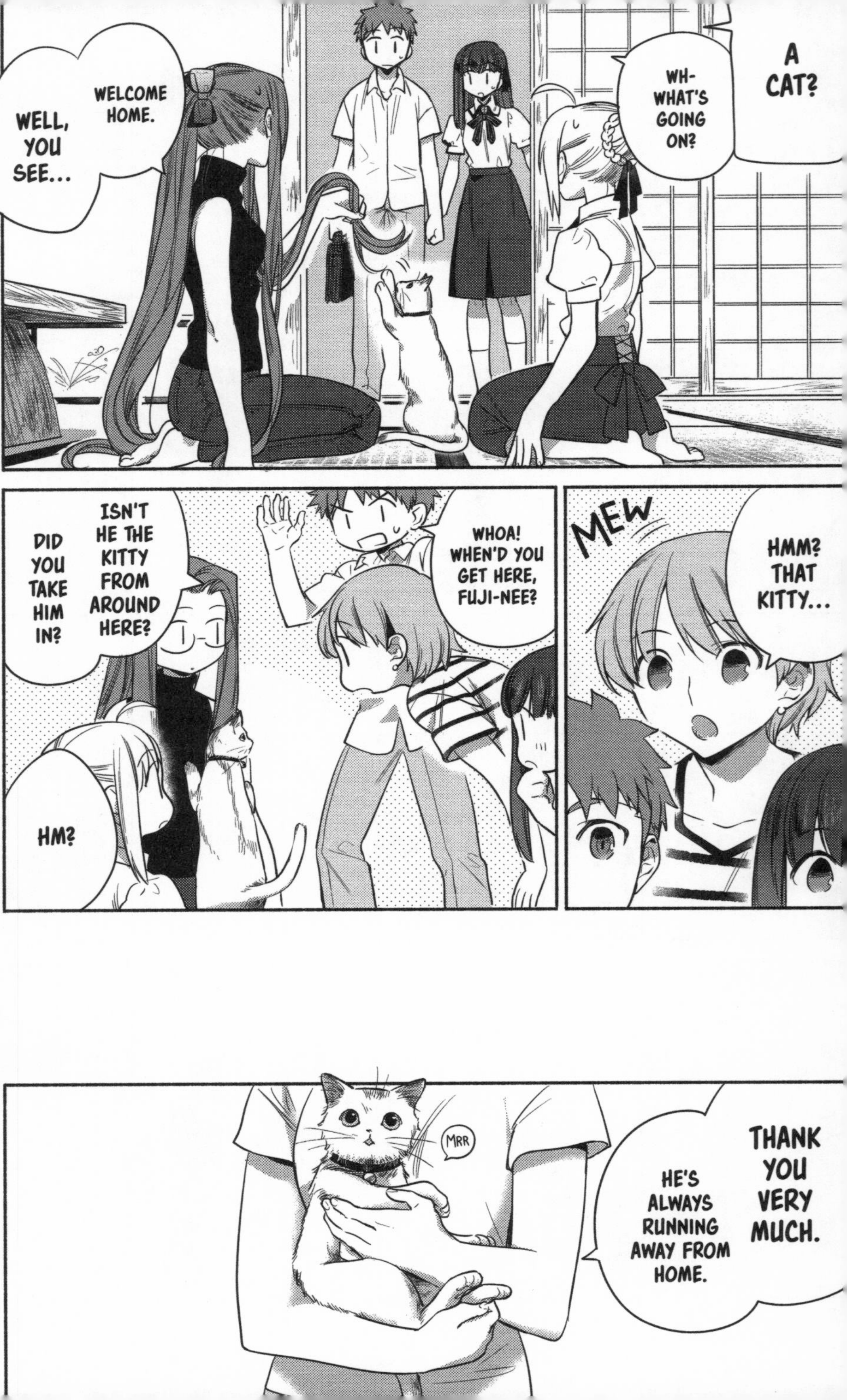
A CAT?
WH- WHAT'S GOING ON?
WELCOME HOME.
WELL, YOU SEE...
MEW
HMM? THAT KITTY...
WHOA! WHEN'D YOU GET HERE, FUJI-NEE?
ISN'T HE THE KITTY FROM AROUND HERE?
DID YOU TAKE HIM IN?
HM?
THANK YOU VERY MUCH.
HE'S ALWAYS RUNNING AWAY FROM HOME.
MRR

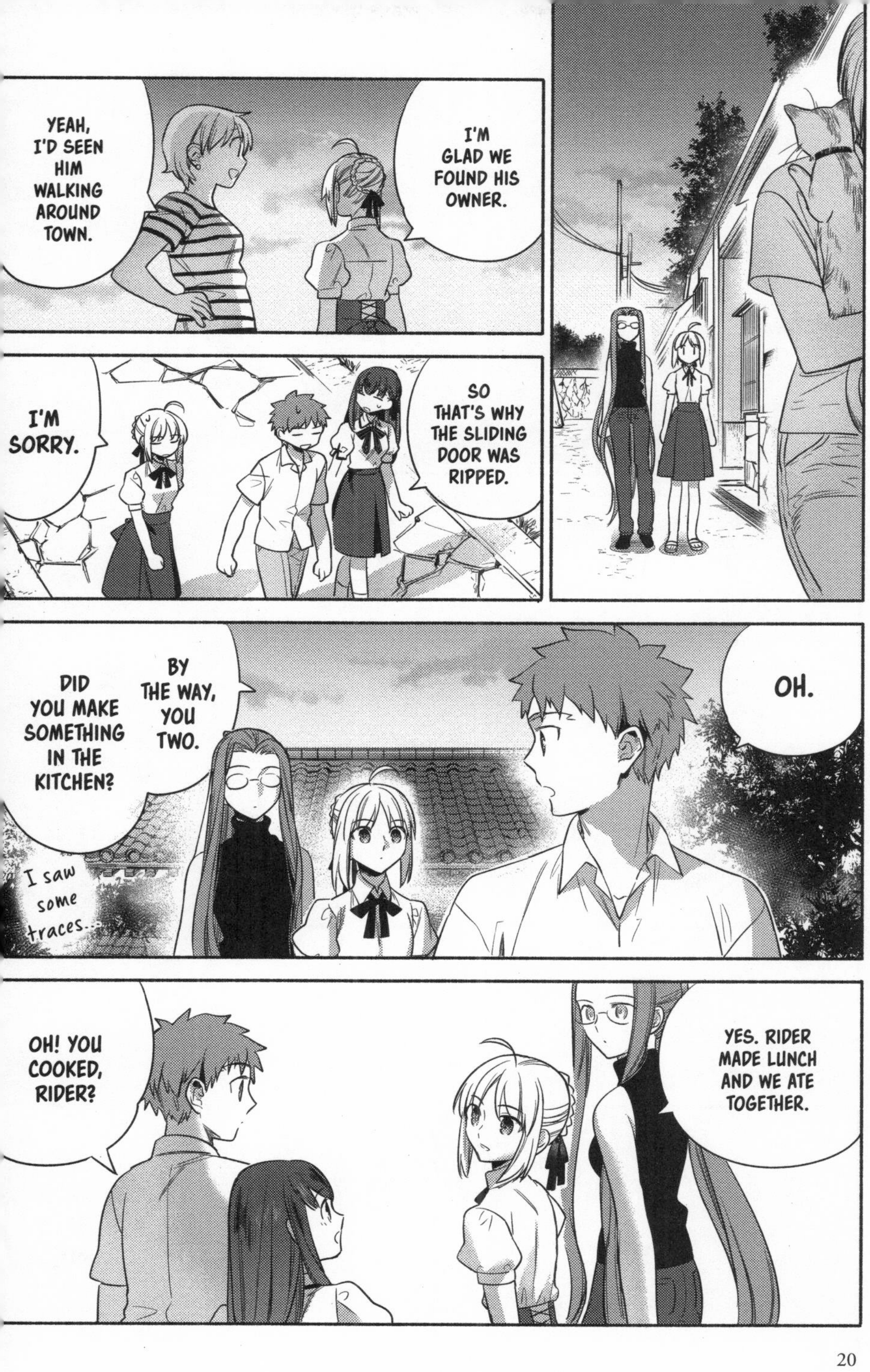
I'M GLAD WE FOUND HIS OWNER.
YEAH, I'D SEEN HIM WALKING AROUND TOWN.
SO THAT'S WHY THE SLIDING DOOR WAS RIPPED.
I'M SORRY.
OH.
BY THE WAY, YOU TWO.
DID YOU MAKE SOMETHING IN THE KITCHEN?
I saw some traces...
YES. RIDER MADE LUNCH AND WE ATE TOGETHER.
OH! YOU COOKED, RIDER?

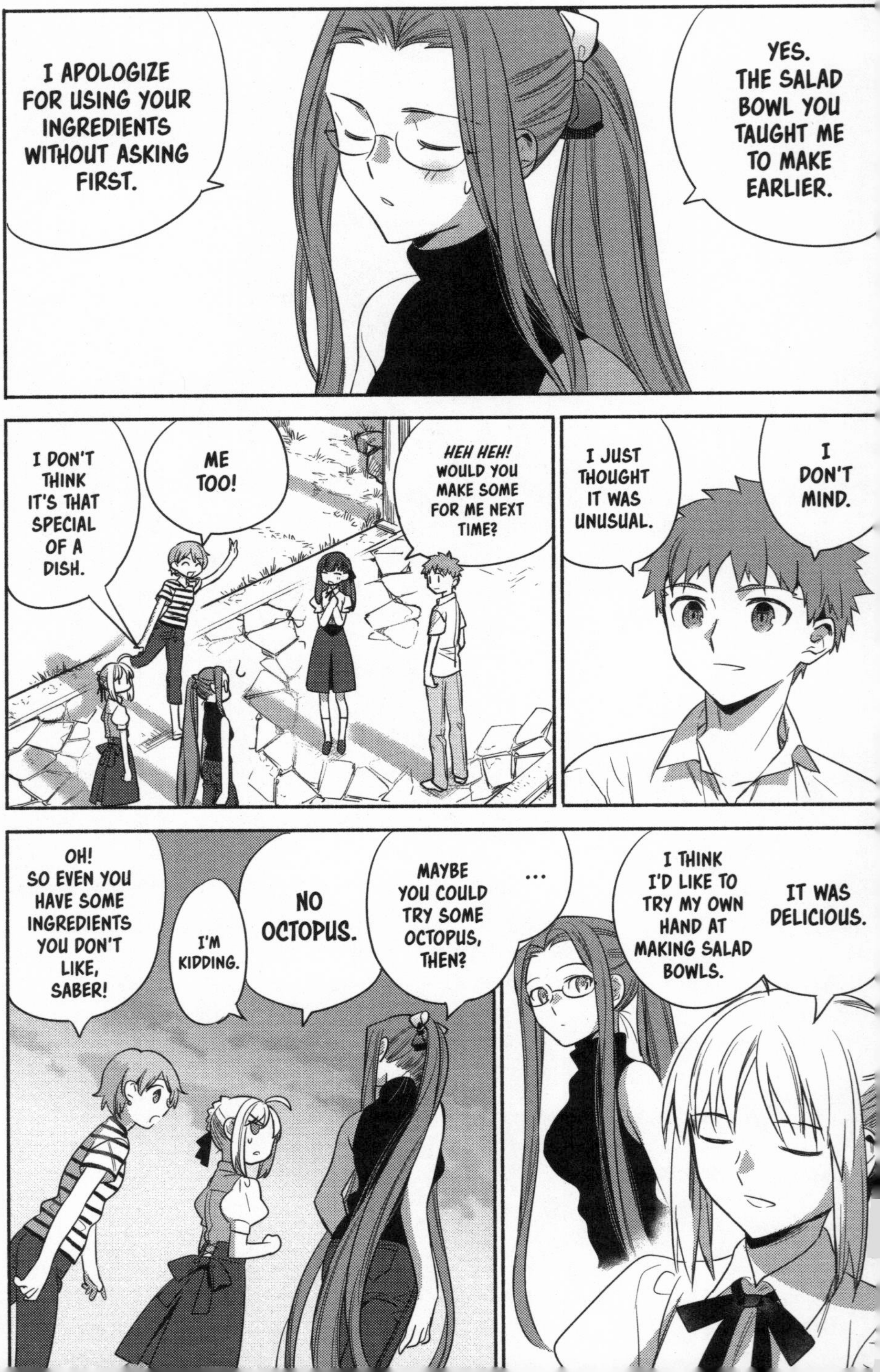
YES. THE SALAD BOWL YOU TAUGHT ME TO MAKE EARLIER.
I APOLOGIZE FOR USING YOUR INGREDIENTS WITHOUT ASKING FIRST.
I DON'T MIND.
I JUST THOUGHT IT WAS UNUSUAL.
HEH HEH! WOULD YOU MAKE SOME FOR ME NEXT TIME?
ME TOO!
I DON'T THINK IT'S THAT SPECIAL OF A DISH.
IT WAS DELICIOUS.
I THINK I'D LIKE TO TRY MY OWN HAND AT MAKING SALAD BOWLS.
...
MAYBE YOU COULD TRY SOME OCTOPUS, THEN?
NO OCTOPUS.
I'M KIDDING.
OH! SO EVEN YOU HAVE SOME INGREDIENTS YOU DON'T LIKE, SABER!

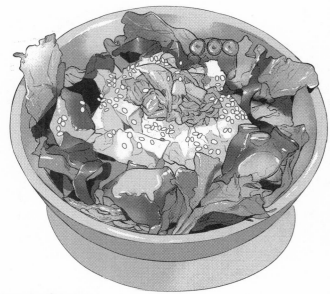

Easy Hand-Torn Salad Bowls

Ingredients - Serves 1

1 bowl of rice
1/4 block (30 g / 1 oz) silken tofu
1/2–1 can (1–2.5 oz) tuna
1–2 leaves (30 g / 1 oz) lettuce
1–2 g dried seaweed mix
White sesame seeds to taste

If desired
  (30 g (1 oz) boiled octopus
    1–3 cherry tomatoes
Asian dressing to taste
Mayonnaise to taste

1. Reconstitute mixed dried seaweed in water, then pat dry.

2. Rip lettuce into bite-sized pieces. (If you like octopus, then cut boiled octopus into bite-sized pieces.)

3. Add rice to your bowls, then put the lettuce and seaweed mix on top, followed by shredded pieces of silken tofu. Add canned tuna and white sesame seeds. If desired, add sliced octopus and cherry tomatoes. Finish it all off with some store-bought Asian dressing and mayonnaise!

*Feel free to use any other kind of dressing, like sesame, ponzu, soy-shiso, and more. Adding wasabi will give it a delicious kick. Try all kinds of other ingredients, like kimchi!

Today's Menu for the Emiya Family

Yes.

Oh!
You're
using it!

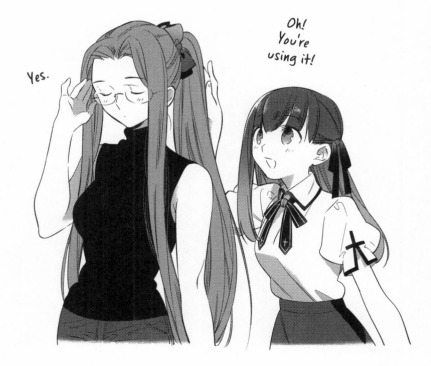

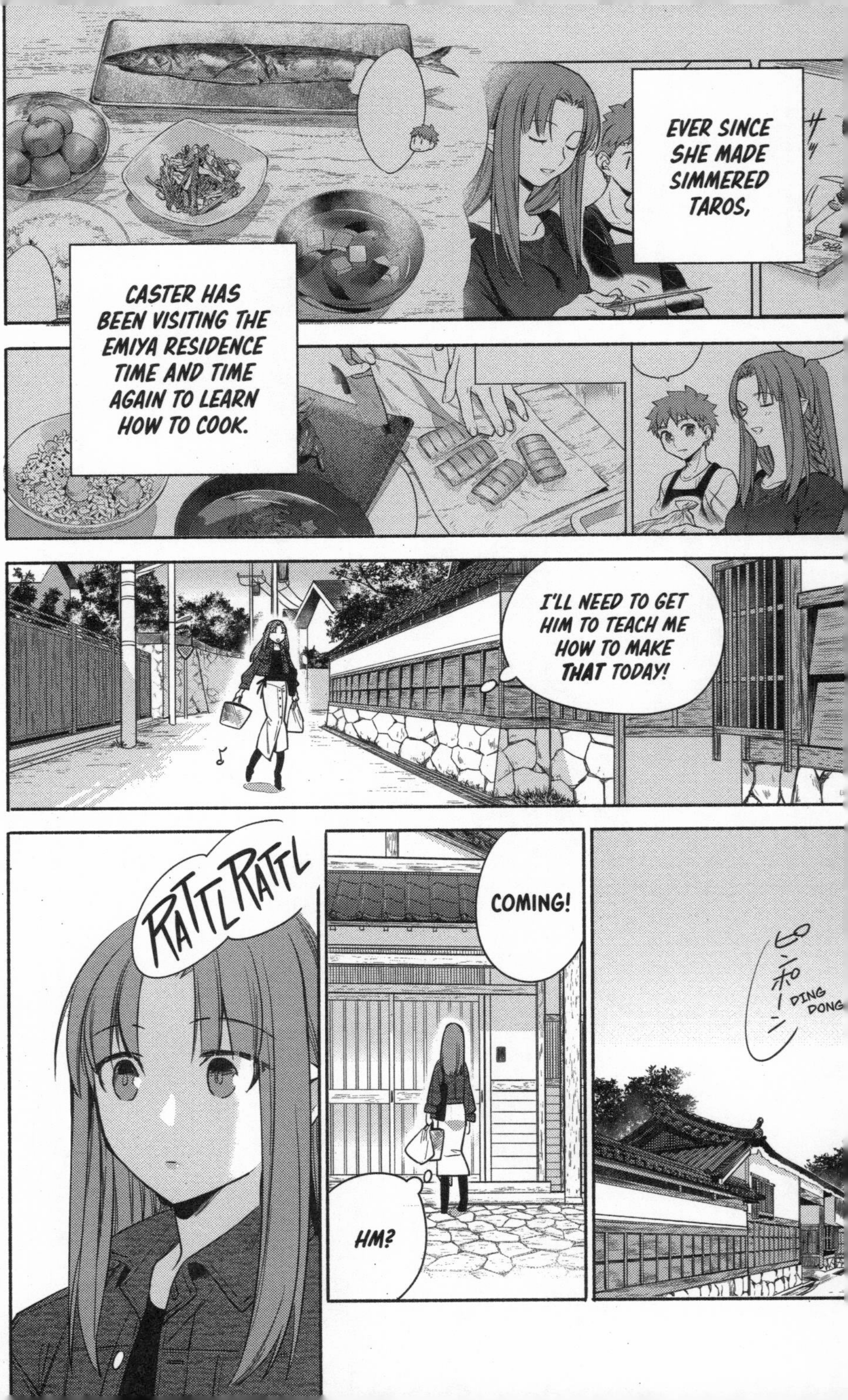

EVER SINCE SHE MADE SIMMERED TAROS,
CASTER HAS BEEN VISITING THE EMIYA RESIDENCE TIME AND TIME AGAIN TO LEARN HOW TO COOK.
I'LL NEED TO GET HIM TO TEACH ME HOW TO MAKE THAT TODAY!
DING DONG
COMING!
HM?
RATTL RATTL

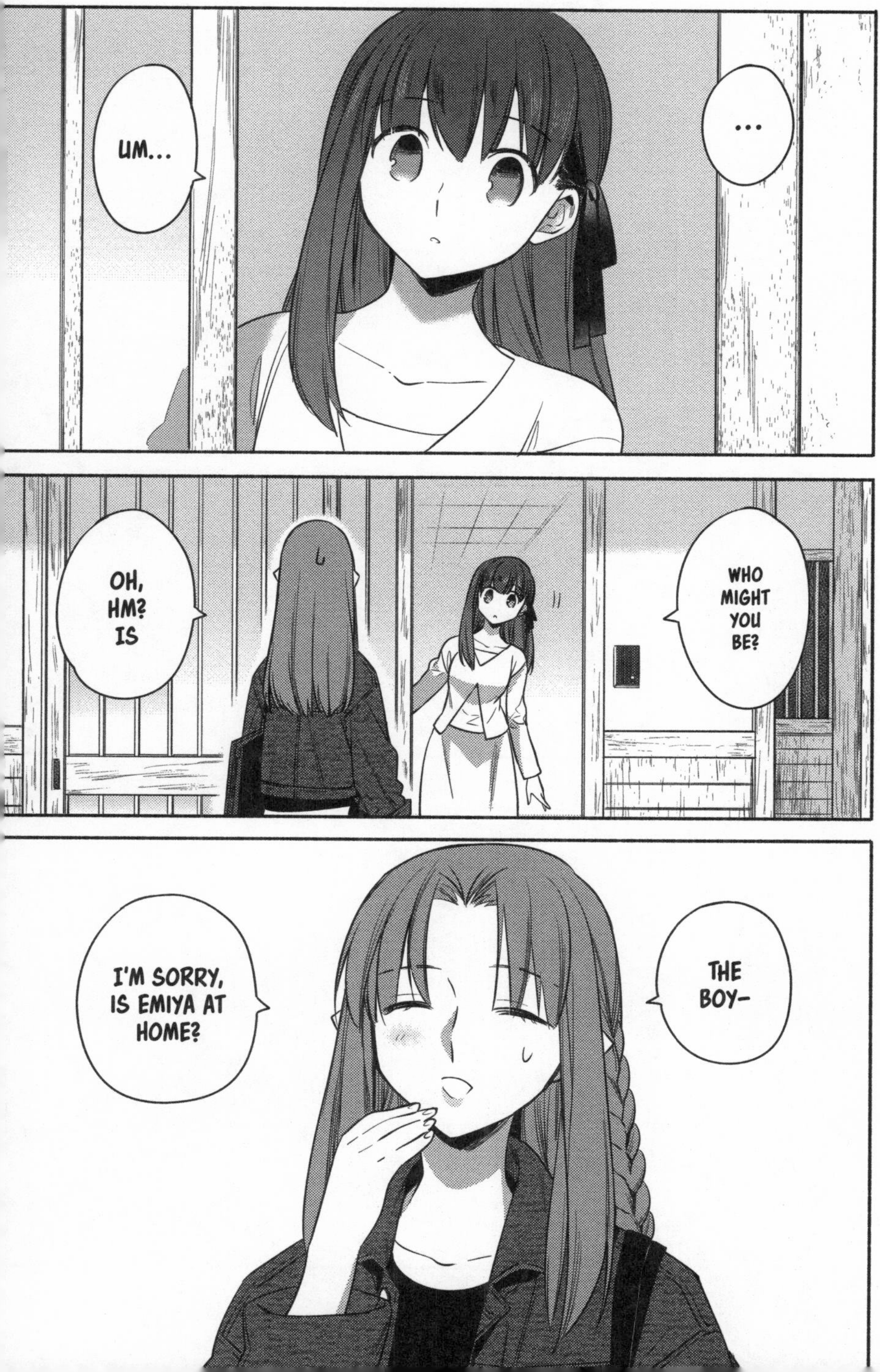
...
UM...
WHO MIGHT YOU BE?
OH, HM? IS
THE BOY-
I'M SORRY, IS EMIYA AT HOME?

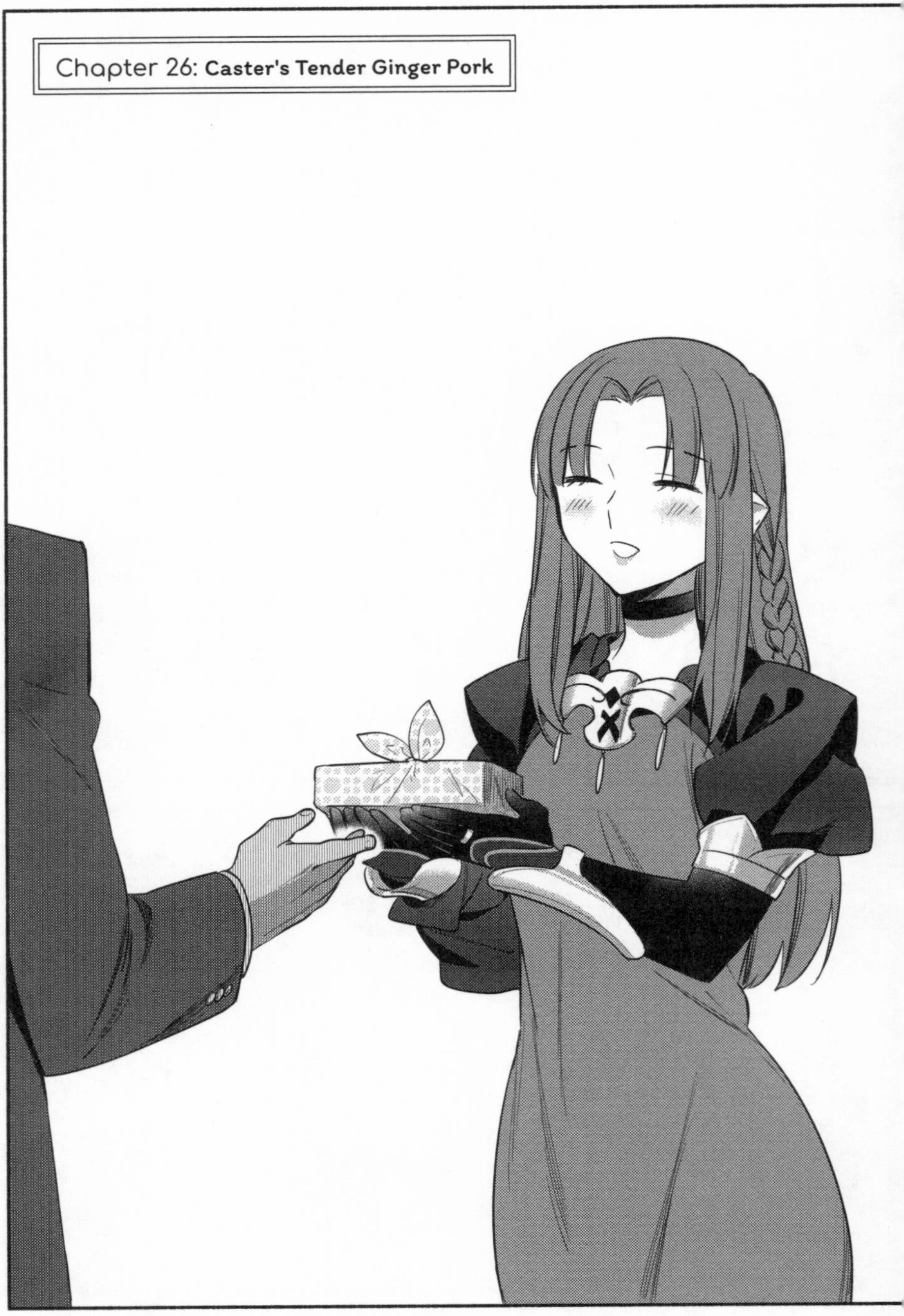
Chapter 26: Caster's Tender Ginger Pork

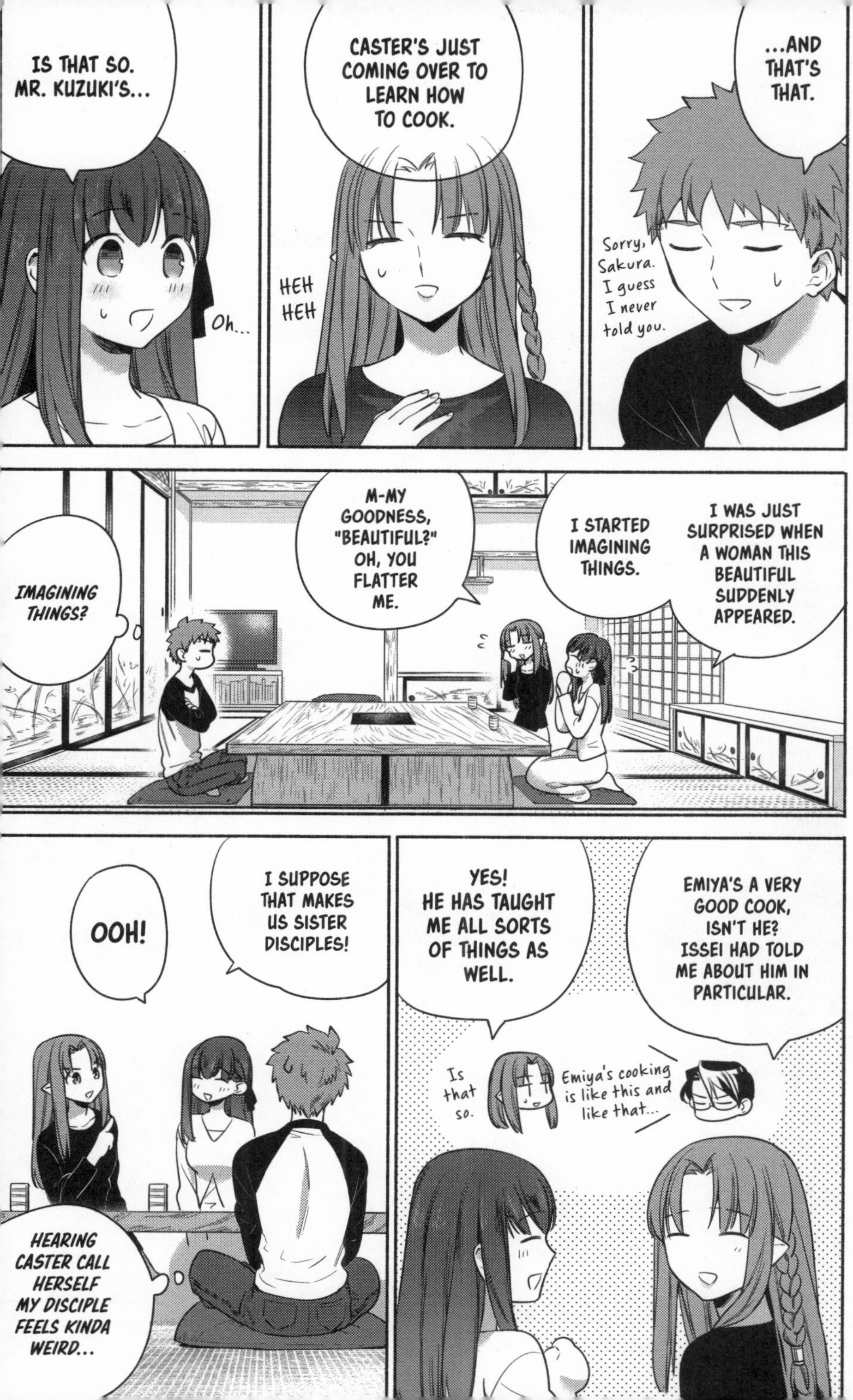
...AND THAT'S THAT.
Sorry, Sakura. I guess I never told you.
CASTER'S JUST COMING OVER TO LEARN HOW TO COOK.
HEH HEH
IS THAT SO. MR. KUZUKI'S...
Oh...
I WAS JUST SURPRISED WHEN A WOMAN THIS BEAUTIFUL SUDDENLY APPEARED.
I STARTED IMAGINING THINGS.
M-MY GOODNESS, "BEAUTIFUL?" OH, YOU FLATTER ME.
IMAGINING THINGS?
EMIYA'S A VERY GOOD COOK, ISN'T HE? ISSEI HAD TOLD ME ABOUT HIM IN PARTICULAR.
YES! HE HAS TAUGHT ME ALL SORTS OF THINGS AS WELL.
Emiya's cooking is like this and like that...
Is that so.
I SUPPOSE THAT MAKES US SISTER DISCIPLES!
OOH!
HEARING CASTER CALL HERSELF MY DISCIPLE FEELS KINDA WEIRD...

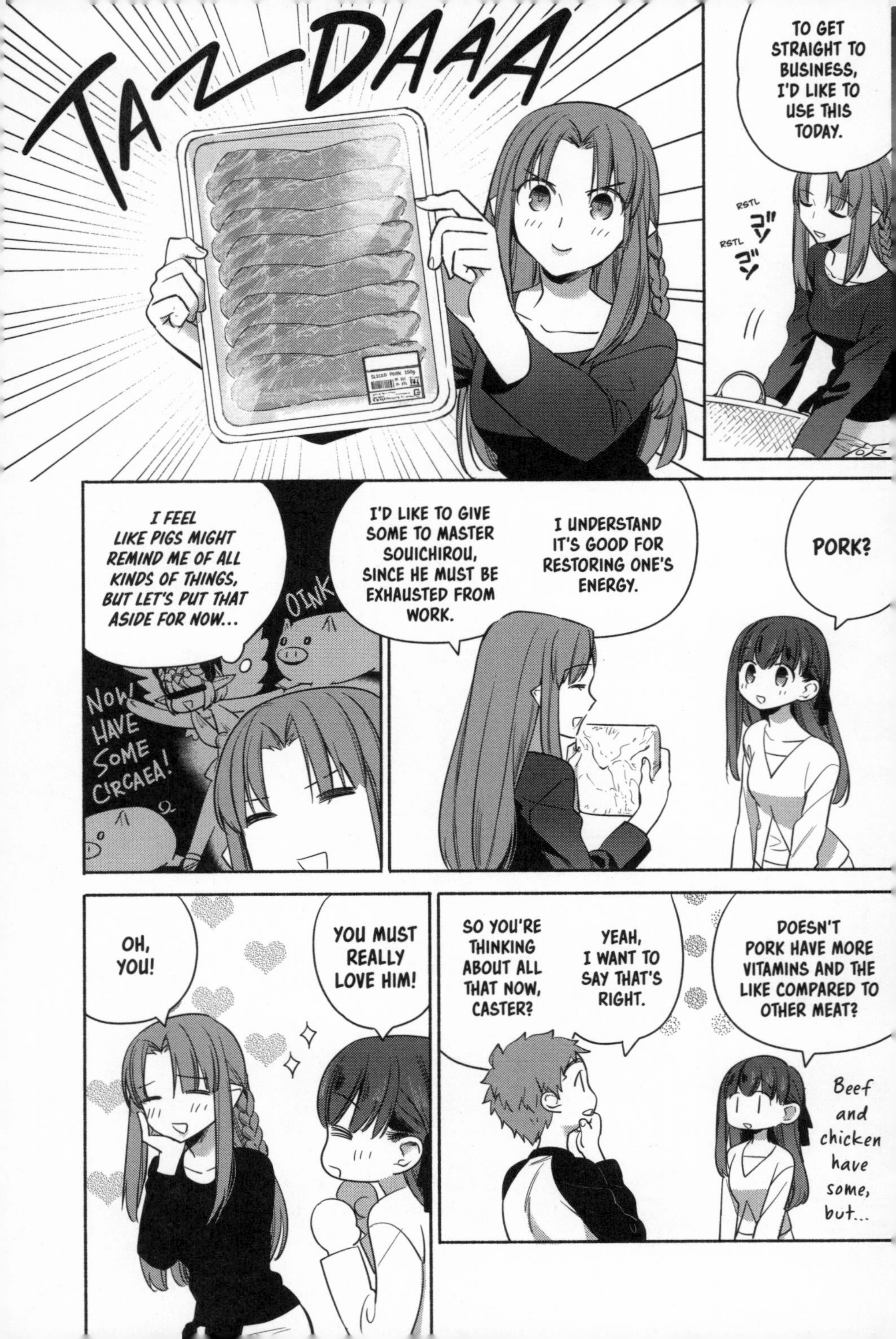
TO GET STRAIGHT TO BUSINESS, I'D LIKE TO USE THIS TODAY.
RSTL ゴソ
RSTL ゴソ
TA-DAAA
SLICED PORK 150g
PORK?
I UNDERSTAND IT'S GOOD FOR RESTORING ONE'S ENERGY.
I'D LIKE TO GIVE SOME TO MASTER SOUICHIROU, SINCE HE MUST BE EXHAUSTED FROM WORK.
I FEEL LIKE PIGS MIGHT REMIND ME OF ALL KINDS OF THINGS, BUT LET'S PUT THAT ASIDE FOR NOW...
OINK
NOW HAVE SOME CIRCAEA!
DOESN'T PORK HAVE MORE VITAMINS AND THE LIKE COMPARED TO OTHER MEAT?
Beef and chicken have some, but...
YEAH, I WANT TO SAY THAT'S RIGHT.
SO YOU'RE THINKING ABOUT ALL THAT NOW, CASTER?
YOU MUST REALLY LOVE HIM!
OH, YOU!

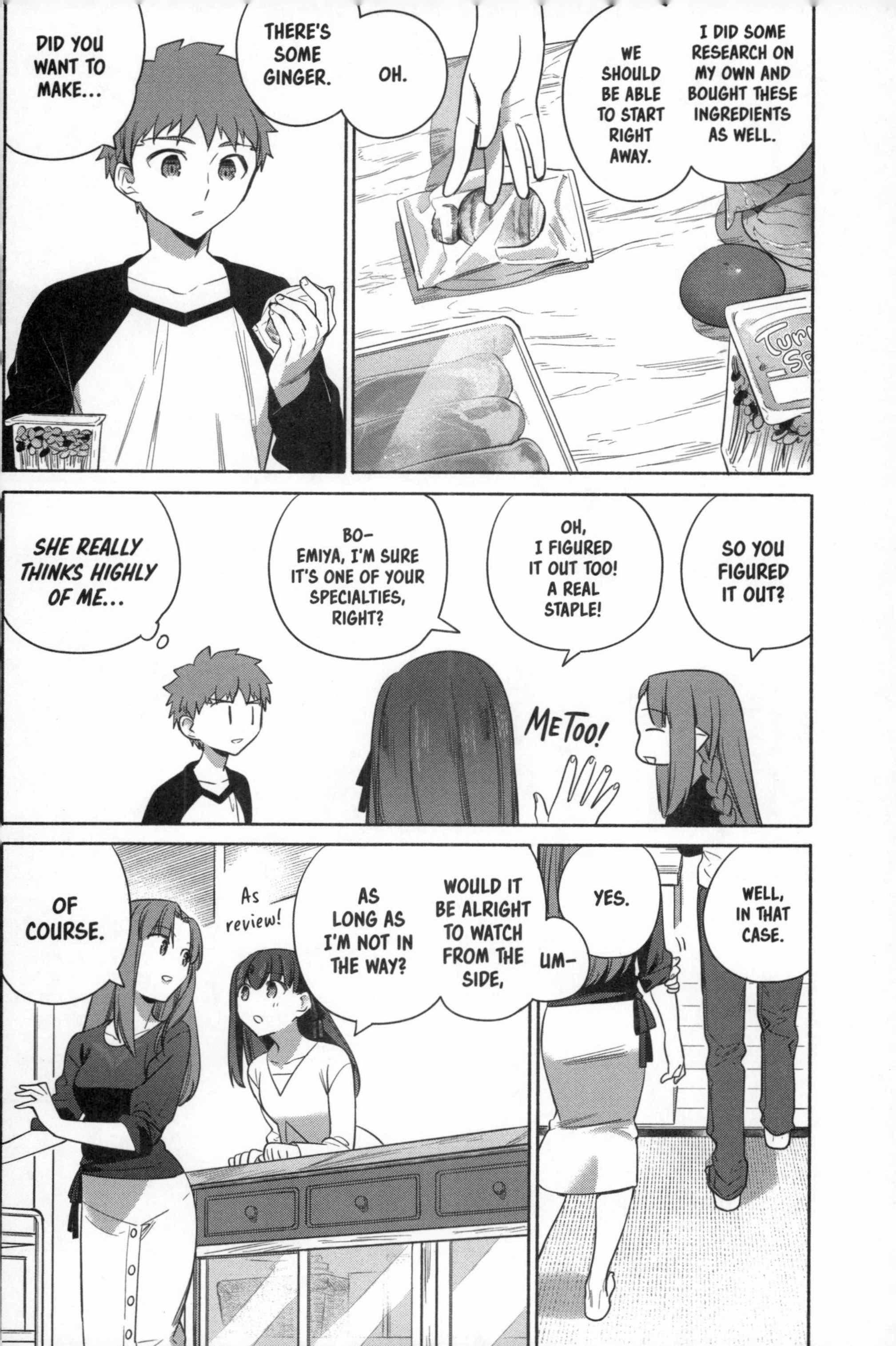
I DID SOME RESEARCH ON MY OWN AND BOUGHT THESE INGREDIENTS AS WELL.
WE SHOULD BE ABLE TO START RIGHT AWAY.
OH.
THERE'S SOME GINGER.
DID YOU WANT TO MAKE...
SO YOU FIGURED IT OUT?
OH, I FIGURED IT OUT TOO! A REAL STAPLE!
ME TOO!
BO- EMIYA, I'M SURE IT'S ONE OF YOUR SPECIALTIES, RIGHT?
SHE REALLY THINKS HIGHLY OF ME...
WELL, IN THAT CASE.
YES.
UM-
WOULD IT BE ALRIGHT TO WATCH FROM THE SIDE,
AS LONG AS I'M NOT IN THE WAY?
As review!
OF COURSE.

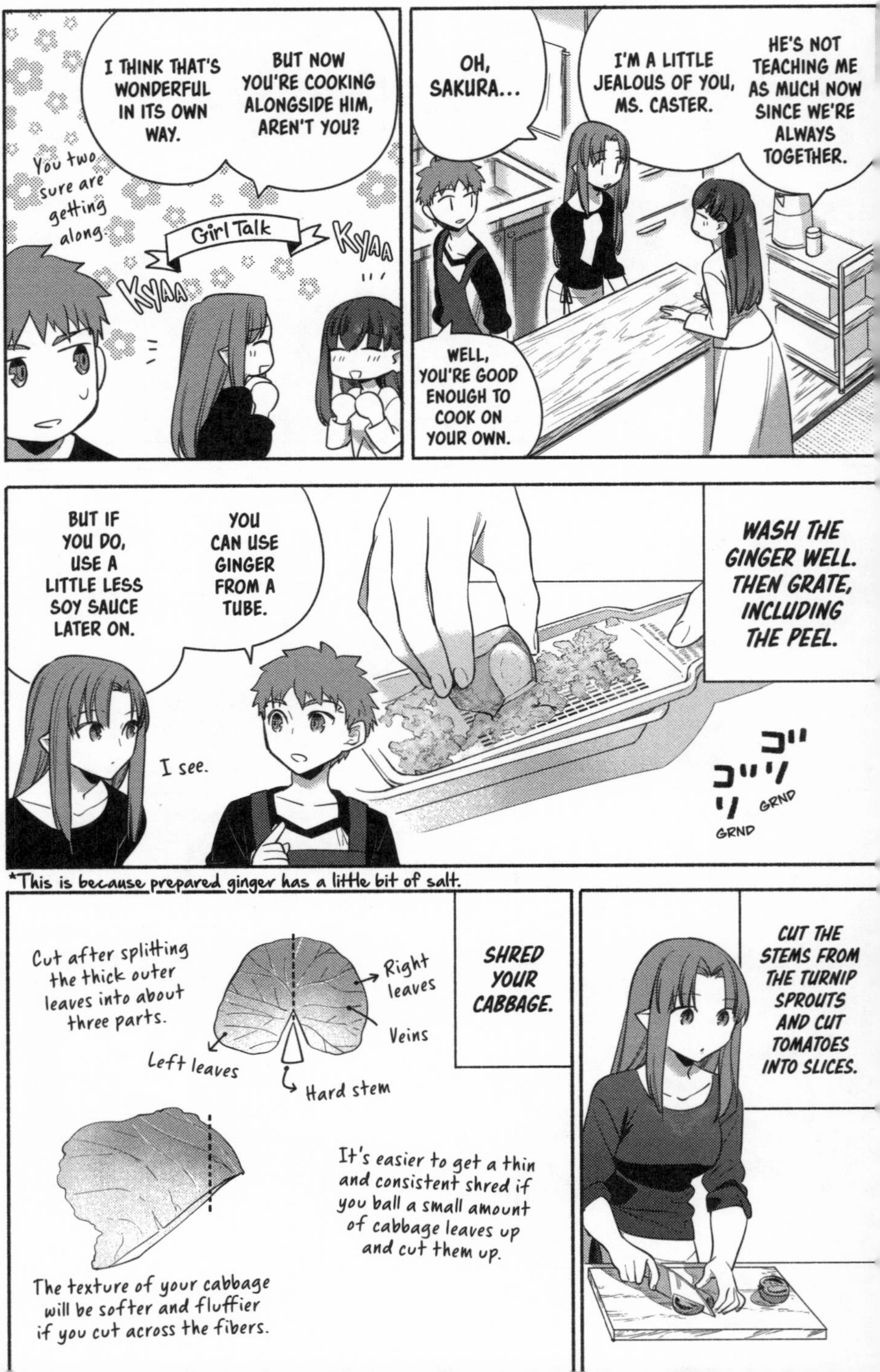
HE'S NOT TEACHING ME AS MUCH NOW SINCE WE'RE ALWAYS TOGETHER.
I'M A LITTLE JEALOUS OF YOU, MS. CASTER.
OH, SAKURA...
WELL, YOU'RE GOOD ENOUGH TO COOK ON YOUR OWN.
BUT NOW YOU'RE COOKING ALONGSIDE HIM, AREN'T YOU?
I THINK THAT'S WONDERFUL IN ITS OWN WAY.
KYAA
Girl Talk
You two sure are getting along.
KYAA
WASH THE GINGER WELL. THEN GRATE, INCLUDING THE PEEL.
ゴリ
GRND
ゴリ
GRND
YOU CAN USE GINGER FROM A TUBE.
BUT IF YOU DO, USE A LITTLE LESS SOY SAUCE LATER ON.
I see.
*This is because prepared ginger has a little bit of salt.
CUT THE STEMS FROM THE TURNIP SPROUTS AND CUT TOMATOES INTO SLICES.
SHRED YOUR CABBAGE.
Cut after splitting the thick outer leaves into about three parts.
Right leaves
Veins
Left leaves
Hard stem
It's easier to get a thin and consistent shred if you ball a small amount of cabbage leaves up and cut them up.
The texture of your cabbage will be softer and fluffier if you cut across the fibers.

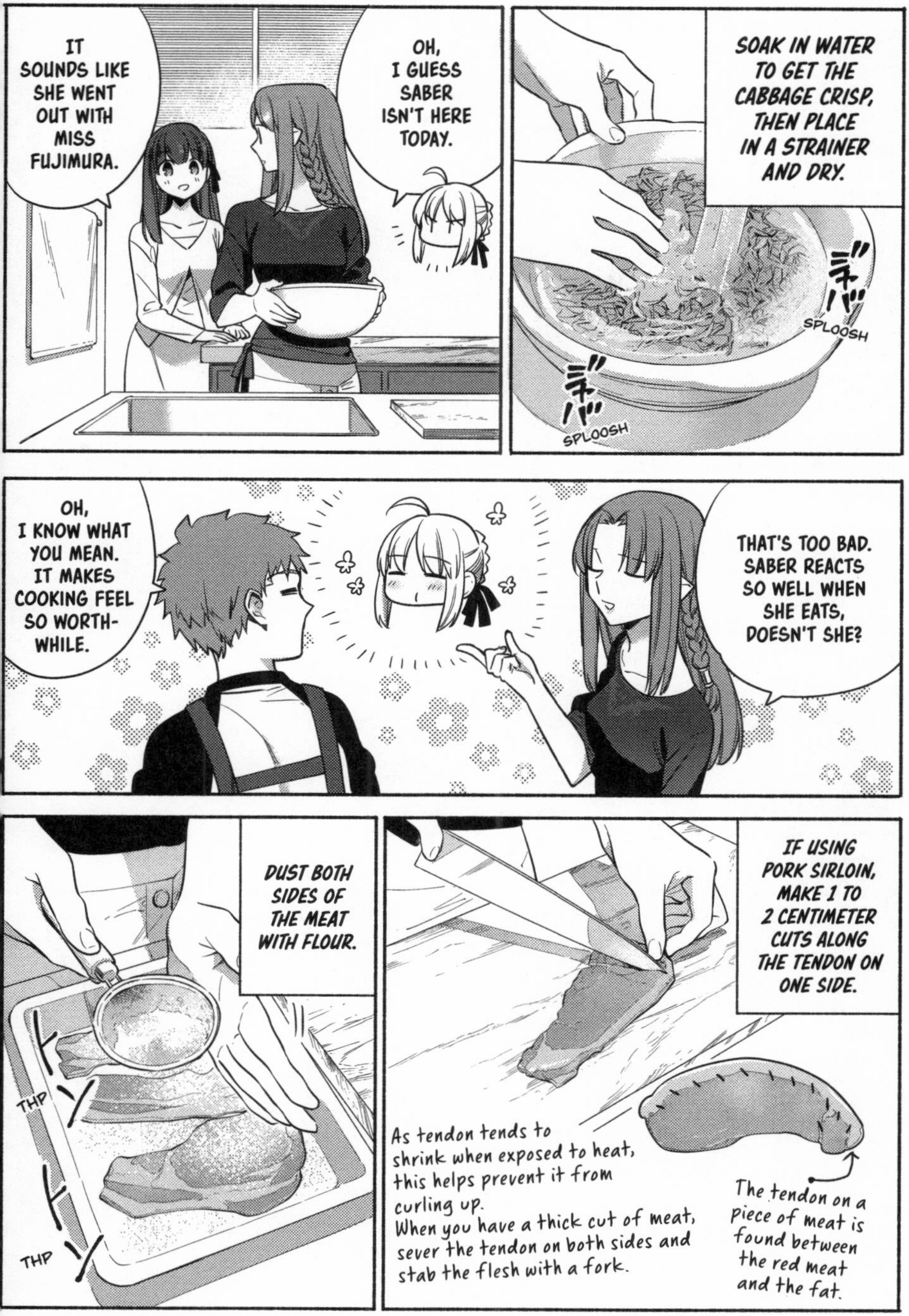
SOAK IN WATER TO GET THE CABBAGE CRISP, THEN PLACE IN A STRAINER AND DRY.
SPLOOSH
SPLOOSH
OH, I GUESS SABER ISN'T HERE TODAY.
IT SOUNDS LIKE SHE WENT OUT WITH MISS FUJIMURA.
THAT'S TOO BAD. SABER REACTS SO WELL WHEN SHE EATS, DOESN'T SHE?
OH, I KNOW WHAT YOU MEAN. IT MAKES COOKING FEEL SO WORTH-WHILE.
IF USING PORK SIRLOIN, MAKE 1 TO 2 CENTIMETER CUTS ALONG THE TENDON ON ONE SIDE.
As tendon tends to shrink when exposed to heat, this helps prevent it from curling up.
When you have a thick cut of meat, sever the tendon on both sides and stab the flesh with a fork.
The tendon on a piece of meat is found between the red meat and the fat.
DUST BOTH SIDES OF THE MEAT WITH FLOUR.
THP
THP

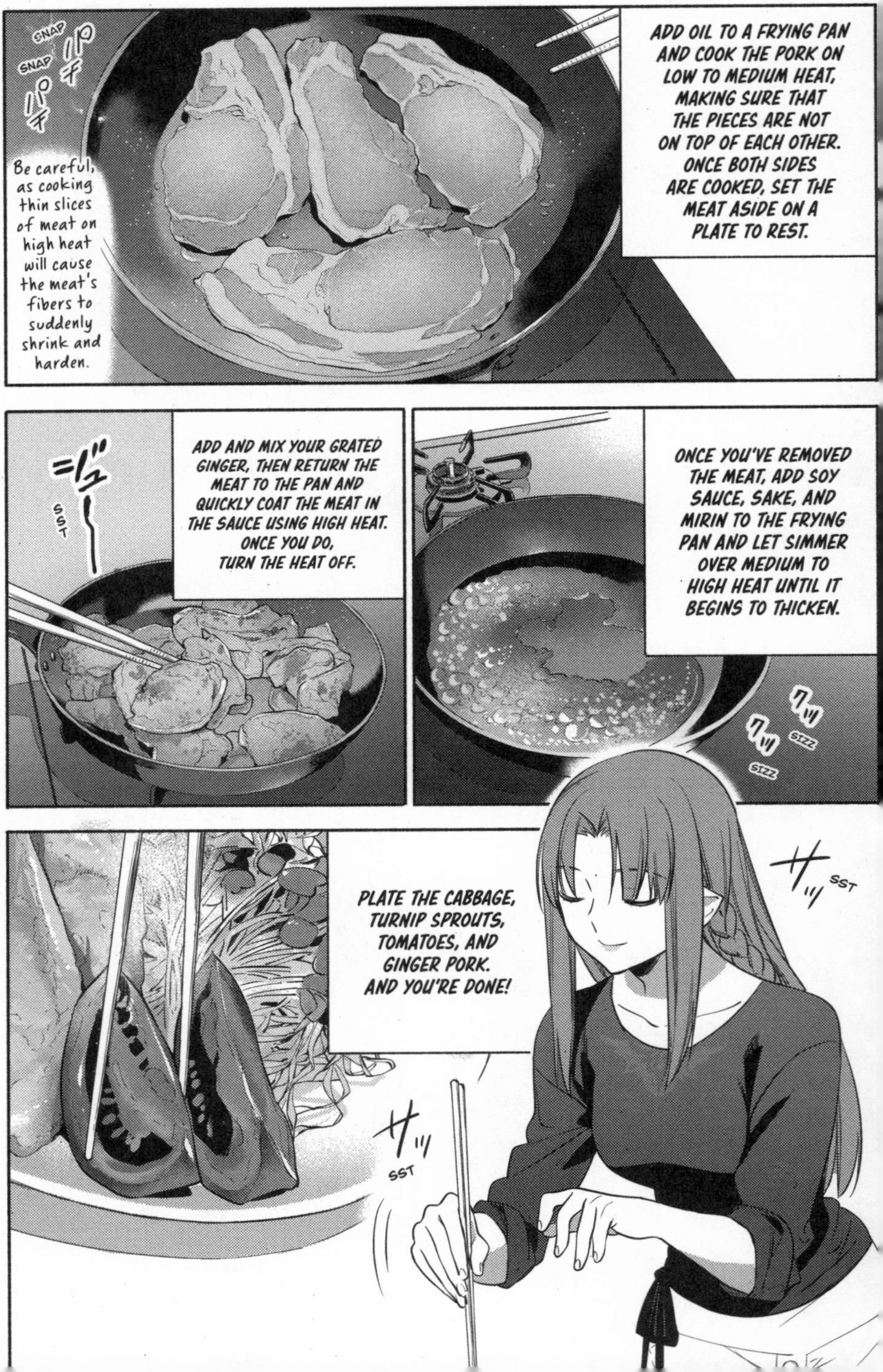
ADD OIL TO A FRYING PAN AND COOK THE PORK ON LOW TO MEDIUM HEAT, MAKING SURE THAT THE PIECES ARE NOT ON TOP OF EACH OTHER. ONCE BOTH SIDES ARE COOKED, SET THE MEAT ASIDE ON A PLATE TO REST.
パチ SNAP
パチ SNAP
Be careful, as cooking thin slices of meat on high heat will cause the meat's fibers to suddenly shrink and harden.
ONCE YOU'VE REMOVED THE MEAT, ADD SOY SAUCE, SAKE, AND MIRIN TO THE FRYING PAN AND LET SIMMER OVER MEDIUM TO HIGH HEAT UNTIL IT BEGINS TO THICKEN.
SIZZ
SIZZ
ADD AND MIX YOUR GRATED GINGER, THEN RETURN THE MEAT TO THE PAN AND QUICKLY COAT THE MEAT IN THE SAUCE USING HIGH HEAT. ONCE YOU DO, TURN THE HEAT OFF.
ジュ～ SST
サッ SST
PLATE THE CABBAGE, TURNIP SPROUTS, TOMATOES, AND GINGER PORK. AND YOU'RE DONE!
サッ SST

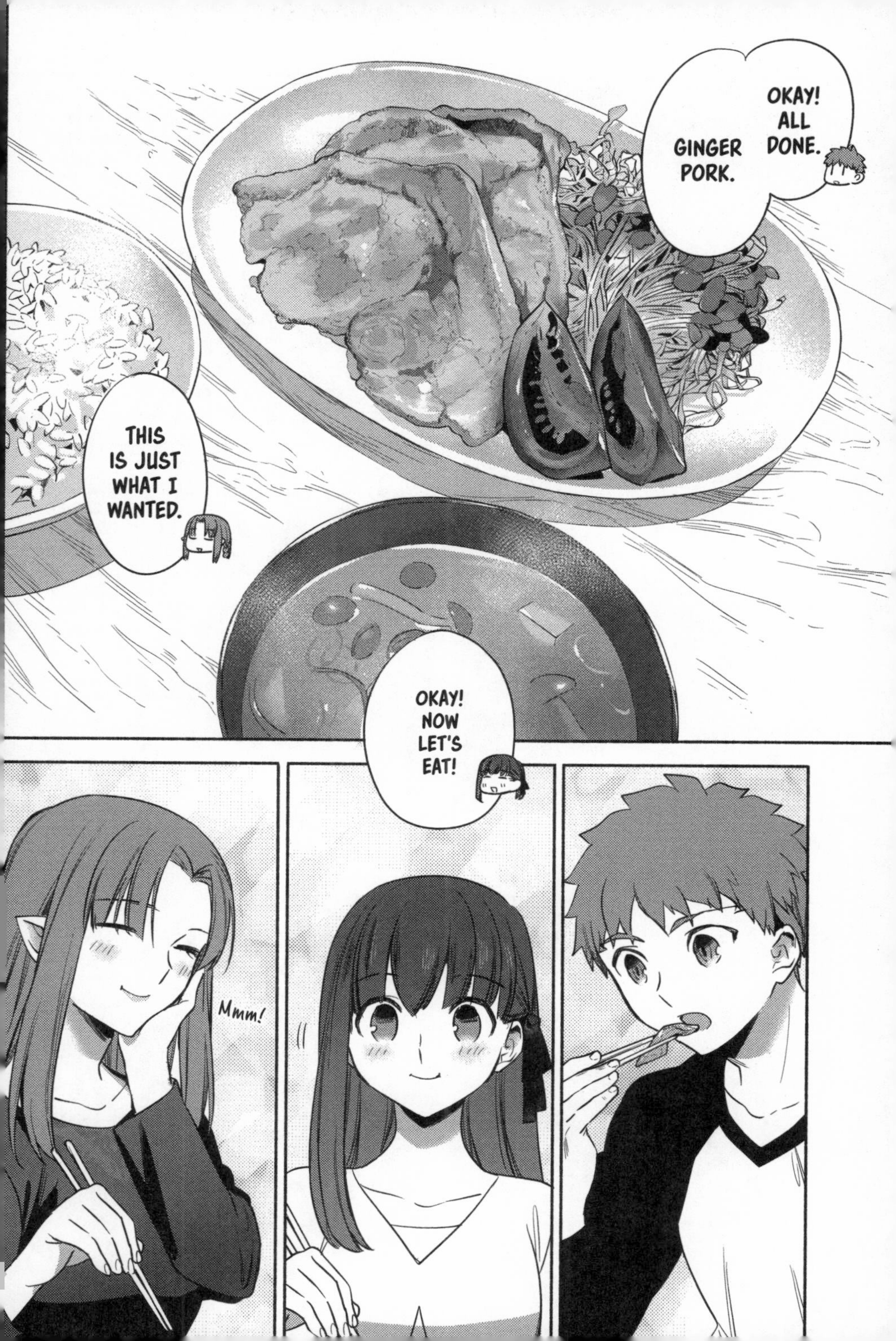
OKAY! ALL DONE.
GINGER PORK.
THIS IS JUST WHAT I WANTED.
OKAY! NOW LET'S EAT!
Mmm!

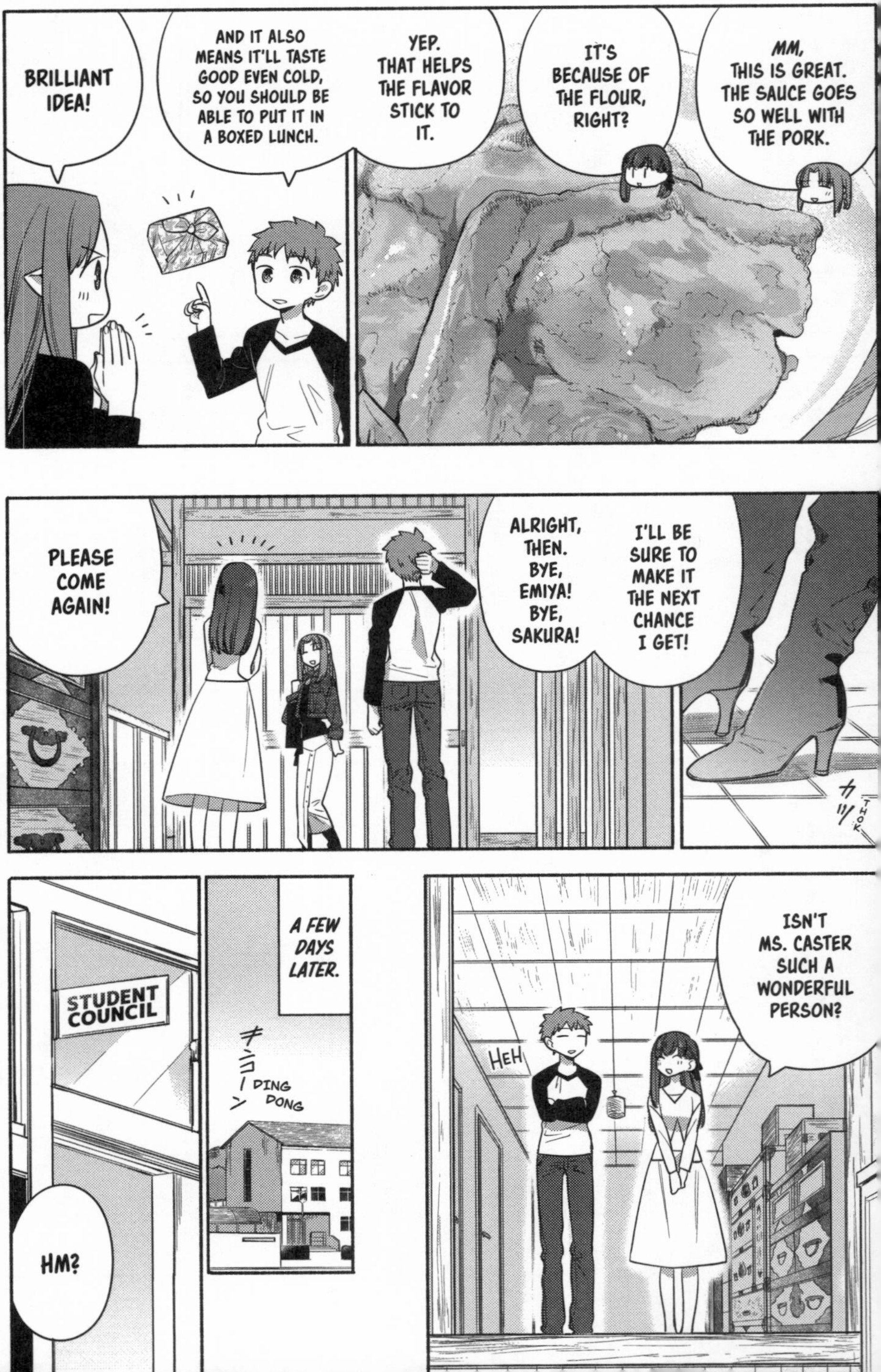
MM, THIS IS GREAT. THE SAUCE GOES SO WELL WITH THE PORK.
IT'S BECAUSE OF THE FLOUR, RIGHT?
YEP. THAT HELPS THE FLAVOR STICK TO IT.
AND IT ALSO MEANS IT'LL TASTE GOOD EVEN COLD, SO YOU SHOULD BE ABLE TO PUT IT IN A BOXED LUNCH.
BRILLIANT IDEA!
カッ THOK
I'LL BE SURE TO MAKE IT THE NEXT CHANCE I GET!
ALRIGHT, THEN. BYE, EMIYA! BYE, SAKURA!
PLEASE COME AGAIN!
ISN'T MS. CASTER SUCH A WONDERFUL PERSON?
HEH
A FEW DAYS LATER.
キンコーン DING DONG
STUDENT COUNCIL
HM?

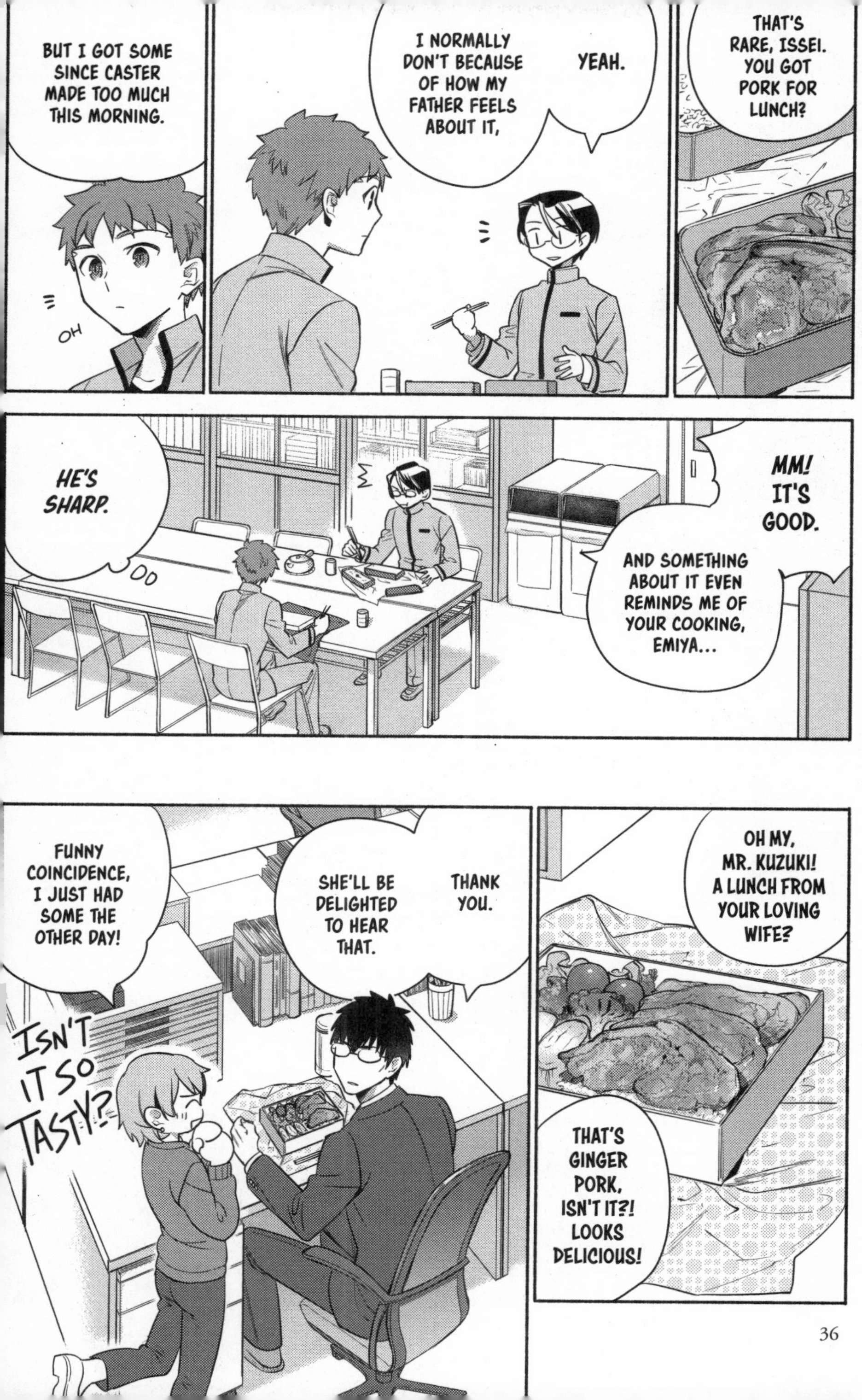
THAT'S RARE, ISSEI. YOU GOT PORK FOR LUNCH?
YEAH.
I NORMALLY DON'T BECAUSE OF HOW MY FATHER FEELS ABOUT IT,
BUT I GOT SOME SINCE CASTER MADE TOO MUCH THIS MORNING.
OH
MM! IT'S GOOD.
AND SOMETHING ABOUT IT EVEN REMINDS ME OF YOUR COOKING, EMIYA...
HE'S SHARP.
OH MY, MR. KUZUKI! A LUNCH FROM YOUR LOVING WIFE?
THAT'S GINGER PORK, ISN'T IT?! LOOKS DELICIOUS!
THANK YOU.
SHE'LL BE DELIGHTED TO HEAR THAT.
FUNNY COINCIDENCE, I JUST HAD SOME THE OTHER DAY!
ISN'T IT SO TASTY?

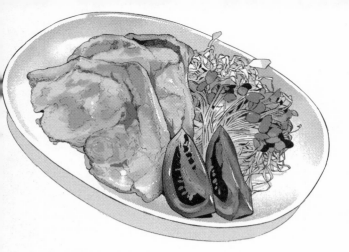

Ginger Pork

Ingredients - Serves 4

400 g (14 oz) pork sirloin (thin cut)

1 stalk grated ginger
(about 40 g / 1.5 oz)

[A] ┌ 3 Tbsp soy sauce
    ├ 3 Tbsp sake
    └ 3 Tbsp mirin

Flour as needed

Vegetable oil as needed

1/4 (200 g / 7 oz) cabbage

1 pack turnip sprouts

1 tomato

*If using ginger from a tube,
use about 3 tablespoons or
3 squirts 4 cm (1.5 in) long.

① Wash the ginger well and then grate, including the peel.
*This is because the ginger close to the peel has a stronger aroma.

② Cut the stems from turnip sprouts, cut tomatoes into slices, and
shred your cabbage. Soak the cabbage so that it's crisp, then place in
a strainer and dry (should take two minutes).

③ Make 1-2 centimeter cuts along the pork's tendon on one side (sever it
on both sides and stab the red meat with a fork in multiple spots when
using a thick cut), then dust a thin coating of flour on both sides.

*Tendon easily shrinks when exposed to heat, so this prevents it from
curling up, resulting in a more evenly cooked piece of meat and a better
visual presentation.

④ Add oil to a frying pan and cook the meat on low to medium heat, making
sure that none of the pieces are on top of each other. Once both sides
are cooked, set the meat aside on a plate or other surface.

*Be careful: Cooking thin slices of meat on high heat will cause the
meat's fibers to suddenly shrink and harden.

⑤ Once you've removed the meat, add [A] to the frying pan and let simmer
over medium to high heat until it begins to thicken (about a minute).
Then then add and mix your grated ginger before returning the meat
to the pan and coating the meat with sauce over high heat.
Once you do, turn the heat off.

⑥ Plate the cabbage, turnip sprouts, tomatoes, and ginger pork.
Then you're done!

Because of the flour coating on the pork, it will still taste good even when cold,
so try adding it to a boxed lunch. If you like your ginger pork less oily, skip the
flour coating in step ③ and go straight to step ④.

Tricks to make sure your meat comes out tender:

① Cut the tendon.

② Don't start by cooking it on high heat.

③ Don't overcook your meat.

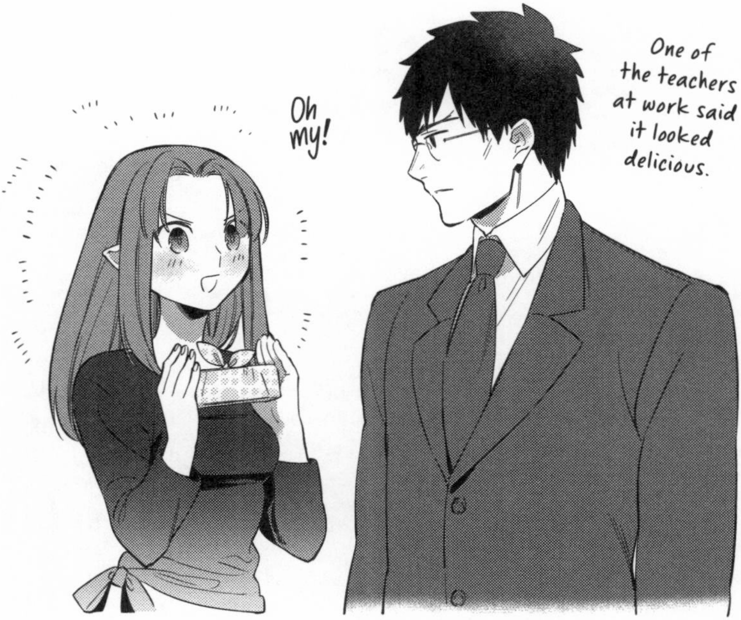
One of the teachers at work said it looked delicious.
Oh my!

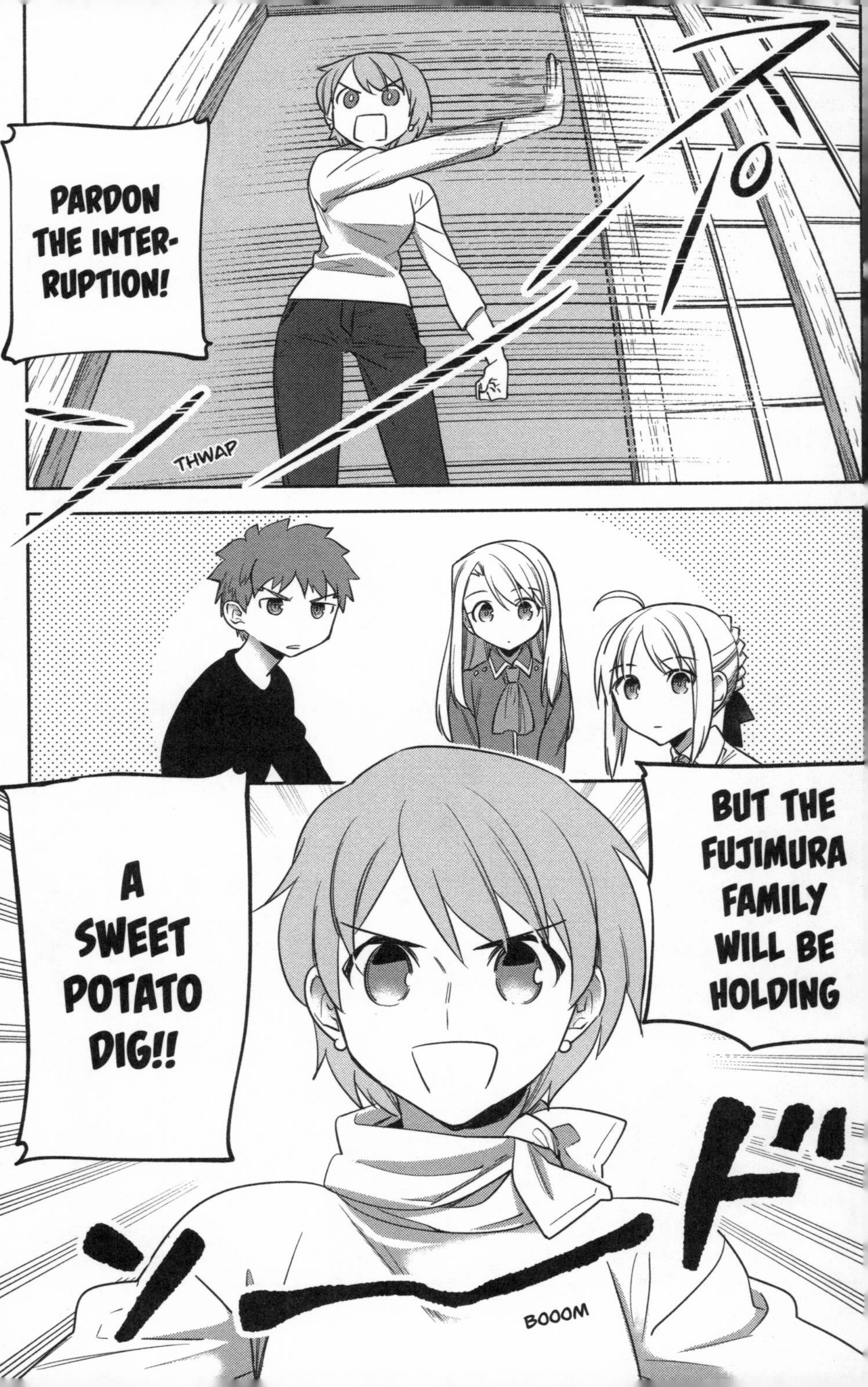
PARDON THE INTER-RUPTION!
THWAP
BUT THE FUJIMURA FAMILY WILL BE HOLDING
A SWEET POTATO DIG!!
BOOOM

Chapter 27: **Sweet Potatoes Two Ways: Candied & Roasted**

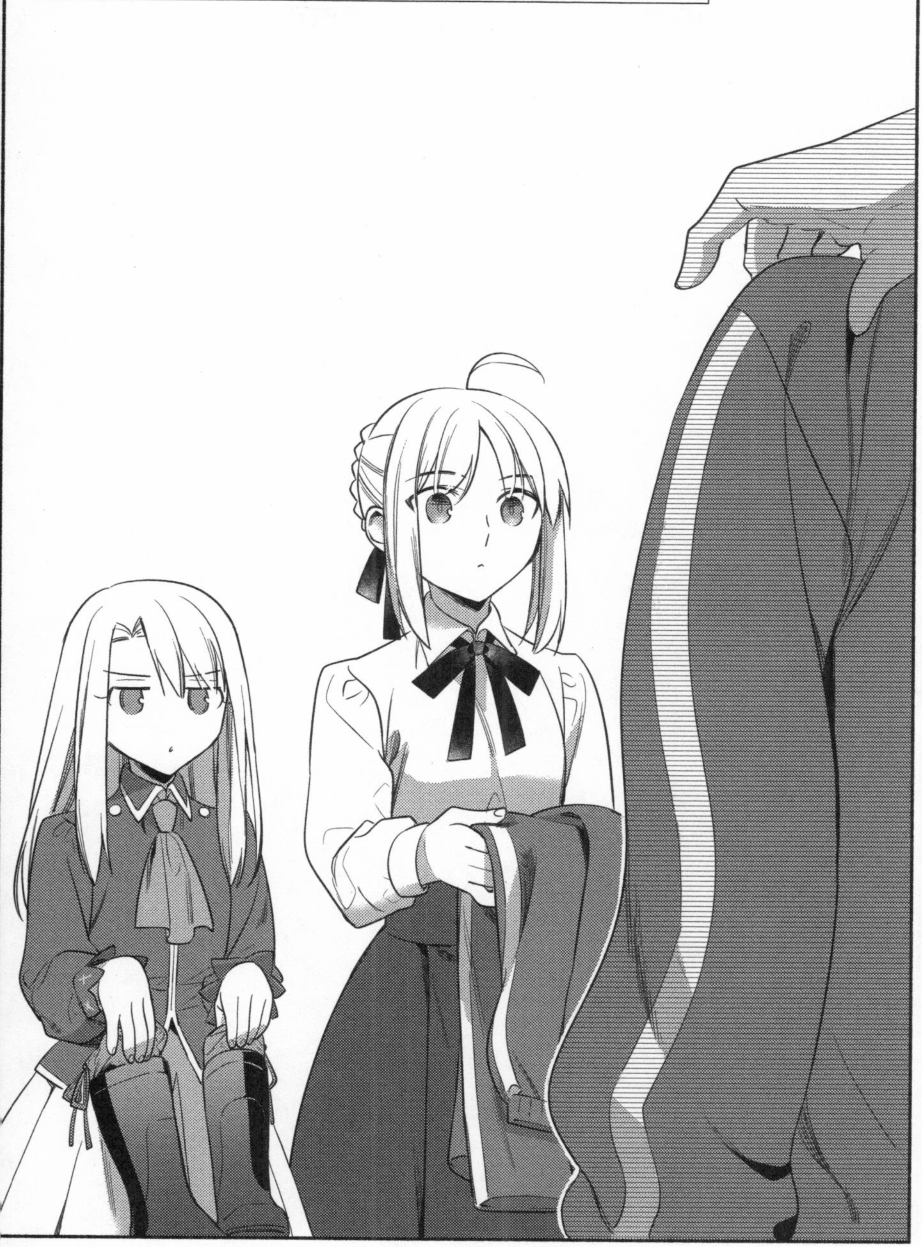

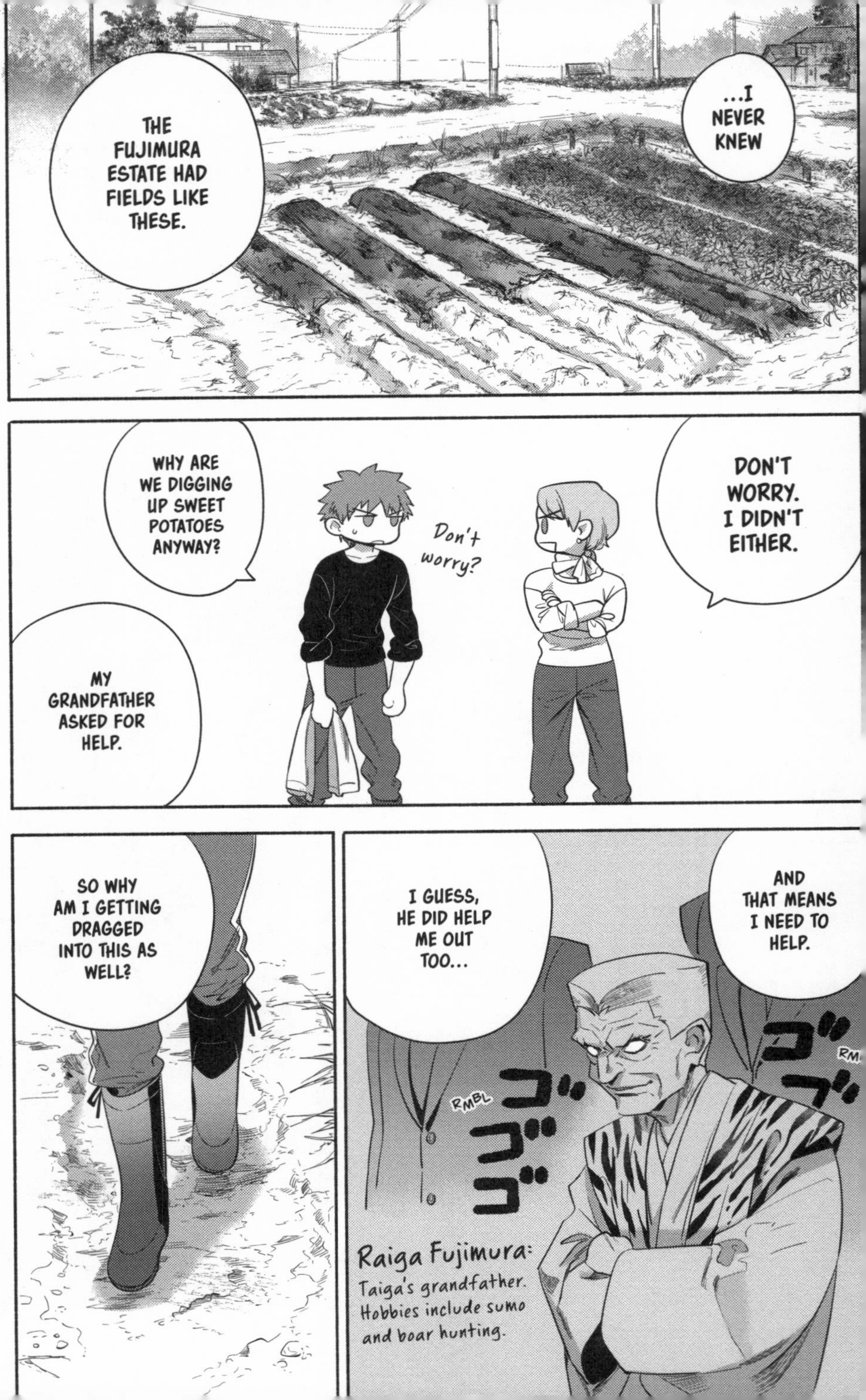

...I NEVER KNEW
THE FUJIMURA ESTATE HAD FIELDS LIKE THESE.
DON'T WORRY. I DIDN'T EITHER.
Don't worry?
WHY ARE WE DIGGING UP SWEET POTATOES ANYWAY?
MY GRANDFATHER ASKED FOR HELP.
AND THAT MEANS I NEED TO HELP.
I GUESS, HE DID HELP ME OUT TOO...
RMBL
ゴゴゴ
Raiga Fujimura:
Taiga's grandfather. Hobbies include sumo and boar hunting.
SO WHY AM I GETTING DRAGGED INTO THIS AS WELL?

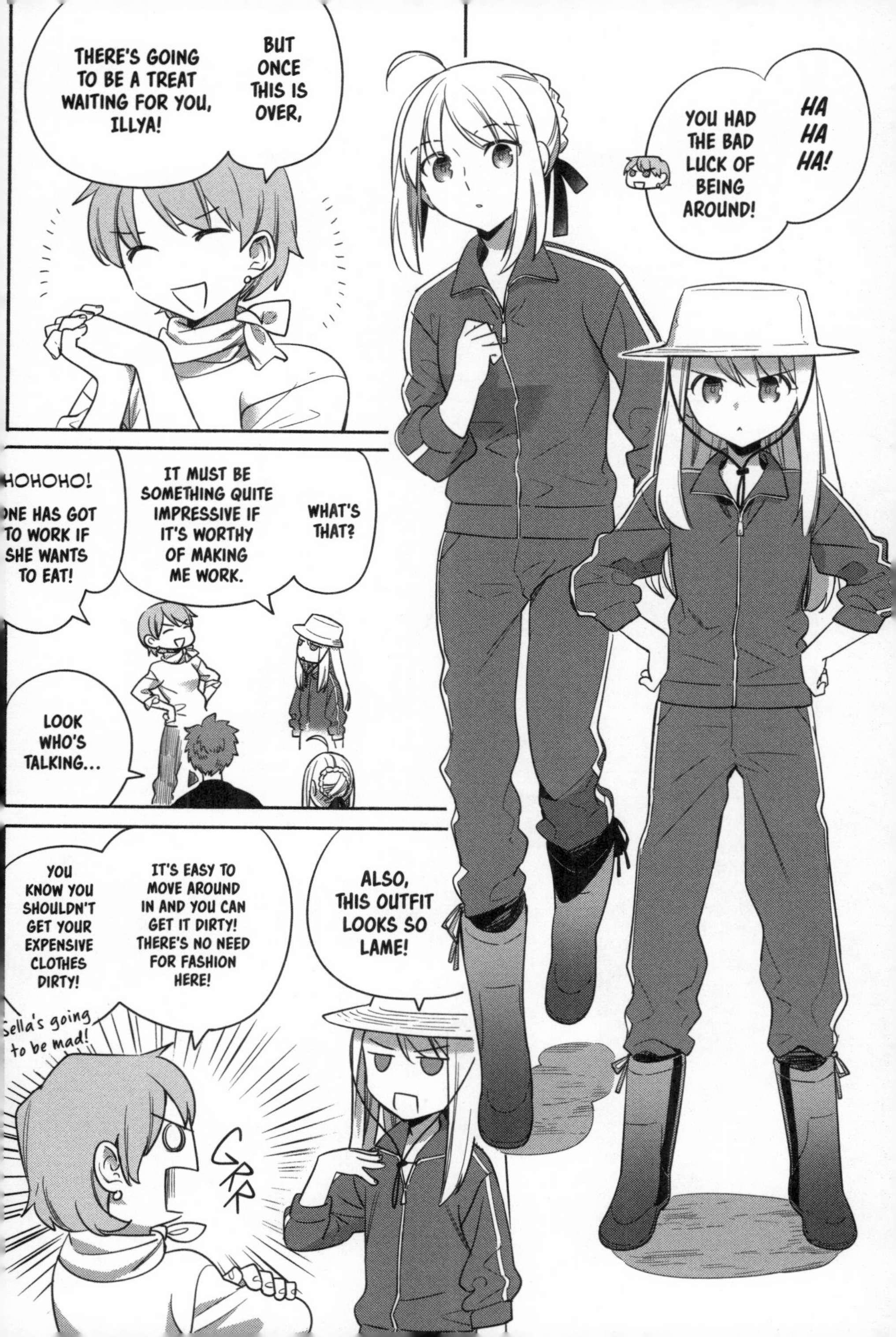
HA HA HA!
YOU HAD THE BAD LUCK OF BEING AROUND!
BUT ONCE THIS IS OVER,
THERE'S GOING TO BE A TREAT WAITING FOR YOU, ILLYA!
WHAT'S THAT?
IT MUST BE SOMETHING QUITE IMPRESSIVE IF IT'S WORTHY OF MAKING ME WORK.
HOHOHO!
ONE HAS GOT TO WORK IF SHE WANTS TO EAT!
LOOK WHO'S TALKING...
ALSO, THIS OUTFIT LOOKS SO LAME!
IT'S EASY TO MOVE AROUND IN AND YOU CAN GET IT DIRTY! THERE'S NO NEED FOR FASHION HERE!
YOU KNOW YOU SHOULDN'T GET YOUR EXPENSIVE CLOTHES DIRTY!
Sella's going to be mad!
GRR

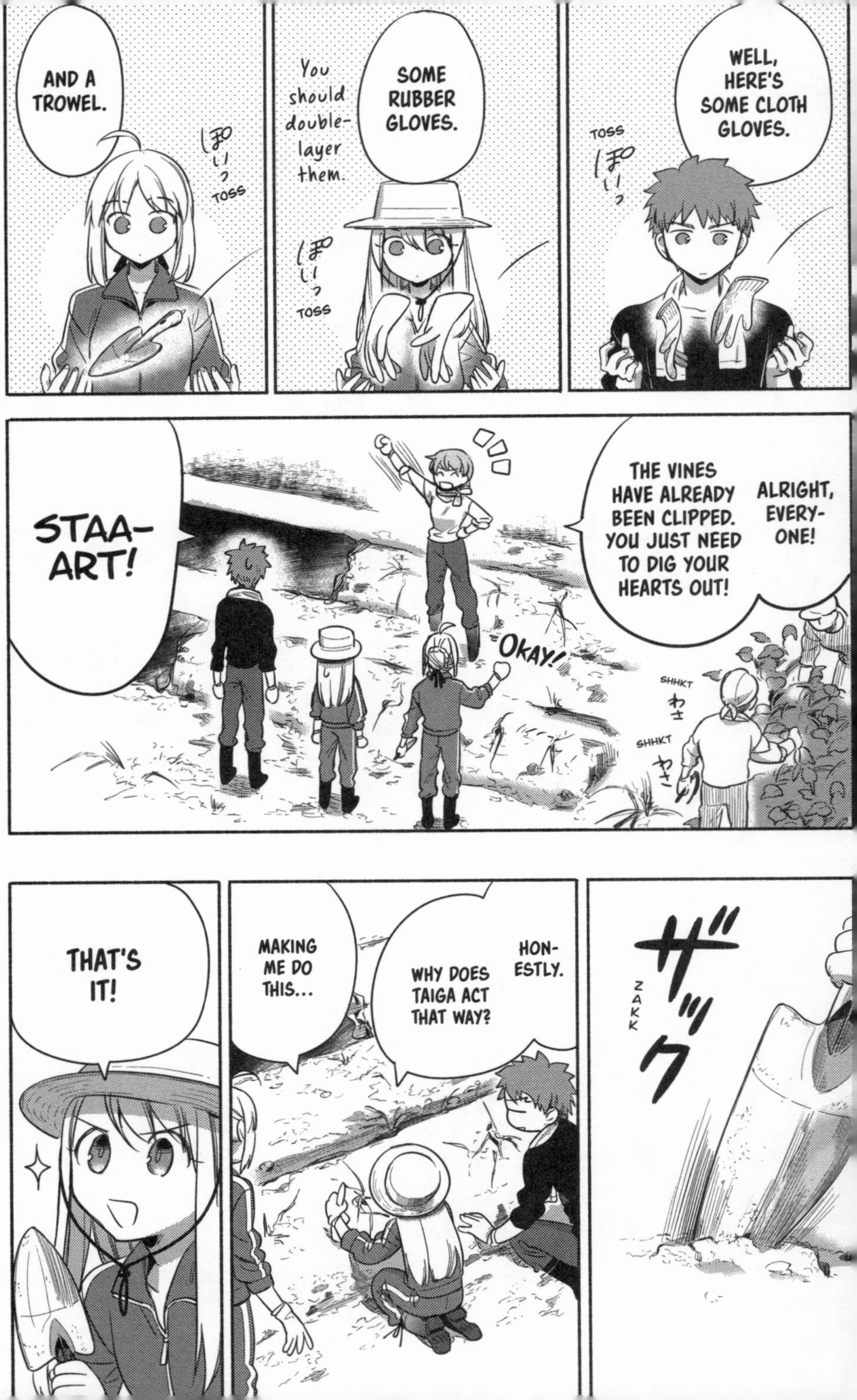
WELL, HERE'S SOME CLOTH GLOVES.
TOSS
ぽいっ
SOME RUBBER GLOVES.
You should double-layer them.
ぽいっ
TOSS
AND A TROWEL.
ぽいっ
TOSS
ALRIGHT, EVERY-ONE!
THE VINES HAVE ALREADY BEEN CLIPPED. YOU JUST NEED TO DIG YOUR HEARTS OUT!
STAA-ART!
OKAY!
SHHKT
わさ
SHHKT
わさ
ザック
ZAKK
HON-ESTLY.
WHY DOES TAIGA ACT THAT WAY?
MAKING ME DO THIS...
THAT'S IT!

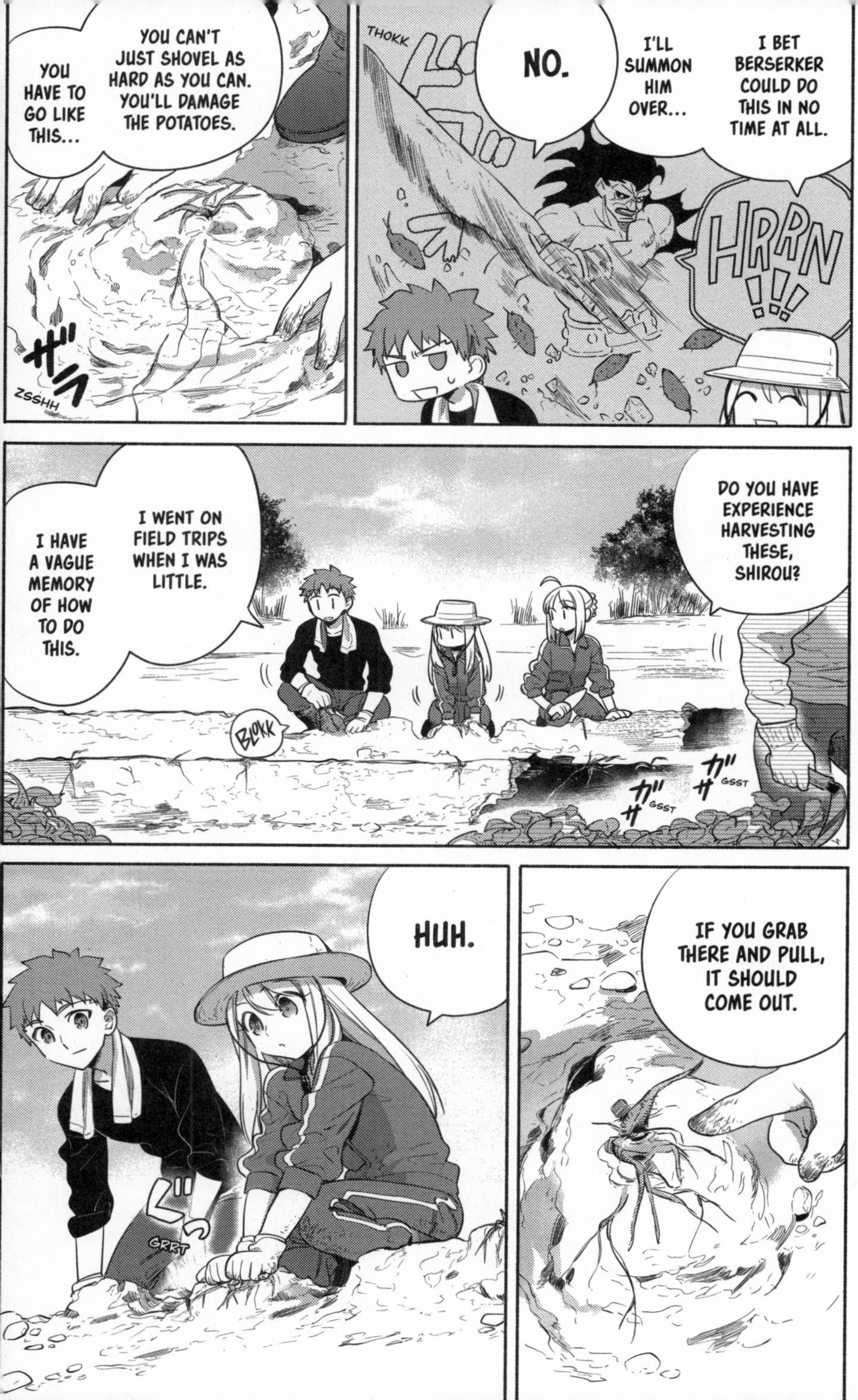
I BET BERSERKER COULD DO THIS IN NO TIME AT ALL.
I'LL SUMMON HIM OVER...
NO.
THOKK
HRRN!!!
YOU CAN'T JUST SHOVEL AS HARD AS YOU CAN. YOU'LL DAMAGE THE POTATOES.
YOU HAVE TO GO LIKE THIS...
ZSSHH
DO YOU HAVE EXPERIENCE HARVESTING THESE, SHIROU?
I WENT ON FIELD TRIPS WHEN I WAS LITTLE.
I HAVE A VAGUE MEMORY OF HOW TO DO THIS.
GSST
GSST
BLOKK
IF YOU GRAB THERE AND PULL, IT SHOULD COME OUT.
HUH.
GRRT

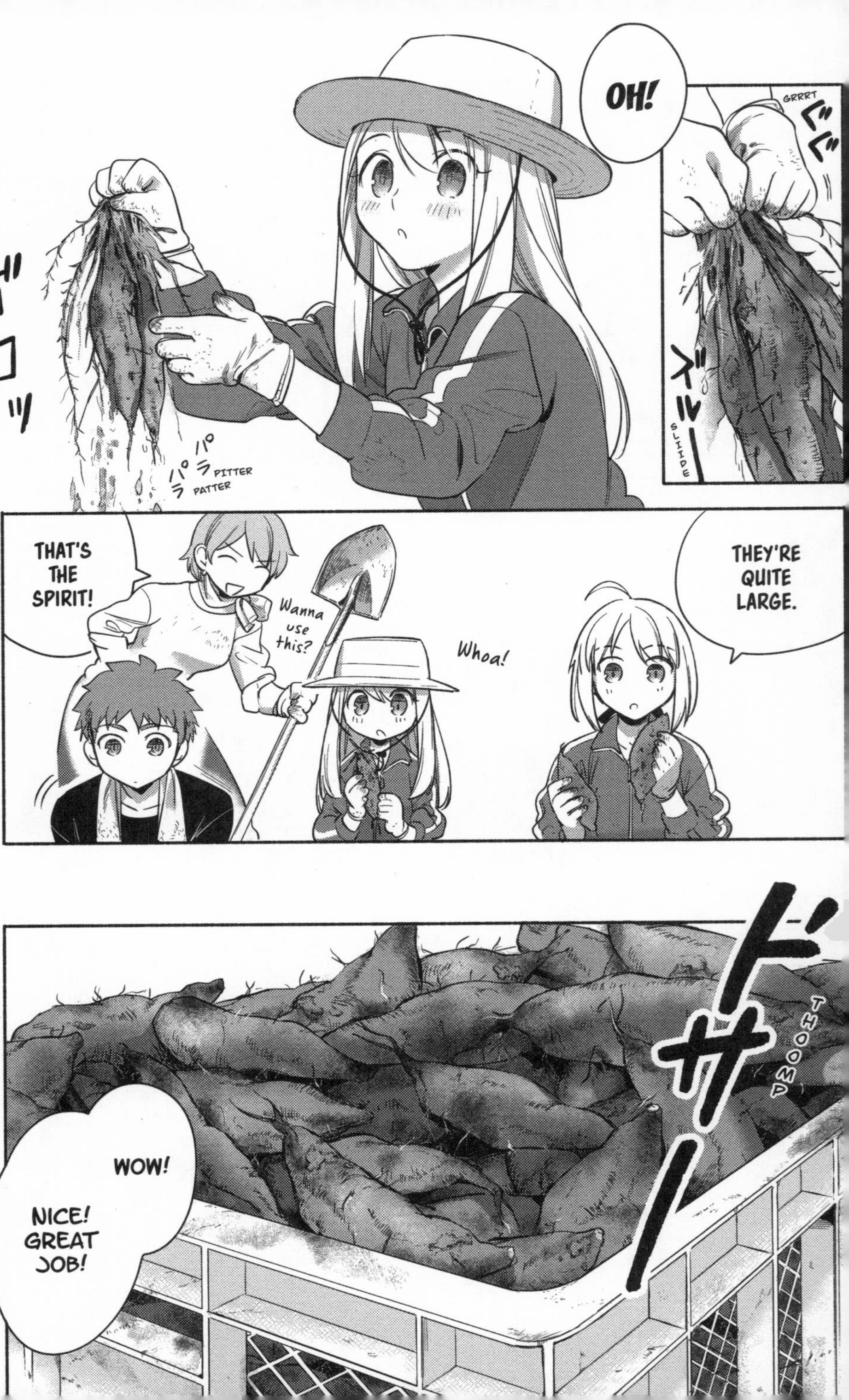

ググ
GRRRT
ズル
SLIIDE
OH!
ボコッ
BLOKK
パラパラ
PITTER PATTER
THEY'RE QUITE LARGE.
Whoa!
Wanna use this?
THAT'S THE SPIRIT!
ドサー
THOOMP
WOW!
NICE! GREAT JOB!

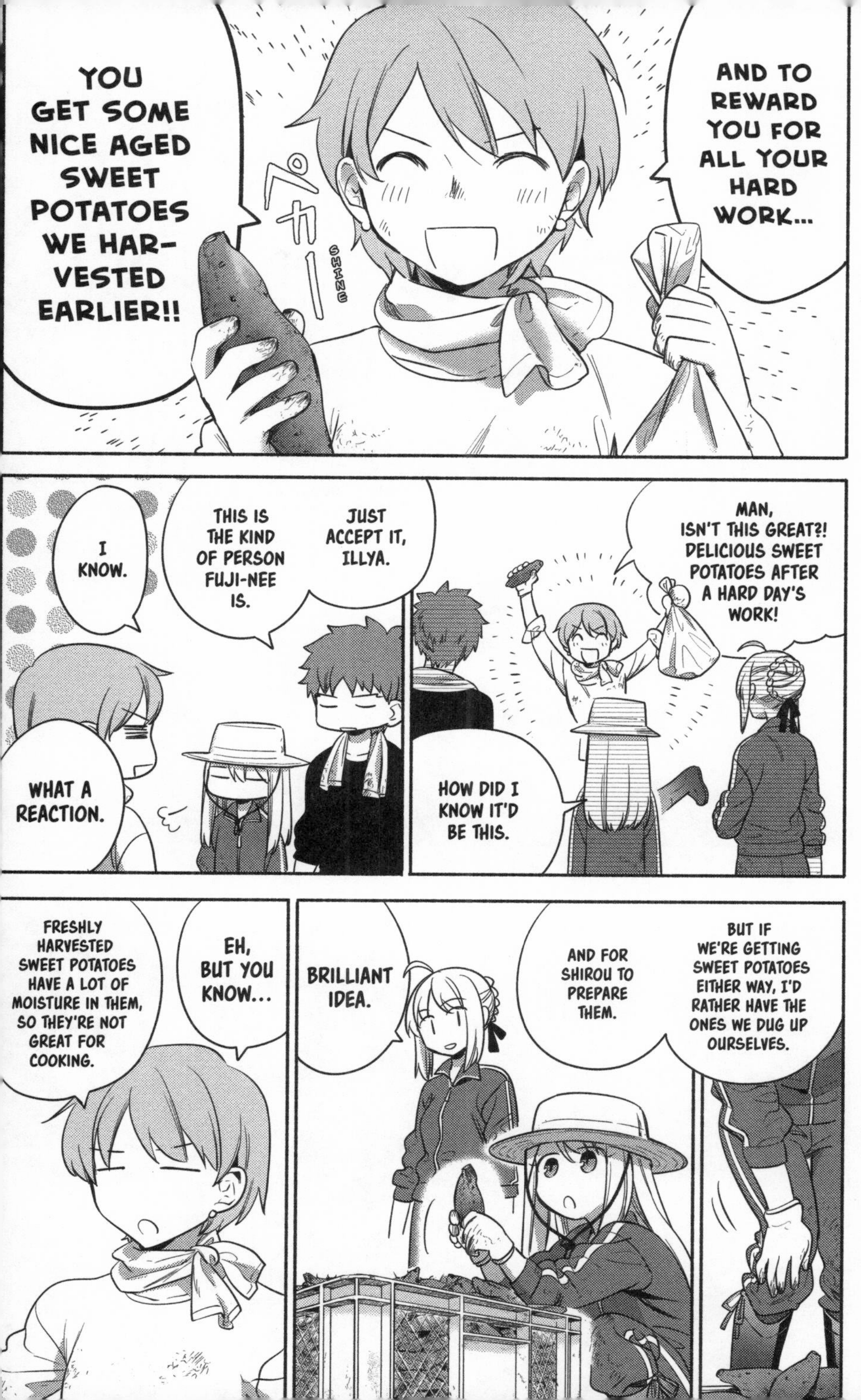
AND TO REWARD YOU FOR ALL YOUR HARD WORK...
ペカー
SHINE
YOU GET SOME NICE AGED SWEET POTATOES WE HAR-VESTED EARLIER!!
MAN, ISN'T THIS GREAT?! DELICIOUS SWEET POTATOES AFTER A HARD DAY'S WORK!
HOW DID I KNOW IT'D BE THIS.
JUST ACCEPT IT, ILLYA.
THIS IS THE KIND OF PERSON FUJI-NEE IS.
I KNOW.
WHAT A REACTION.
BUT IF WE'RE GETTING SWEET POTATOES EITHER WAY, I'D RATHER HAVE THE ONES WE DUG UP OURSELVES.
AND FOR SHIROU TO PREPARE THEM.
BRILLIANT IDEA.
EH, BUT YOU KNOW...
FRESHLY HARVESTED SWEET POTATOES HAVE A LOT OF MOISTURE IN THEM, SO THEY'RE NOT GREAT FOR COOKING.

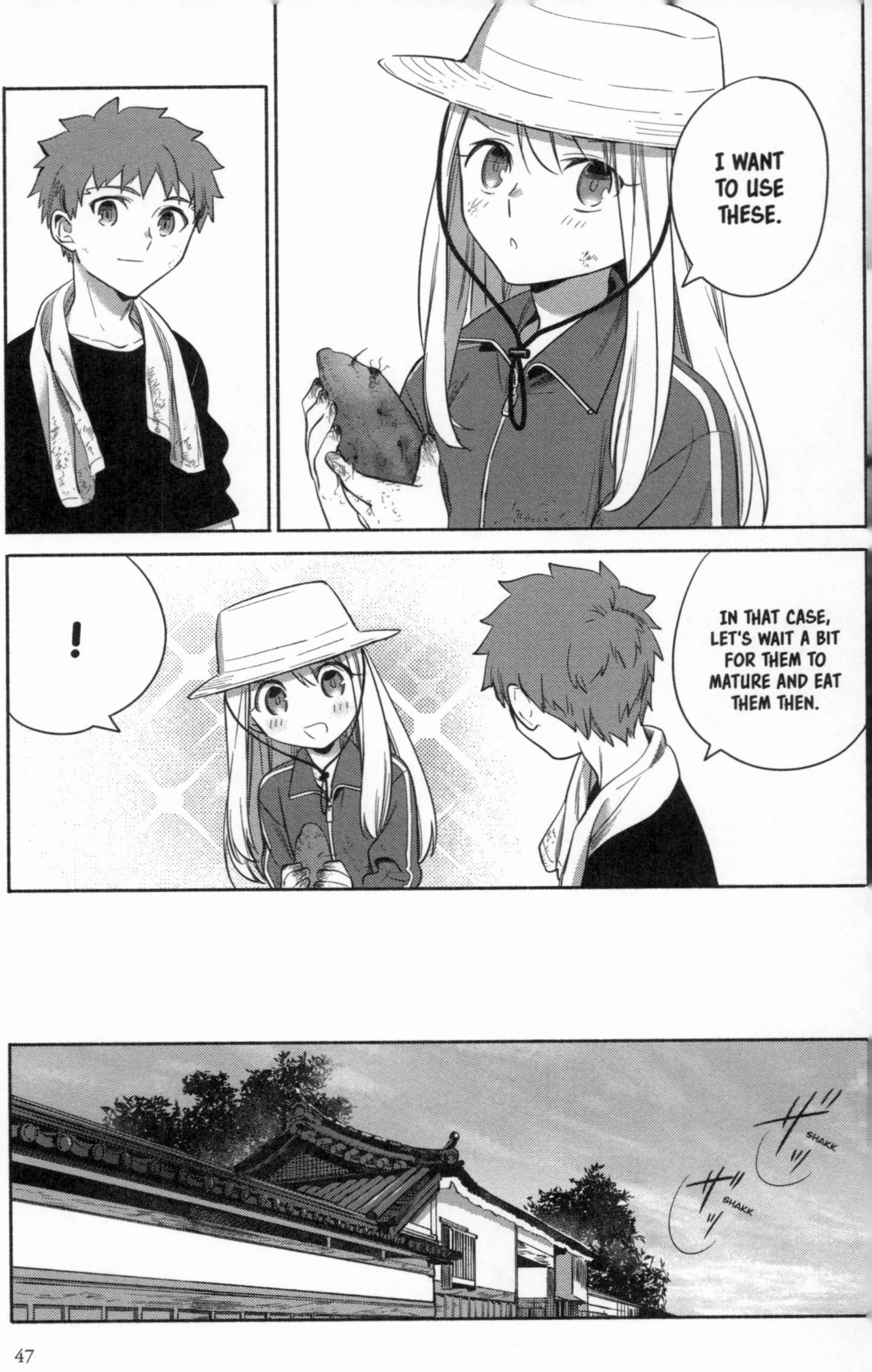
I WANT TO USE THESE.
IN THAT CASE, LET'S WAIT A BIT FOR THEM TO MATURE AND EAT THEM THEN.
!
SHAKK
SHAKK

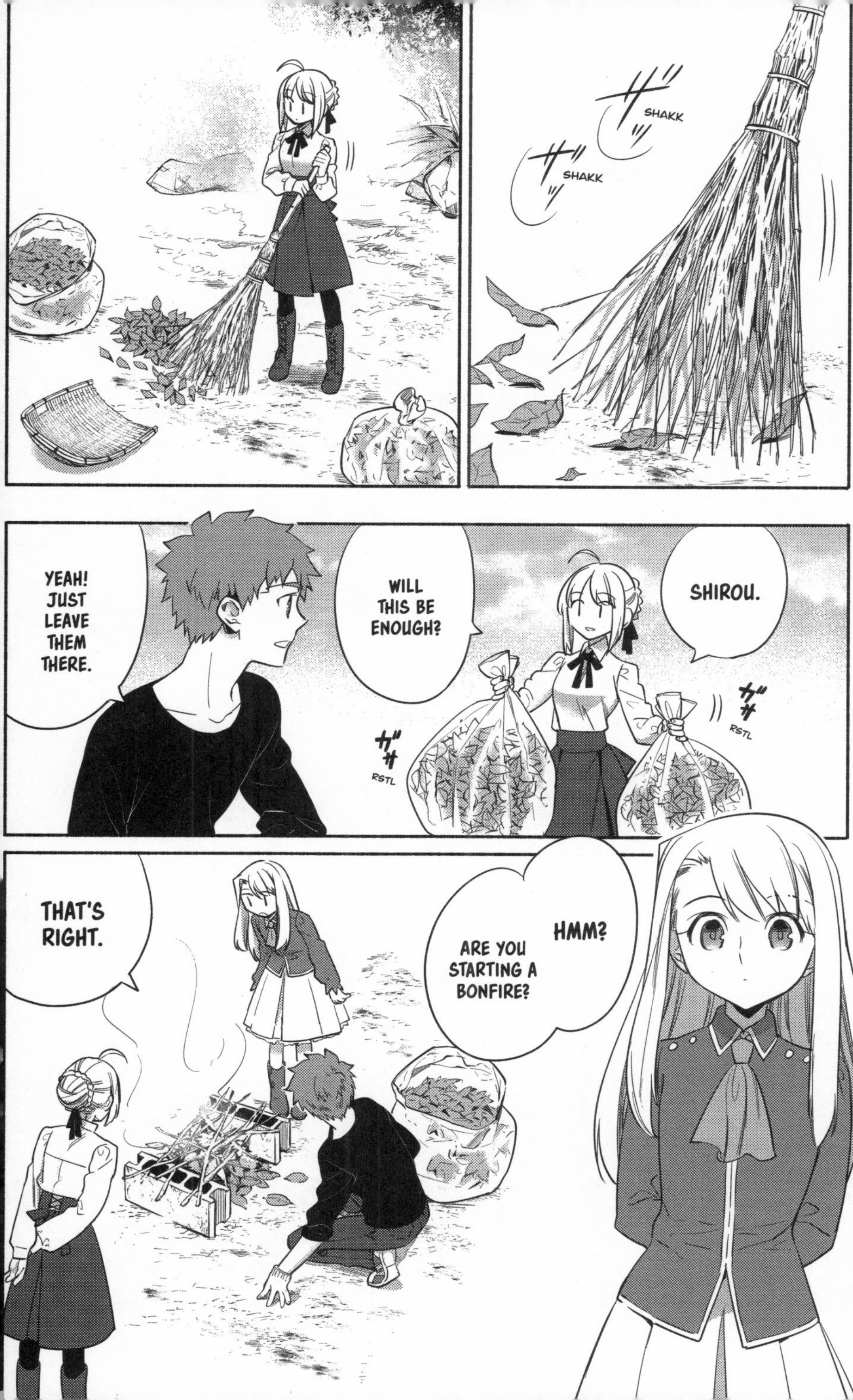

ザッ
SHAKK
ザッ
SHAKK
SHIROU.
ガサ
RSTL
WILL THIS BE ENOUGH?
ガサ
RSTL
YEAH! JUST LEAVE THEM THERE.
HMM?
ARE YOU STARTING A BONFIRE?
THAT'S RIGHT.

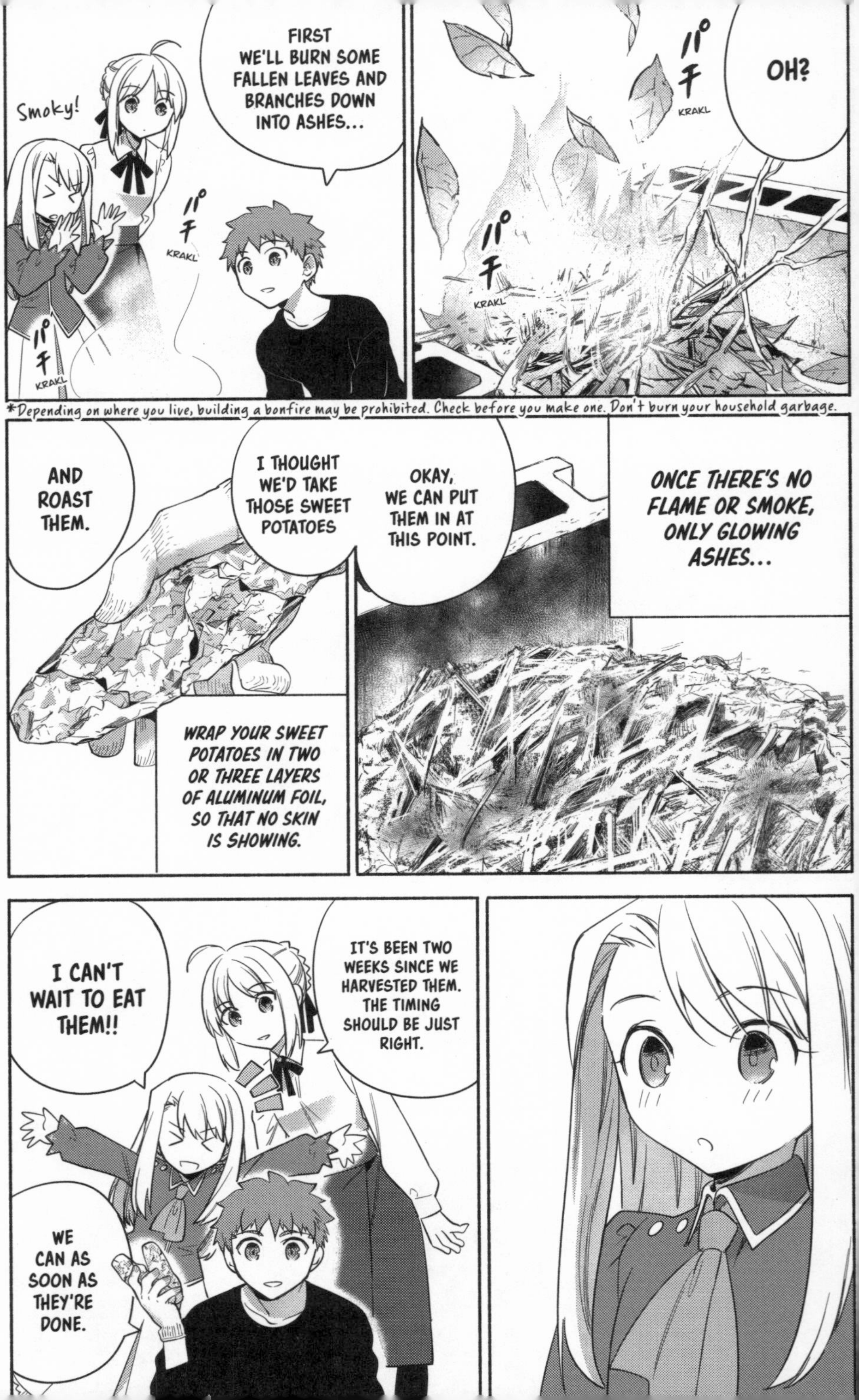
パチ
KRAKL
OH?
パチ
KRAKL
FIRST WE'LL BURN SOME FALLEN LEAVES AND BRANCHES DOWN INTO ASHES...
Smoky!
パチ
KRAKL
パチ
KRAKL
*Depending on where you live, building a bonfire may be prohibited. Check before you make one. Don't burn your household garbage.
ONCE THERE'S NO FLAME OR SMOKE, ONLY GLOWING ASHES...
OKAY, WE CAN PUT THEM IN AT THIS POINT.
I THOUGHT WE'D TAKE THOSE SWEET POTATOES
AND ROAST THEM.
WRAP YOUR SWEET POTATOES IN TWO OR THREE LAYERS OF ALUMINUM FOIL, SO THAT NO SKIN IS SHOWING.
IT'S BEEN TWO WEEKS SINCE WE HARVESTED THEM. THE TIMING SHOULD BE JUST RIGHT.
I CAN'T WAIT TO EAT THEM!!
WE CAN AS SOON AS THEY'RE DONE.

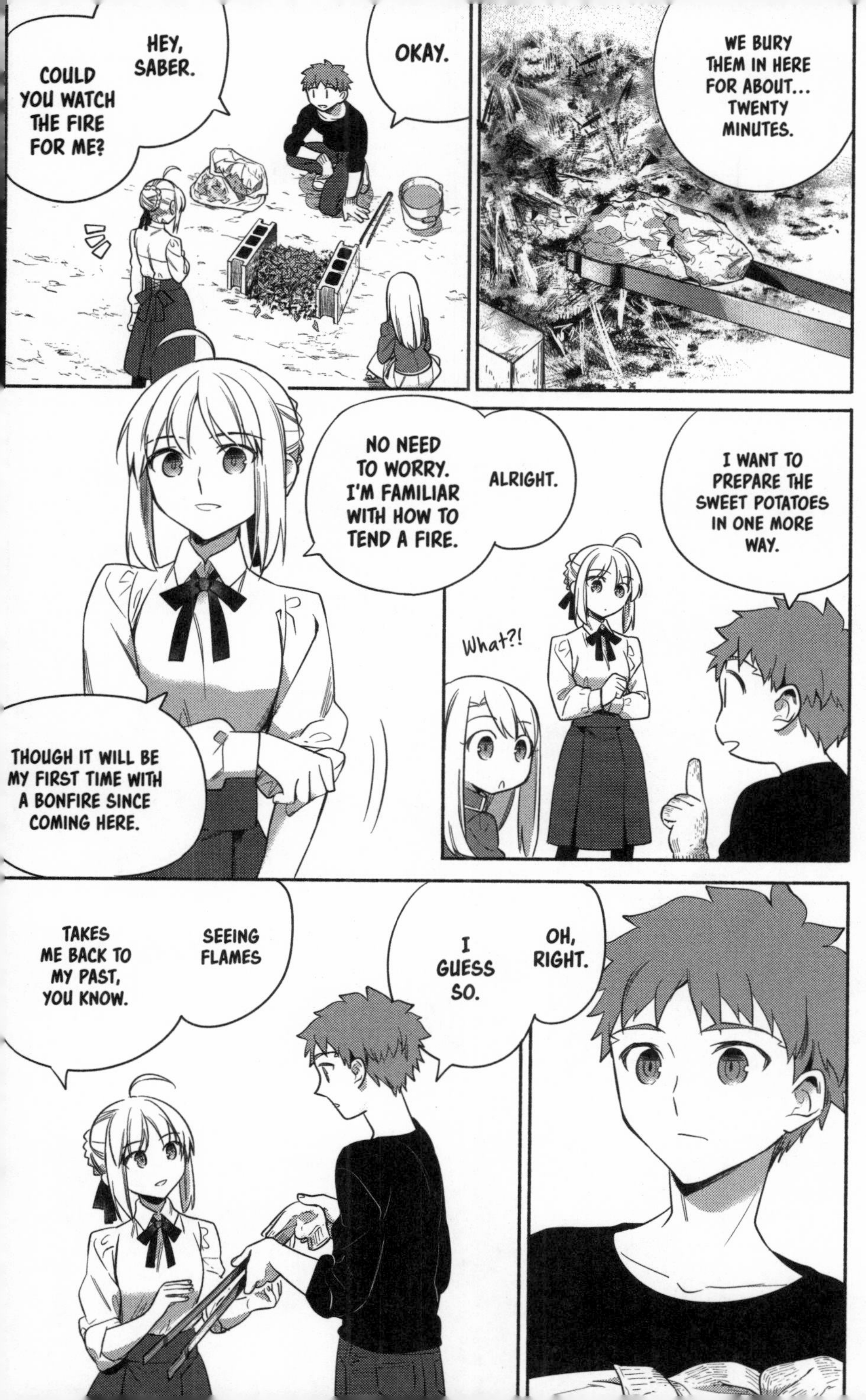
WE BURY THEM IN HERE FOR ABOUT... TWENTY MINUTES.
HEY, SABER. COULD YOU WATCH THE FIRE FOR ME?
OKAY.
I WANT TO PREPARE THE SWEET POTATOES IN ONE MORE WAY.
What?!
ALRIGHT.
NO NEED TO WORRY. I'M FAMILIAR WITH HOW TO TEND A FIRE.
THOUGH IT WILL BE MY FIRST TIME WITH A BONFIRE SINCE COMING HERE.
OH, RIGHT.
I GUESS SO.
SEEING FLAMES
TAKES ME BACK TO MY PAST, YOU KNOW.

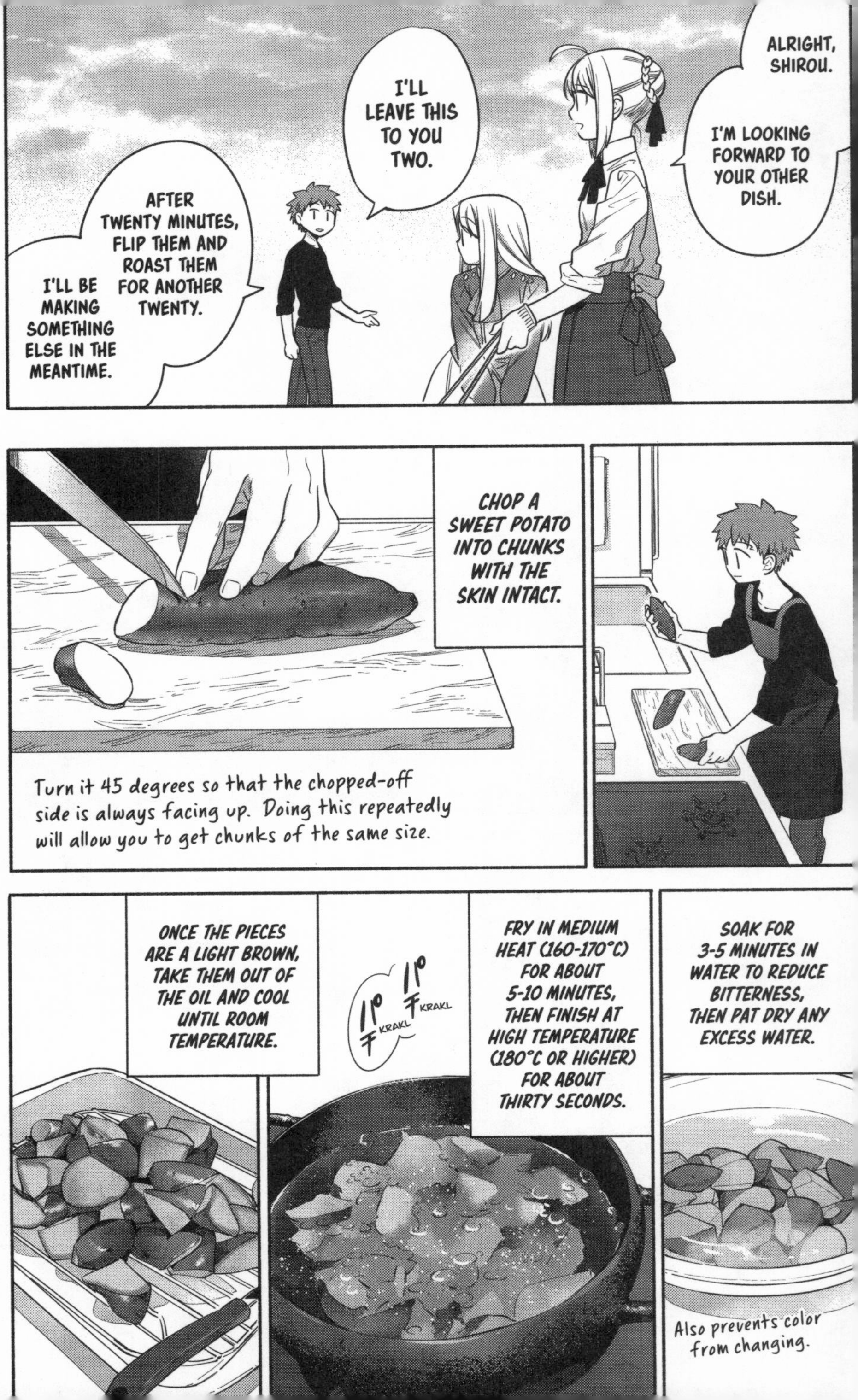
ALRIGHT, SHIROU.
I'M LOOKING FORWARD TO YOUR OTHER DISH.
I'LL LEAVE THIS TO YOU TWO.
AFTER TWENTY MINUTES, FLIP THEM AND ROAST THEM FOR ANOTHER TWENTY.
I'LL BE MAKING SOMETHING ELSE IN THE MEANTIME.
CHOP A SWEET POTATO INTO CHUNKS WITH THE SKIN INTACT.
Turn it 45 degrees so that the chopped-off side is always facing up. Doing this repeatedly will allow you to get chunks of the same size.
SOAK FOR 3-5 MINUTES IN WATER TO REDUCE BITTERNESS, THEN PAT DRY ANY EXCESS WATER.
Also prevents color from changing.
FRY IN MEDIUM HEAT (160-170°C) FOR ABOUT 5-10 MINUTES, THEN FINISH AT HIGH TEMPERATURE (180°C OR HIGHER) FOR ABOUT THIRTY SECONDS.
KRAKL
KRAKL
ONCE THE PIECES ARE A LIGHT BROWN, TAKE THEM OUT OF THE OIL AND COOL UNTIL ROOM TEMPERATURE.

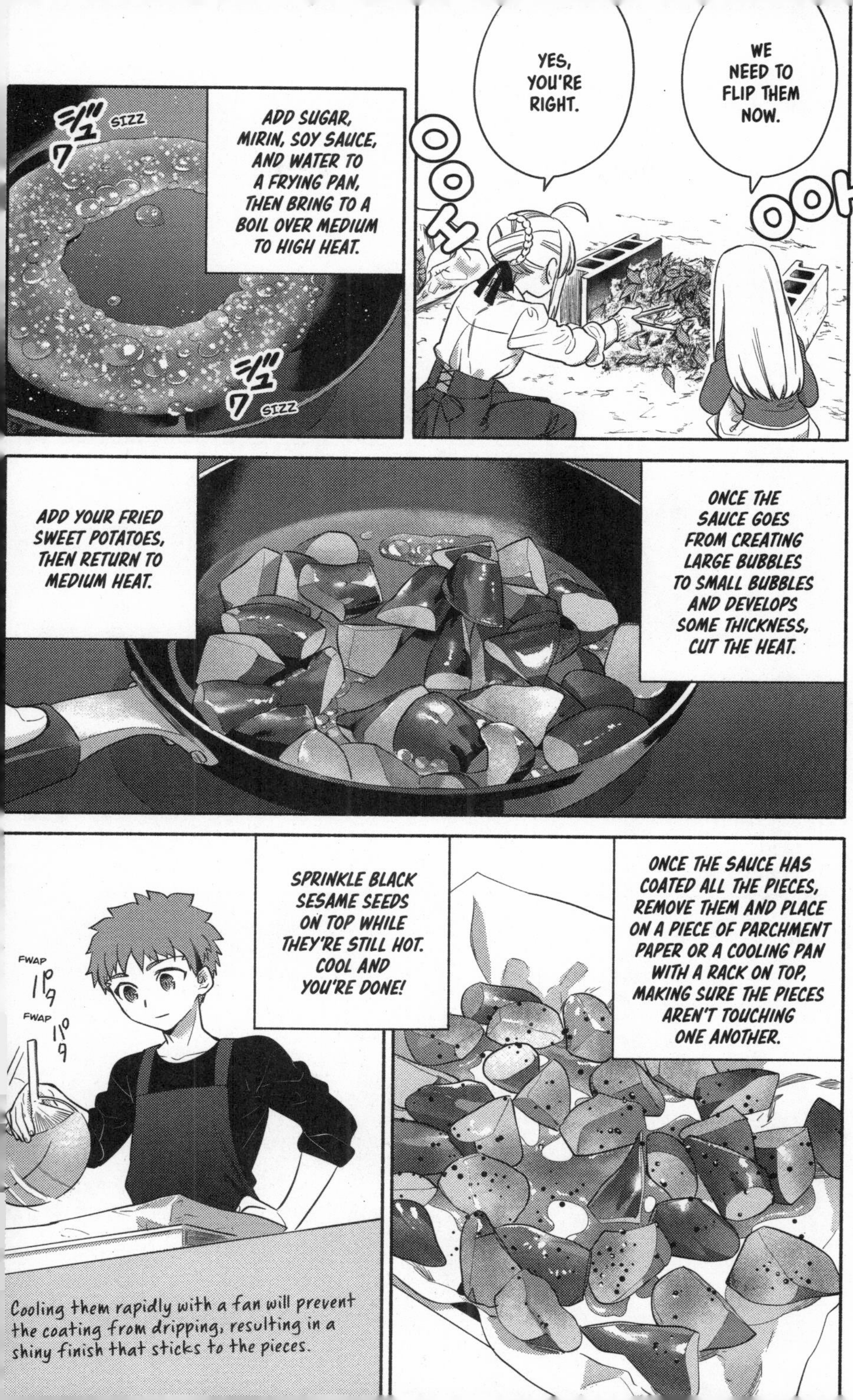
WE NEED TO FLIP THEM NOW.
YES, YOU'RE RIGHT.
OOH
OOH
ADD SUGAR, MIRIN, SOY SAUCE, AND WATER TO A FRYING PAN, THEN BRING TO A BOIL OVER MEDIUM TO HIGH HEAT.
ジュワ
SIZZ
ジュワ
SIZZ
ONCE THE SAUCE GOES FROM CREATING LARGE BUBBLES TO SMALL BUBBLES AND DEVELOPS SOME THICKNESS, CUT THE HEAT.
ADD YOUR FRIED SWEET POTATOES, THEN RETURN TO MEDIUM HEAT.
ONCE THE SAUCE HAS COATED ALL THE PIECES, REMOVE THEM AND PLACE ON A PIECE OF PARCHMENT PAPER OR A COOLING PAN WITH A RACK ON TOP, MAKING SURE THE PIECES AREN'T TOUCHING ONE ANOTHER.
SPRINKLE BLACK SESAME SEEDS ON TOP WHILE THEY'RE STILL HOT. COOL AND YOU'RE DONE!
パタ
FWAP
パタ
FWAP
Cooling them rapidly with a fan will prevent the coating from dripping, resulting in a shiny finish that sticks to the pieces.

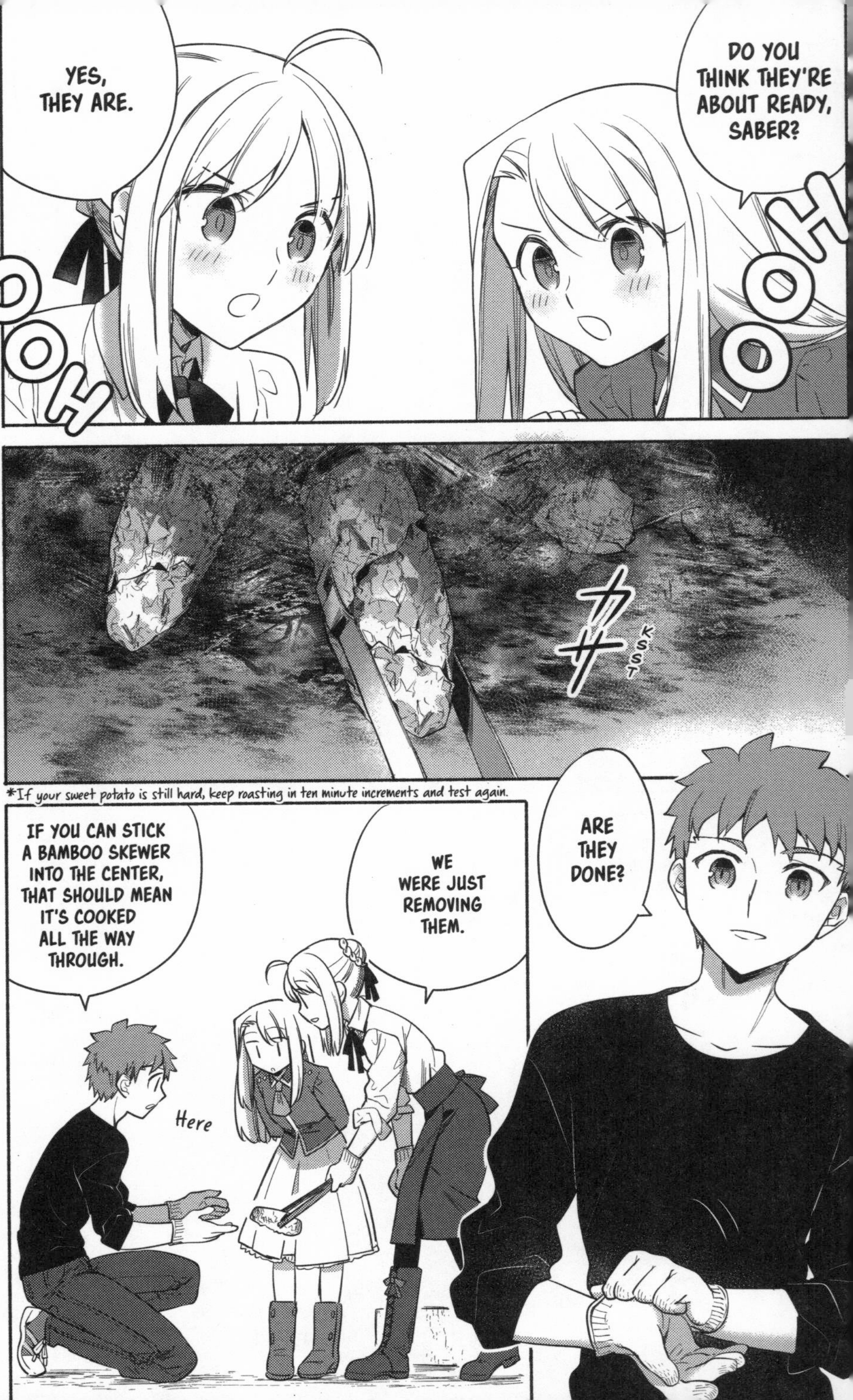
DO YOU THINK THEY'RE ABOUT READY, SABER?
OOH
YES, THEY ARE.
OOH
KSST
ARE THEY DONE?
WE WERE JUST REMOVING THEM.
IF YOU CAN STICK A BAMBOO SKEWER INTO THE CENTER, THAT SHOULD MEAN IT'S COOKED ALL THE WAY THROUGH.
Here

*If your sweet potato is still hard, keep roasting in ten minute increments and test again.

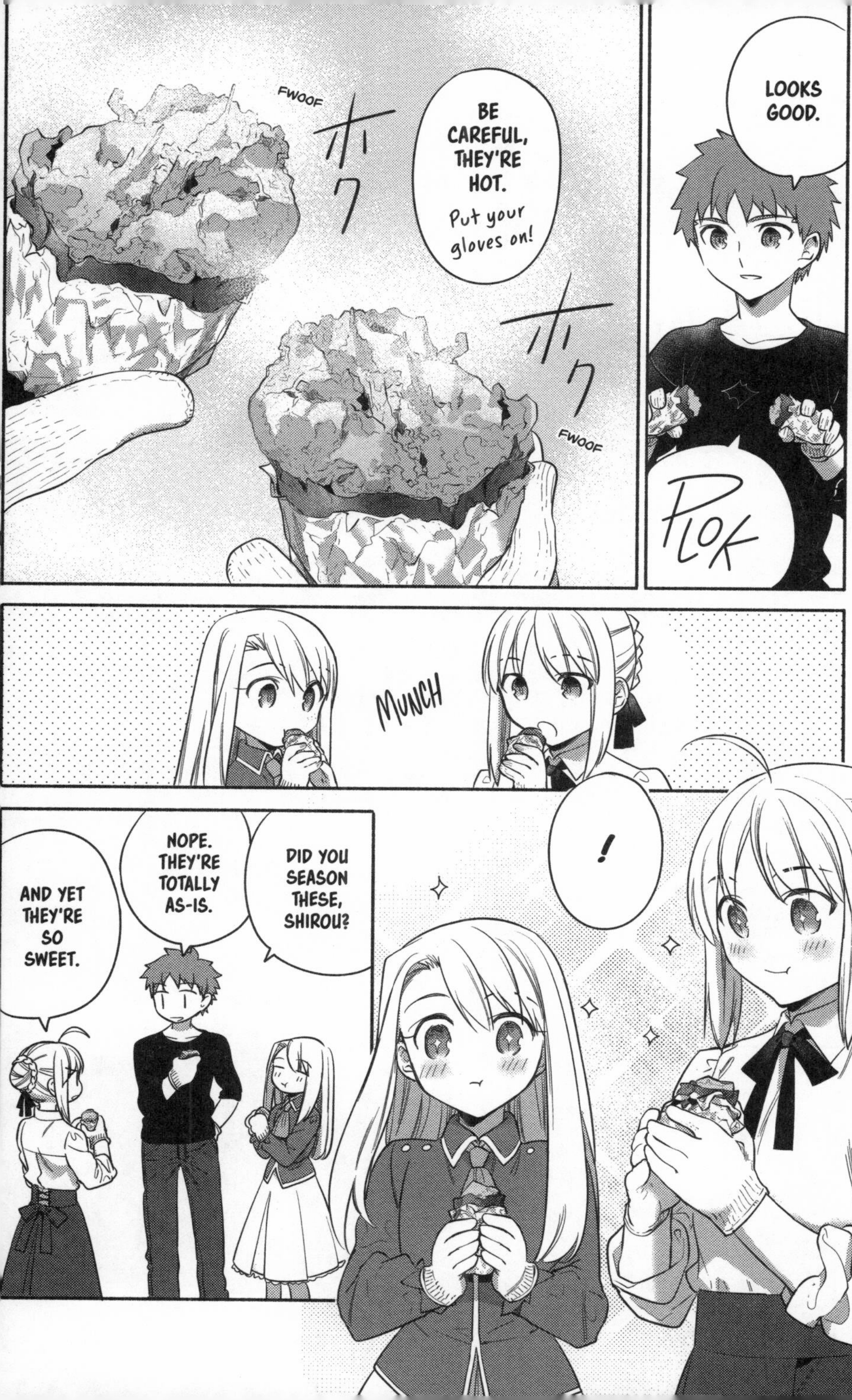
LOOKS GOOD.
PLOK
BE CAREFUL, THEY'RE HOT.
Put your gloves on!
FWOOF
ホク
ホク
FWOOF
MUNCH
!
DID YOU SEASON THESE, SHIROU?
NOPE. THEY'RE TOTALLY AS-IS.
AND YET THEY'RE SO SWEET.

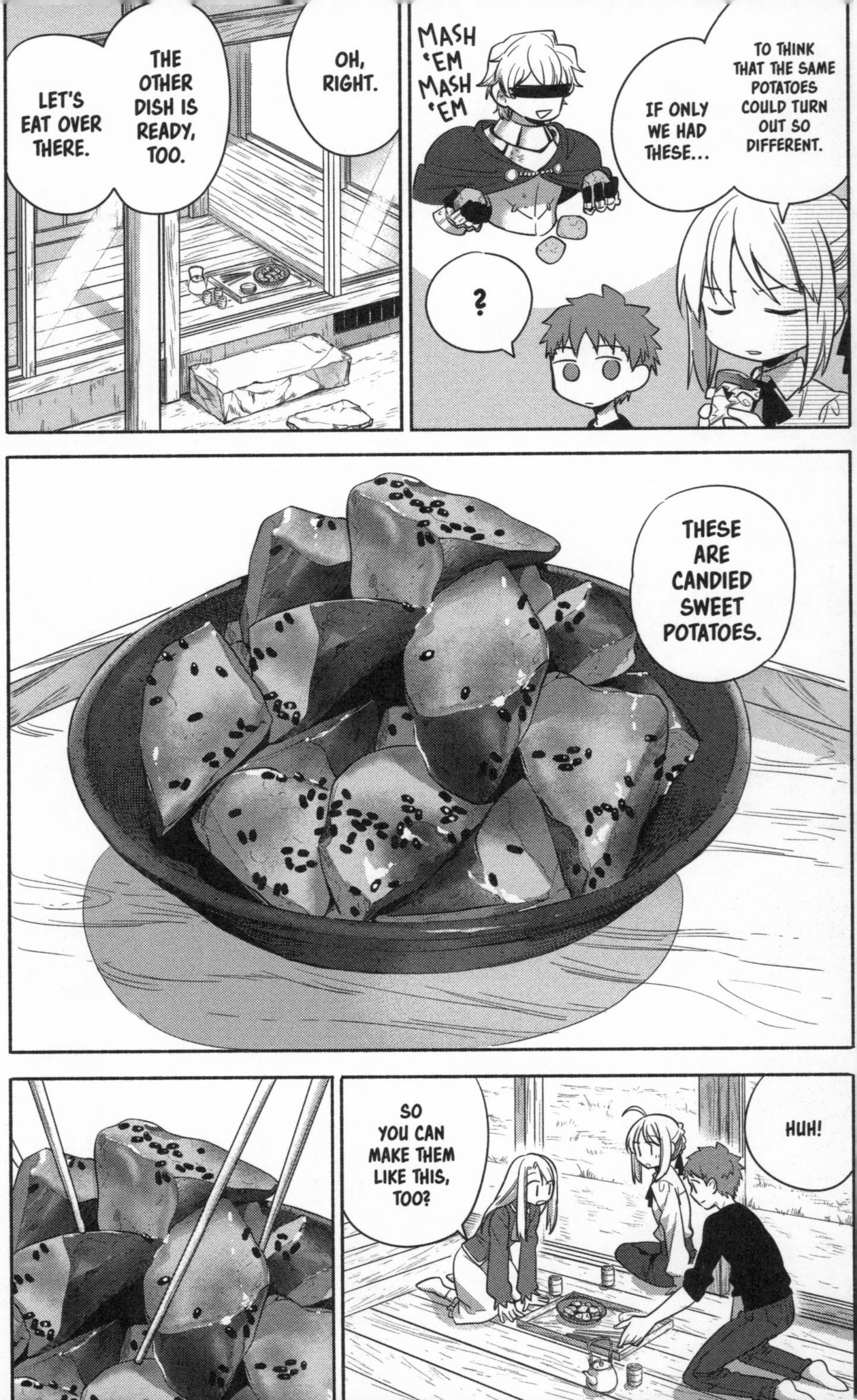
TO THINK THAT THE SAME POTATOES COULD TURN OUT SO DIFFERENT.
IF ONLY WE HAD THESE...
MASH 'EM MASH 'EM
?
OH, RIGHT.
THE OTHER DISH IS READY, TOO.
LET'S EAT OVER THERE.
THESE ARE CANDIED SWEET POTATOES.
HUH!
SO YOU CAN MAKE THEM LIKE THIS, TOO?

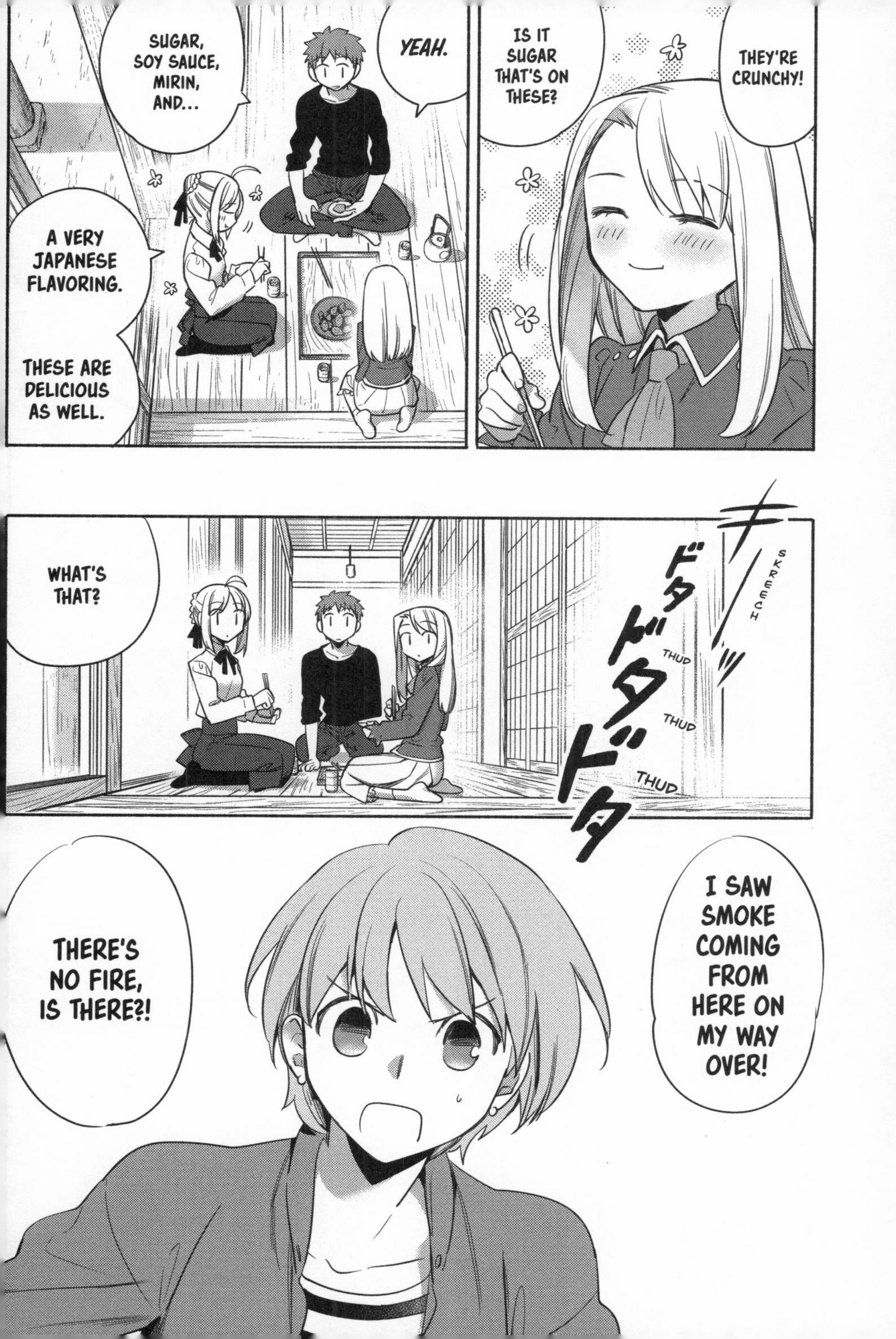
THEY'RE CRUNCHY!
IS IT SUGAR THAT'S ON THESE?
YEAH.
SUGAR, SOY SAUCE, MIRIN, AND...
A VERY JAPANESE FLAVORING.
THESE ARE DELICIOUS AS WELL.
キ—
SKREECH
ドタドタドタ
THUD
THUD
THUD
WHAT'S THAT?
I SAW SMOKE COMING FROM HERE ON MY WAY OVER!
THERE'S NO FIRE, IS THERE?!

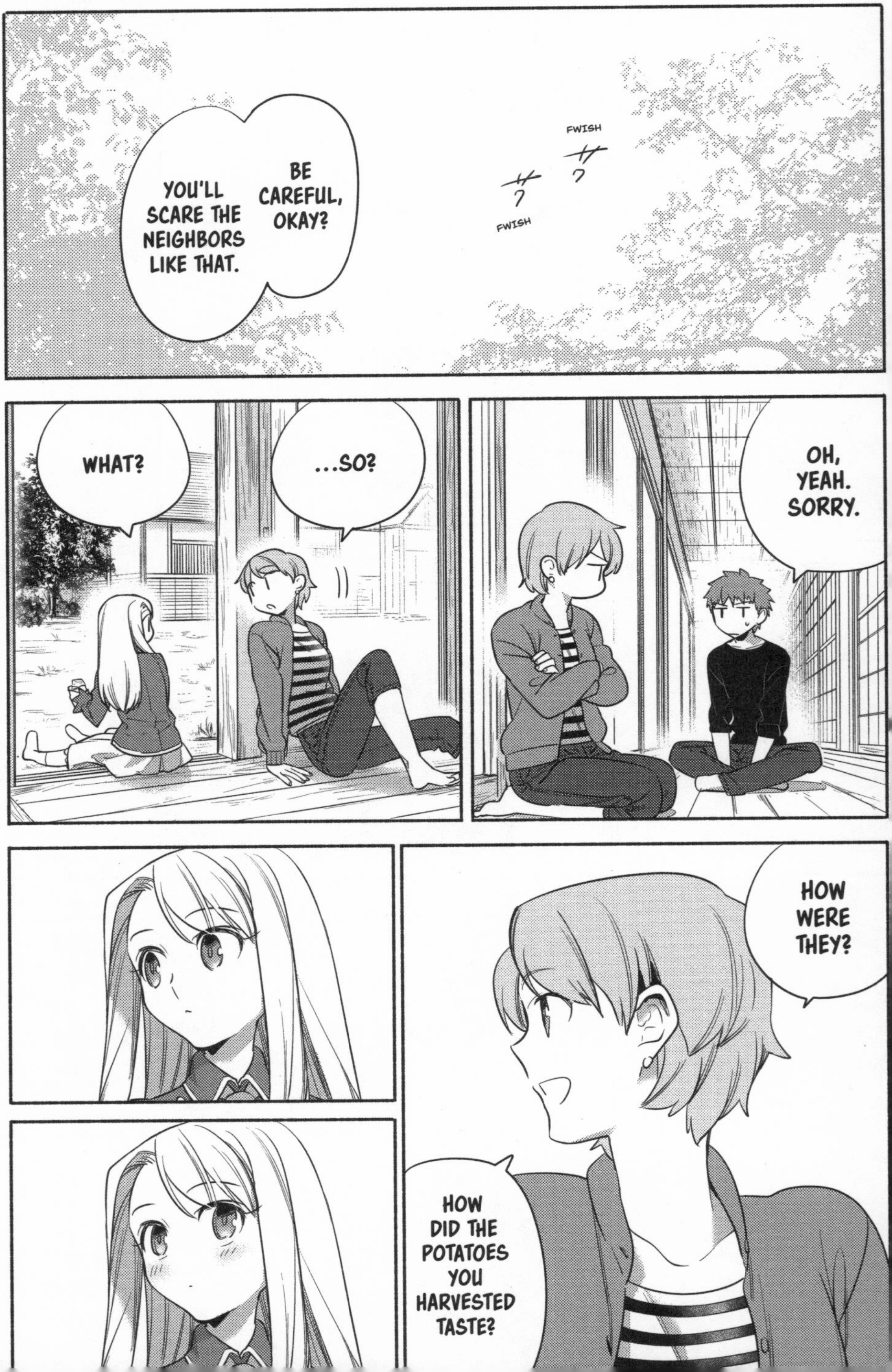
FWISH
FWISH
BE CAREFUL, OKAY?
YOU'LL SCARE THE NEIGHBORS LIKE THAT.
OH, YEAH. SORRY.
...SO?
WHAT?
HOW WERE THEY?
HOW DID THE POTATOES YOU HARVESTED TASTE?

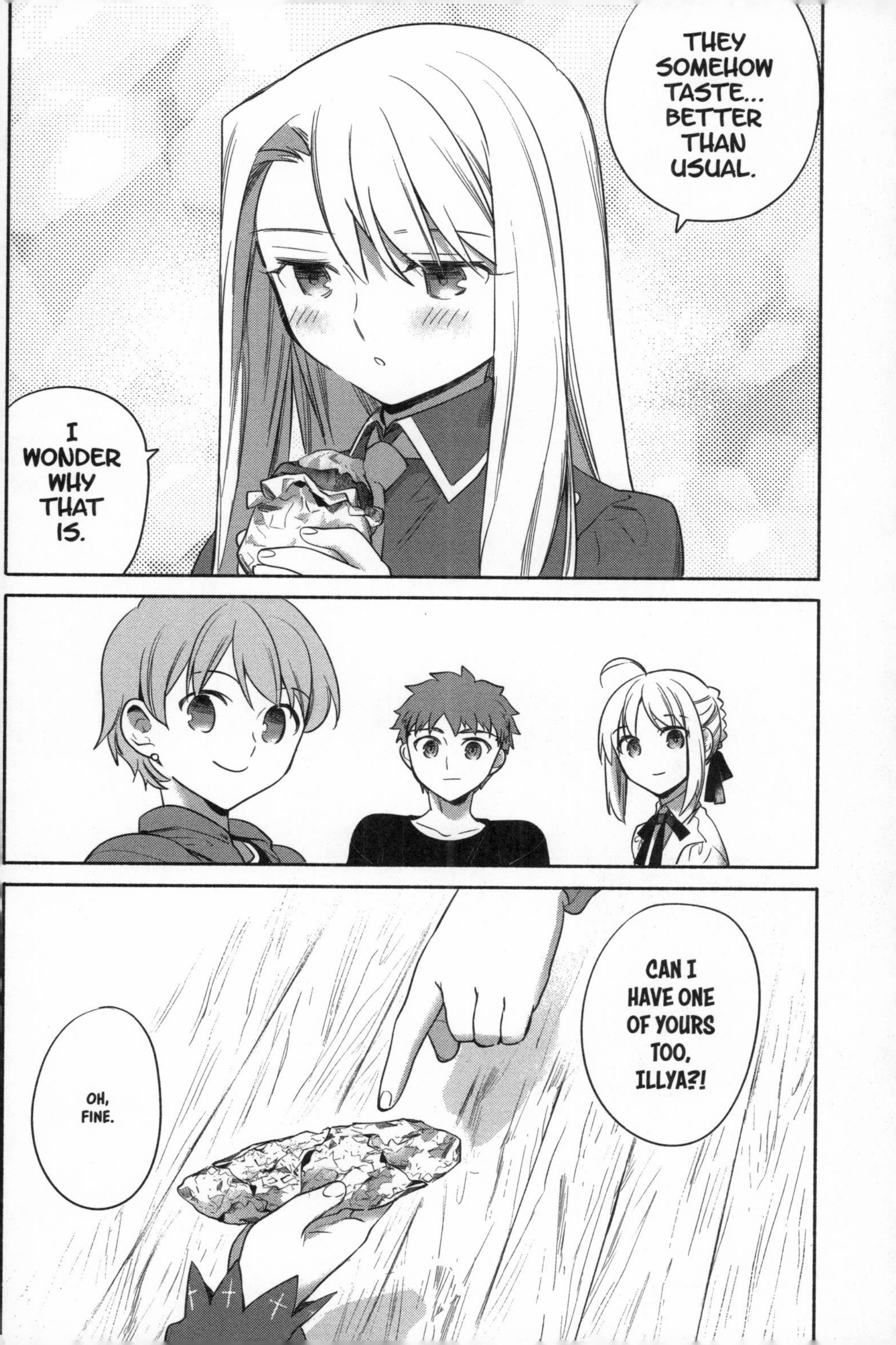
THEY SOMEHOW TASTE... BETTER THAN USUAL.
I WONDER WHY THAT IS.
CAN I HAVE ONE OF YOURS TOO, ILLYA?!
OH, FINE.

Roasted Sweet Potatoes

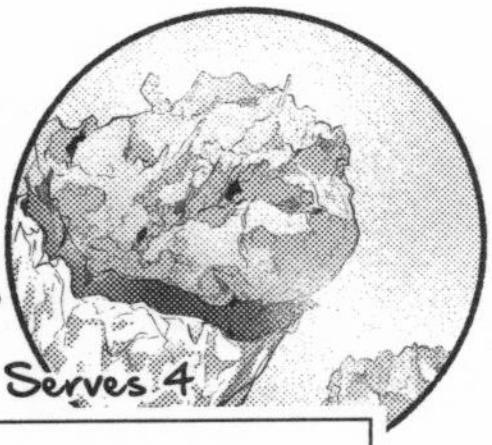

Ingredients - Serves 4

- 2-4 sweet potatoes
- Aluminum foil
- Bamboo skewers

In a Bonfire

1. Cover your sweet potatoes with two to three layers of aluminum foil so that you can't see any of the potato.
2. Burn some fallen leaves and branches down into ashes (where there's no flame or smoke, only glowing ashes), then bury the sweet potatoes from step 1 underneath and cook for 20 minutes. After that, flip and cook for another 20 minutes.
3. If you can pierce a potato to its center with a bamboo skewer and there's no resistance, you're done! (If it's still hard, keep cooking 10 minutes at a time and checking again.)

In a Toaster Oven

1. Cover your sweet potatoes with one or two layers of aluminum foil so that you can't see any of the potato.
   *This is to make sure enough moisture leaves the potato.
2. Cook for 15-20 minutes in your toaster oven, then flip and cook for another 15-20 minutes.
3. If you can pierce it to the center with a bamboo skewer and there's no resistance, you're done! (If it's still hard, keep cooking 10 minutes at a time and checking again.)

Candied Sweet Potatoes (Daigaku-imo)

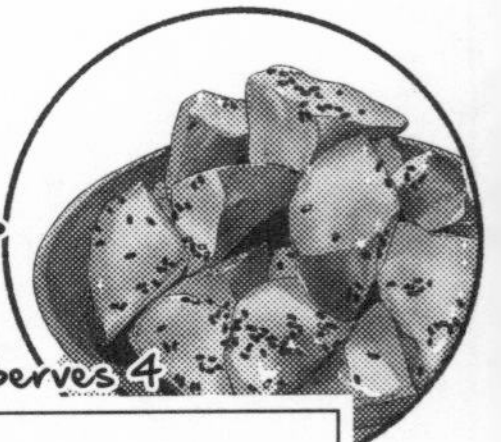

Ingredients - Serves 4

- 2-3 sweet potatoes (500 g / 17.5 oz)
- Black sesame seeds to taste
- Frying oil as needed
- [A]
  - 4-6 Tbsp sugar
  - 1 Tbsp mirin
  - 1 Tbsp soy sauce
  - 3 Tbsp water

1. Chop a sweet potato into chunks with the skin intact.
2. Soak for 3-5 minutes in water to reduce bitterness, then pat dry with a paper towel.
   *This allso prevents the color from changing.
3. Fry in medium heat (160-170°C / 320-338°F) for about 5-10 minutes, then finish at high temperature (180°C / 356°F or higher) for about thirty seconds. Once the pieces are a light brown, take them out of the oil onto a cooling pan with a rack and cool to room temperature.
   *The high heat at the end is to help make sure the potatoes aren't too greasy.
4. Add [A] to a frying pan and bring to a boil over medium to high heat. Once the sauce goes from creating large bubbles to small bubbles and thickens, cut the heat.
5. Add your fried sweet potatoes, then return to medium heat. Once the sauce has coated all the pieces, remove them and place on a piece of parchment paper or a cooling pan with a rack on top, making sure the pieces aren't touching one another. Sprinkle black sesame seeds on top while they're still hot. Cool and you're done.
   *Cooling them rapidly with a fan or other tool will prevent the coating from dripping, resulting in a shiny finish that sticks to the pieces.

★ Even if the sauce hardens on your frying pan or your other utensils, just add some hot water and it will easily melt away.

Types of sweet potatoes

Lots of different breeds of sweet potatoes exist. Try using your favorite!

Fluffy:	Naruto Kintoki, Beniazuma
Fluffy & Sticky:	Tosabeni
Sticky:	Anno, Beni Harukai

*Fluffy and Fluffy & Sticky are also recommended for tempura and candied sweet potatoes

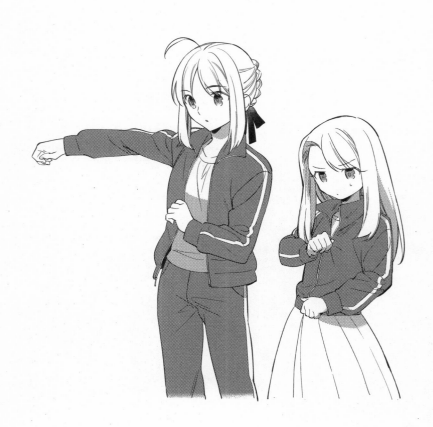

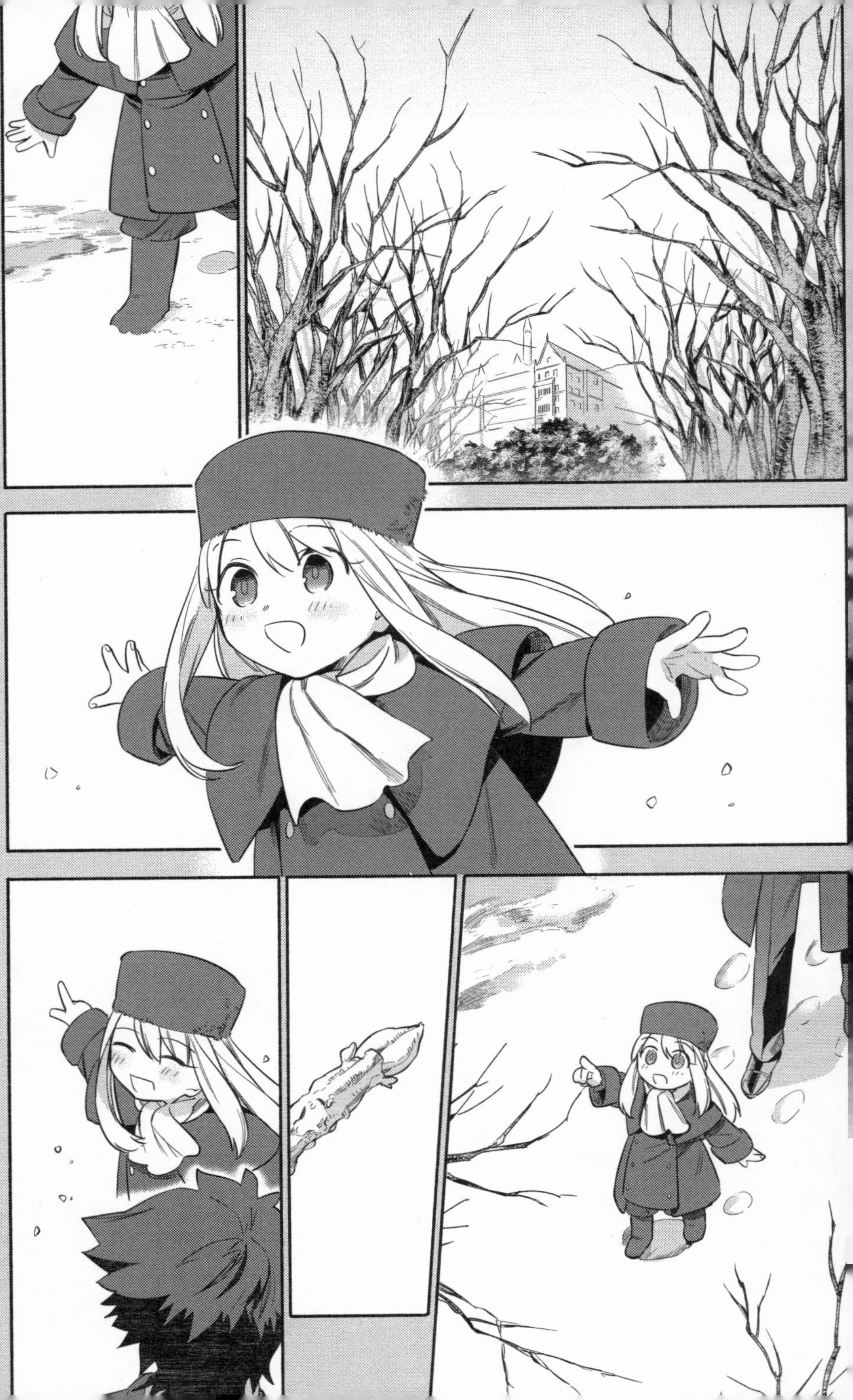

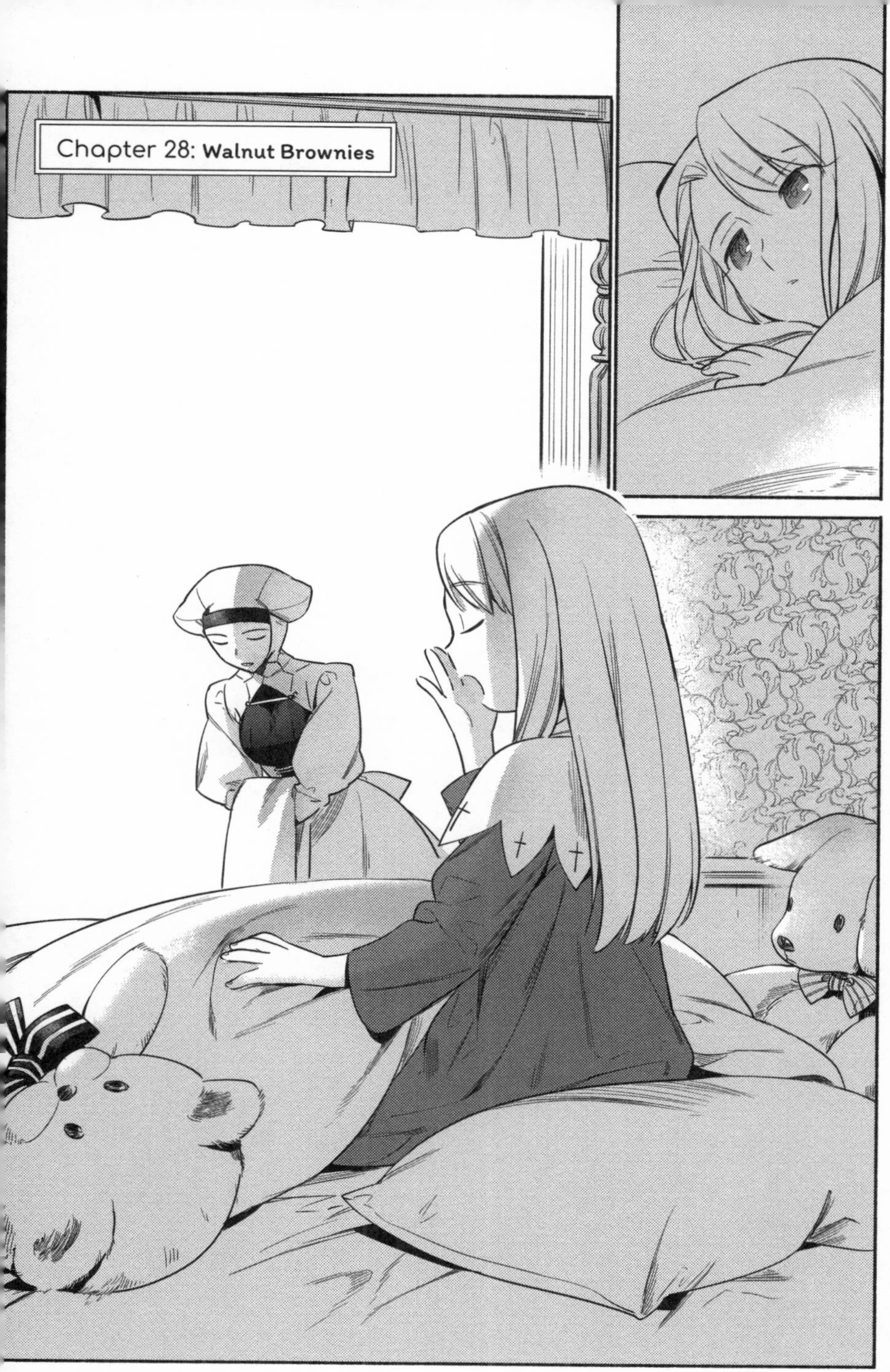
Chapter 28: Walnut Brownies

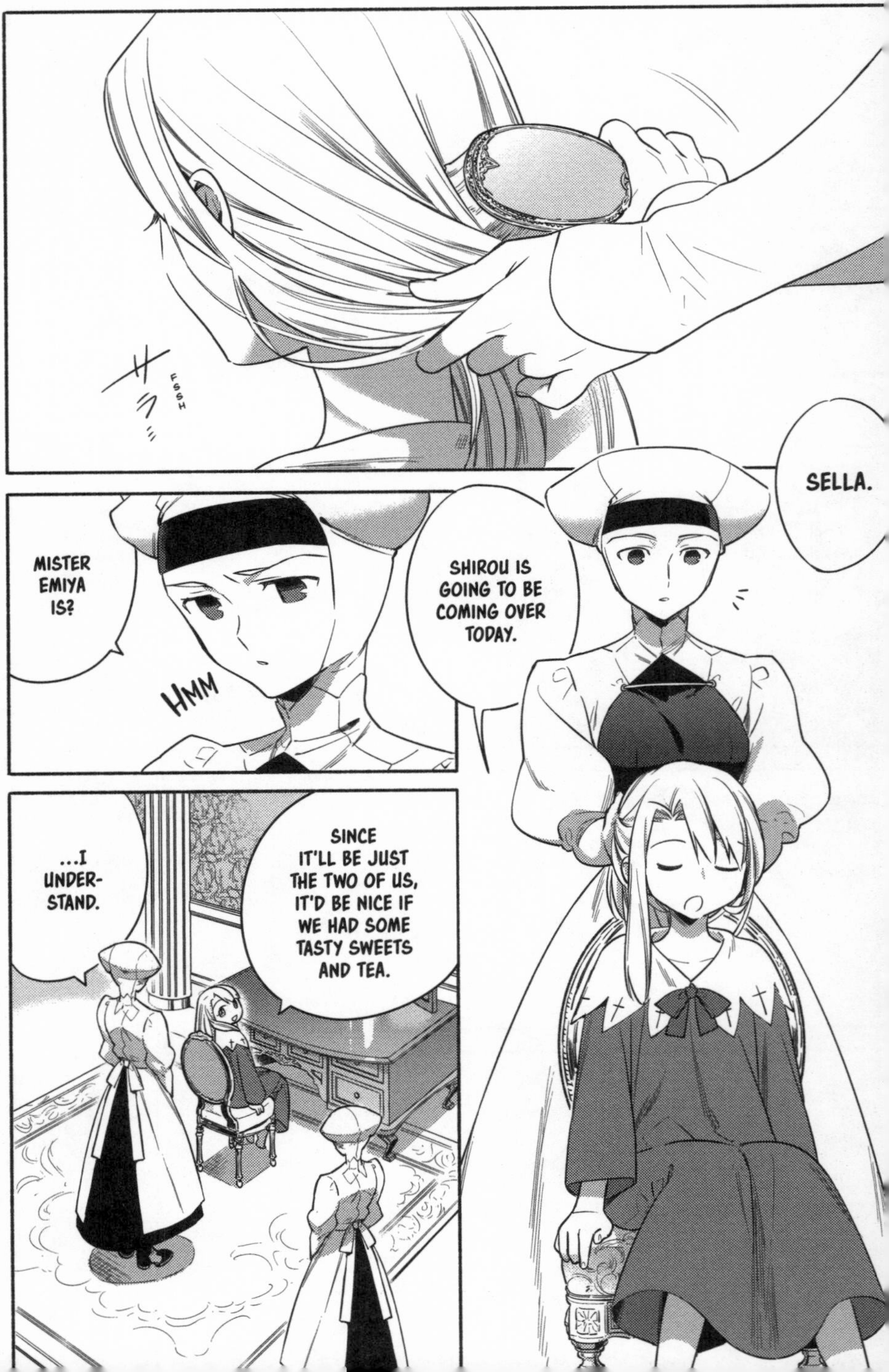
FSSH
SELLA.
SHIROU IS GOING TO BE COMING OVER TODAY.
MISTER EMIYA IS?
HMM
SINCE IT'LL BE JUST THE TWO OF US, IT'D BE NICE IF WE HAD SOME TASTY SWEETS AND TEA.
...I UNDER-STAND.

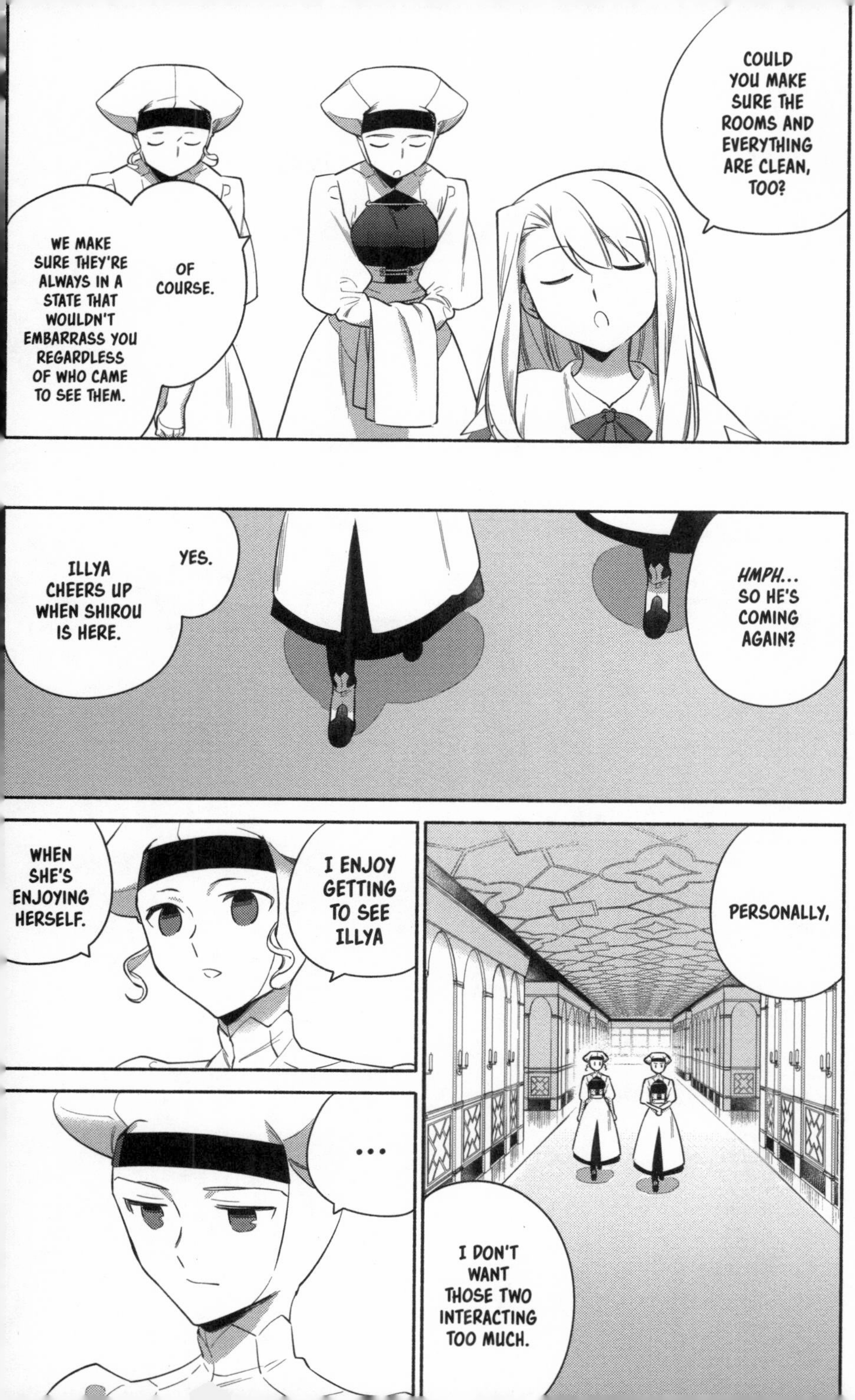
COULD YOU MAKE SURE THE ROOMS AND EVERYTHING ARE CLEAN, TOO?
OF COURSE.
WE MAKE SURE THEY'RE ALWAYS IN A STATE THAT WOULDN'T EMBARRASS YOU REGARDLESS OF WHO CAME TO SEE THEM.
HMPH... SO HE'S COMING AGAIN?
YES.
ILLYA CHEERS UP WHEN SHIROU IS HERE.
PERSONALLY,
I DON'T WANT THOSE TWO INTERACTING TOO MUCH.
I ENJOY GETTING TO SEE ILLYA
WHEN SHE'S ENJOYING HERSELF.
...

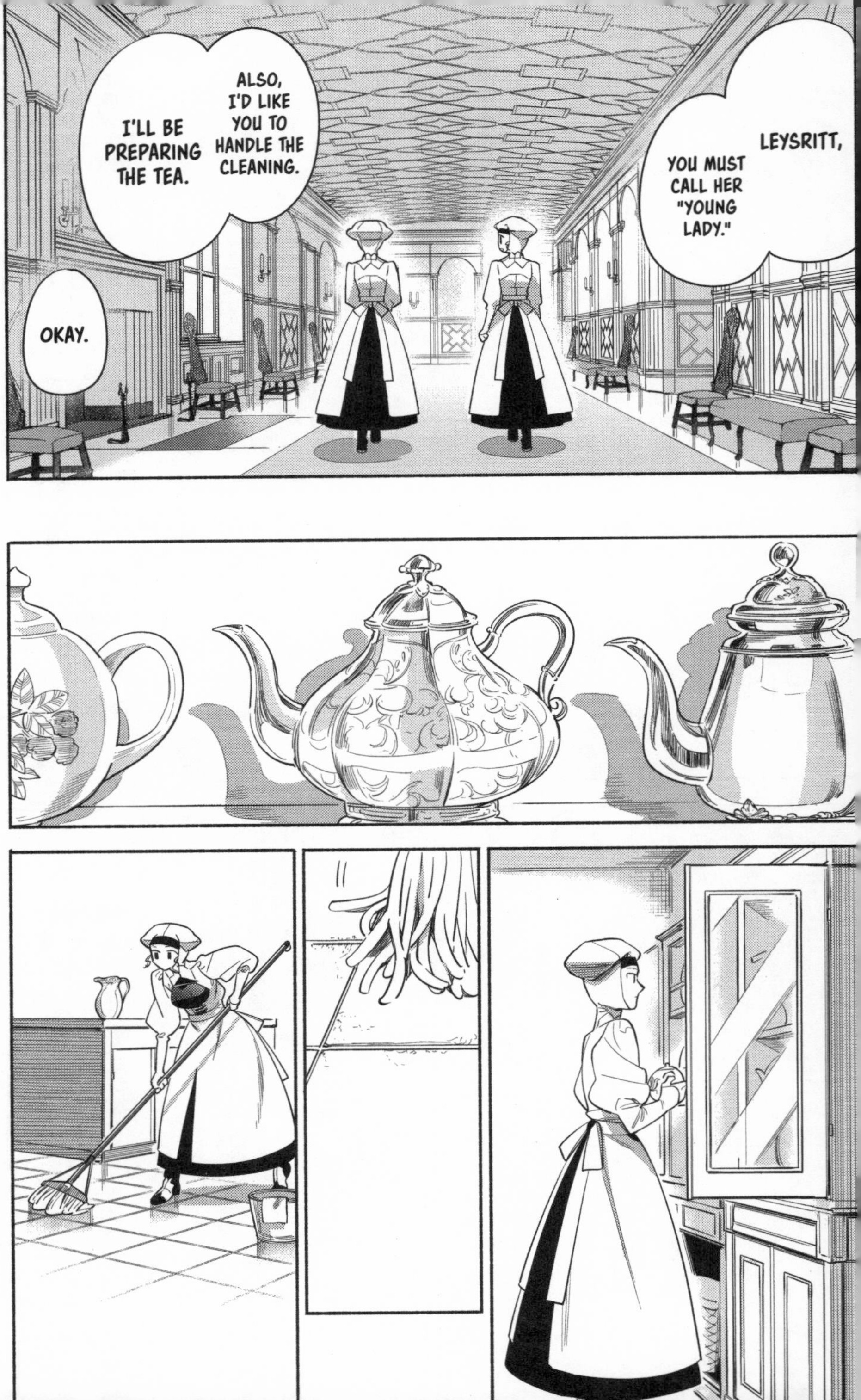
LEYSRITT, YOU MUST CALL HER "YOUNG LADY."
I'LL BE PREPARING THE TEA. ALSO, I'D LIKE YOU TO HANDLE THE CLEANING.
OKAY.

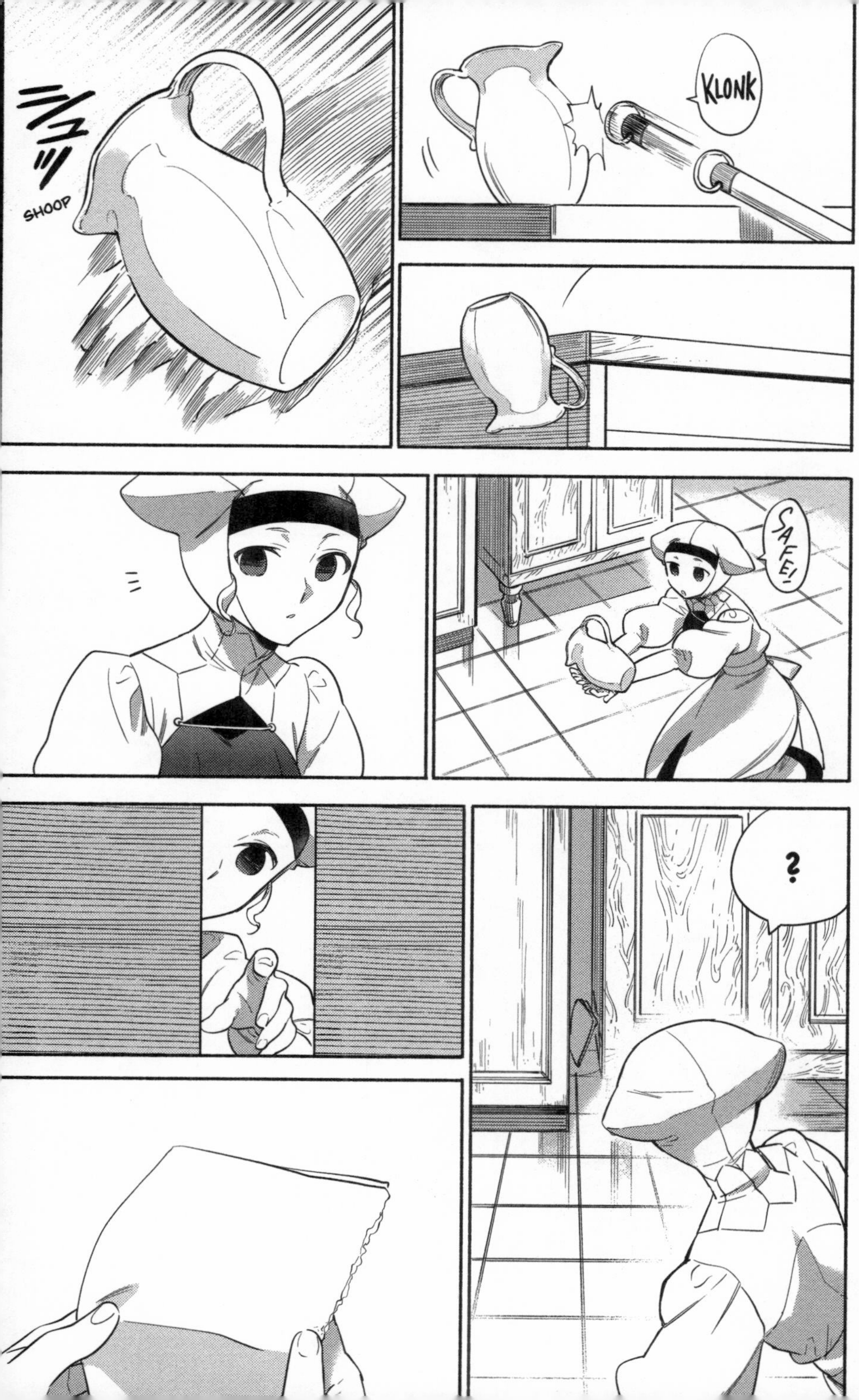
KLONK
シュッ
SHOOP
SAFE!
?

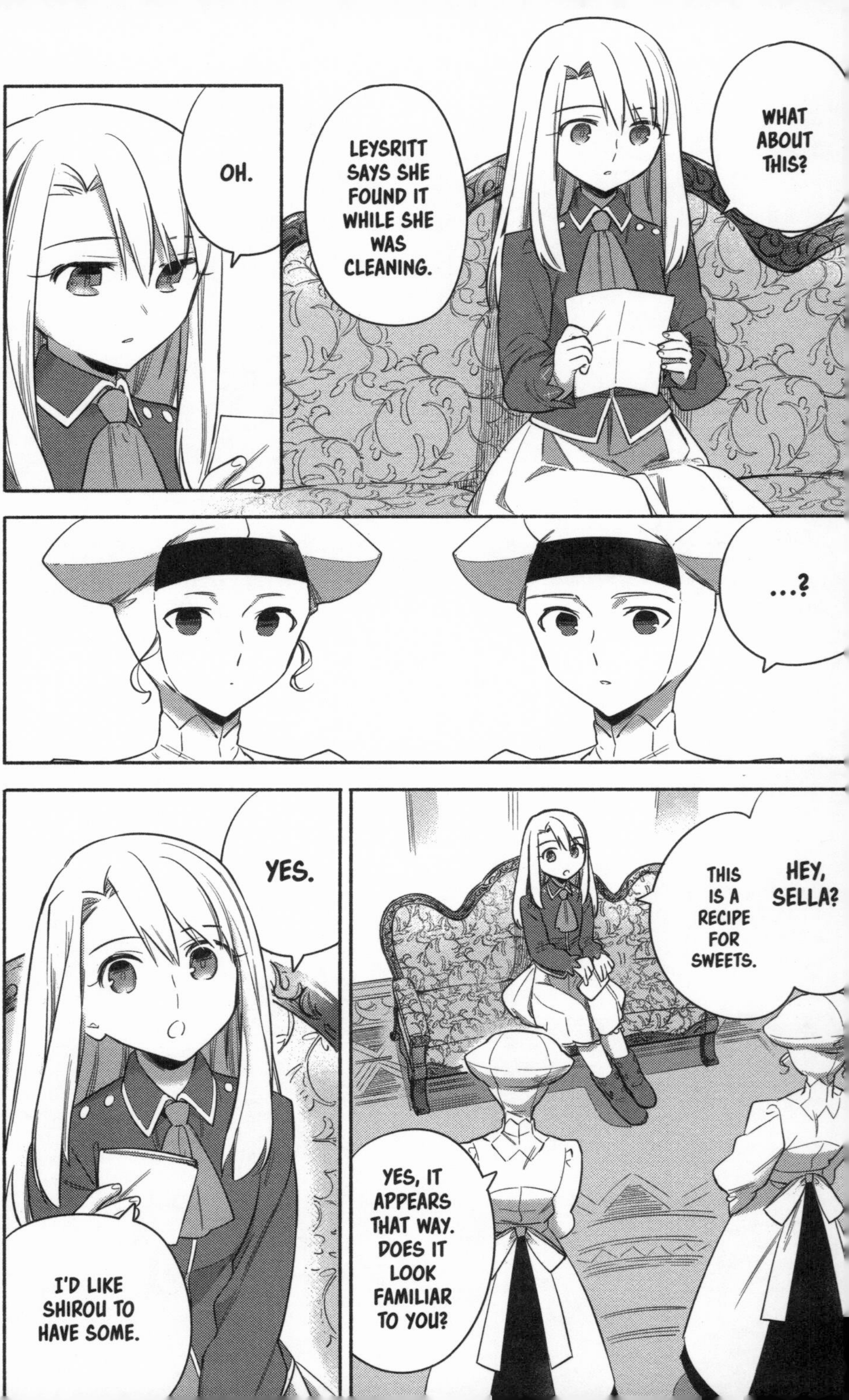
WHAT ABOUT THIS?
LEYSRITT SAYS SHE FOUND IT WHILE SHE WAS CLEANING.
OH.
...?
HEY, SELLA?
THIS IS A RECIPE FOR SWEETS.
YES, IT APPEARS THAT WAY. DOES IT LOOK FAMILIAR TO YOU?
YES.
I'D LIKE SHIROU TO HAVE SOME.

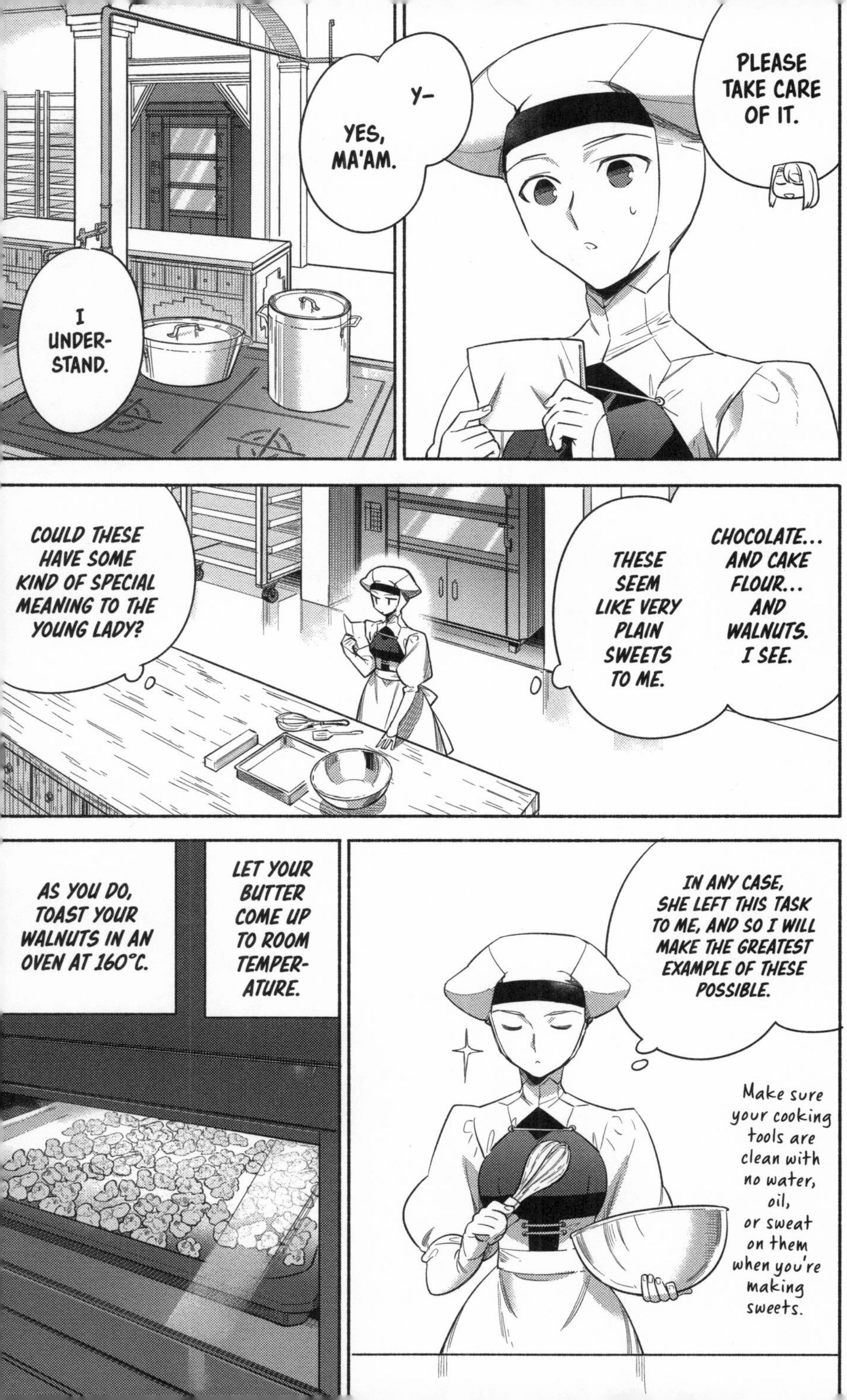
PLEASE TAKE CARE OF IT.
Y– YES, MA'AM.
I UNDER-STAND.
CHOCOLATE... AND CAKE FLOUR... AND WALNUTS. I SEE.
THESE SEEM LIKE VERY PLAIN SWEETS TO ME.
COULD THESE HAVE SOME KIND OF SPECIAL MEANING TO THE YOUNG LADY?
IN ANY CASE, SHE LEFT THIS TASK TO ME, AND SO I WILL MAKE THE GREATEST EXAMPLE OF THESE POSSIBLE.
Make sure your cooking tools are clean with no water, oil, or sweat on them when you're making sweets.
LET YOUR BUTTER COME UP TO ROOM TEMPER-ATURE.
AS YOU DO, TOAST YOUR WALNUTS IN AN OVEN AT 160°C.

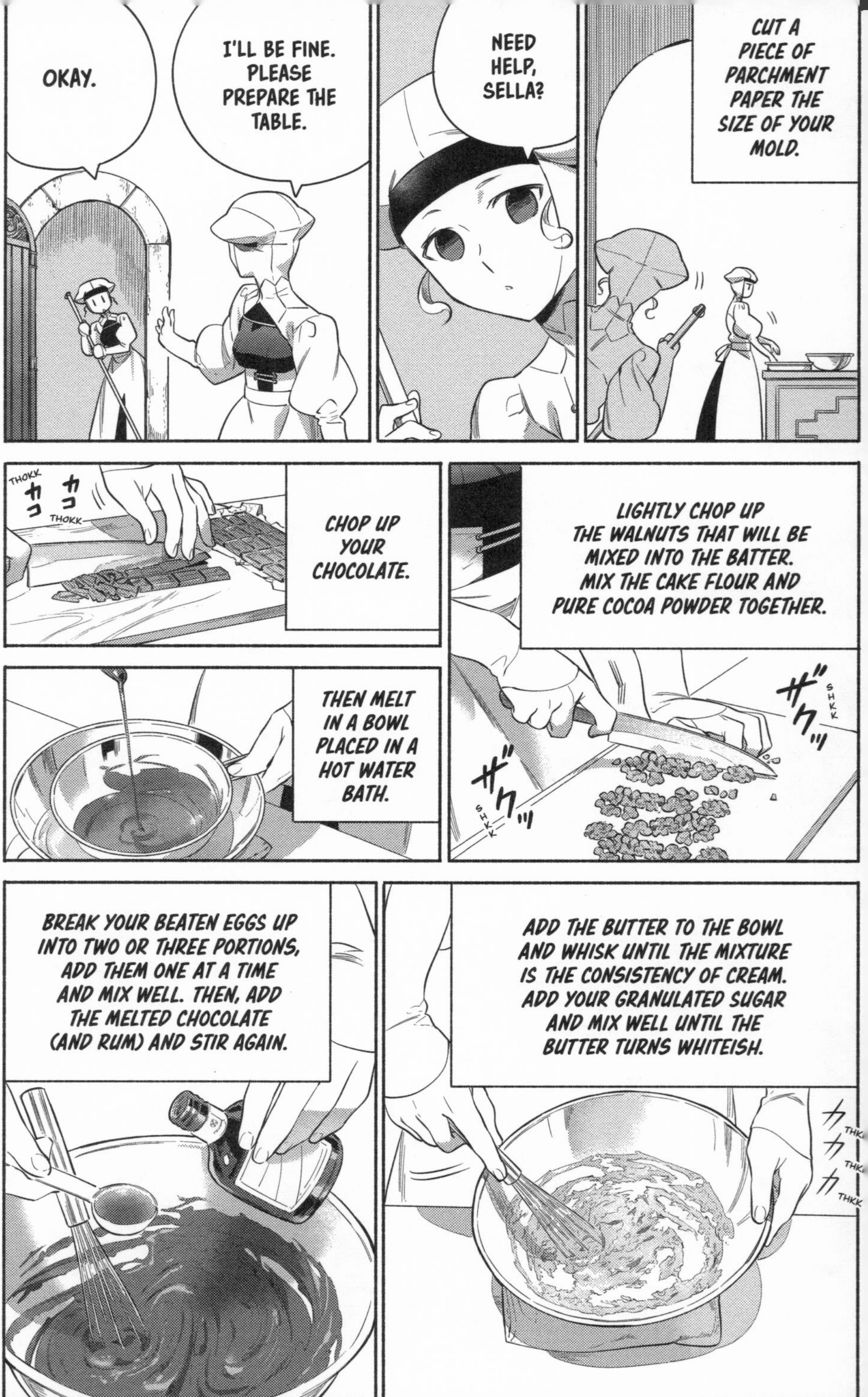
CUT A PIECE OF PARCHMENT PAPER THE SIZE OF YOUR MOLD.
NEED HELP, SELLA?
I'LL BE FINE. PLEASE PREPARE THE TABLE.
OKAY.
LIGHTLY CHOP UP THE WALNUTS THAT WILL BE MIXED INTO THE BATTER. MIX THE CAKE FLOUR AND PURE COCOA POWDER TOGETHER.
CHOP UP YOUR CHOCOLATE.
THOKK
THOKK
SHKK
SHKK
THEN MELT IN A BOWL PLACED IN A HOT WATER BATH.
ADD THE BUTTER TO THE BOWL AND WHISK UNTIL THE MIXTURE IS THE CONSISTENCY OF CREAM. ADD YOUR GRANULATED SUGAR AND MIX WELL UNTIL THE BUTTER TURNS WHITEISH.
THK
THK
THK
BREAK YOUR BEATEN EGGS UP INTO TWO OR THREE PORTIONS, ADD THEM ONE AT A TIME AND MIX WELL. THEN, ADD THE MELTED CHOCOLATE (AND RUM) AND STIR AGAIN.

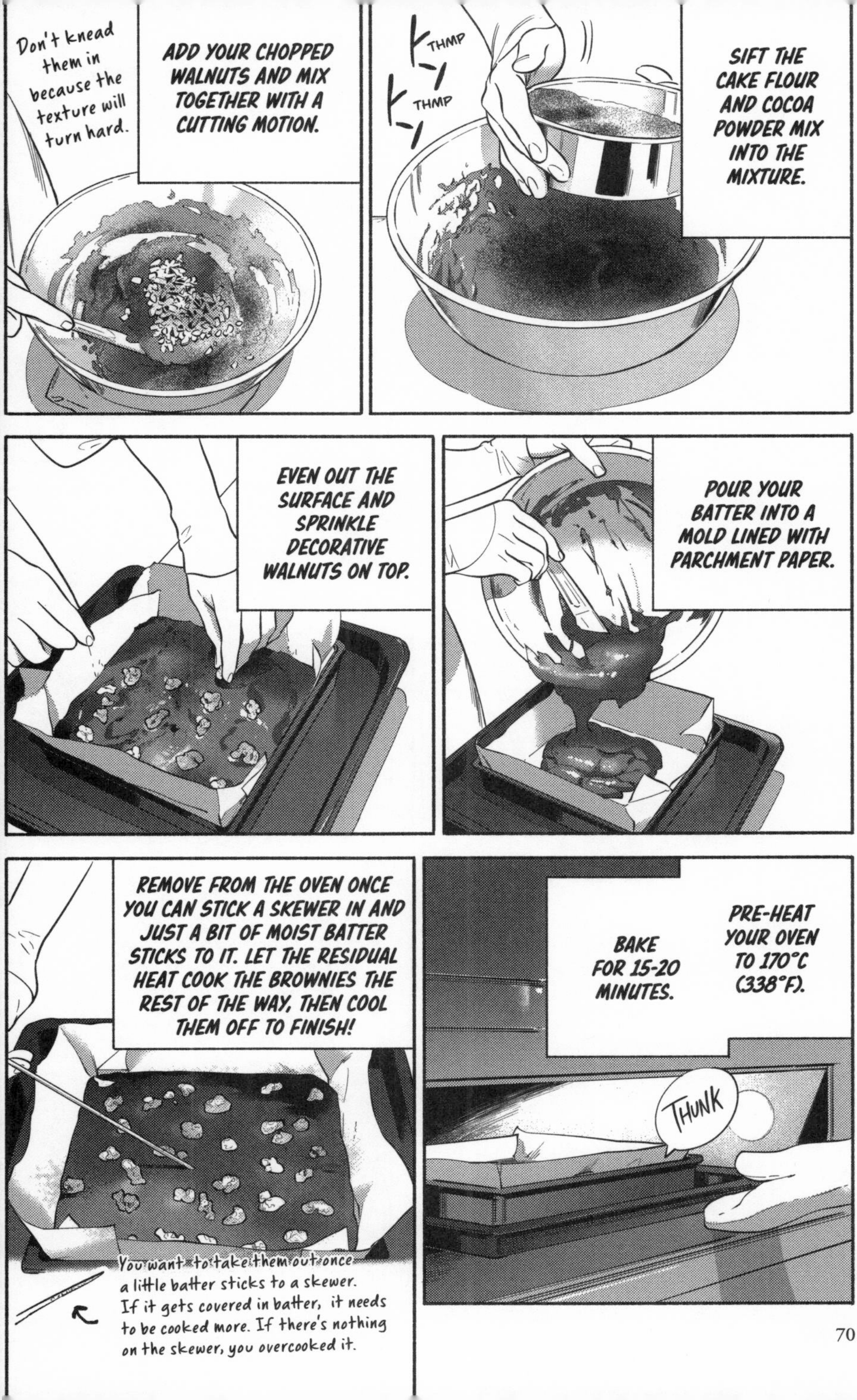
SIFT THE CAKE FLOUR AND COCOA POWDER MIX INTO THE MIXTURE.
THMP
THMP
ADD YOUR CHOPPED WALNUTS AND MIX TOGETHER WITH A CUTTING MOTION.
Don't knead them in because the texture will turn hard.
POUR YOUR BATTER INTO A MOLD LINED WITH PARCHMENT PAPER.
EVEN OUT THE SURFACE AND SPRINKLE DECORATIVE WALNUTS ON TOP.
PRE-HEAT YOUR OVEN TO 170°C (338°F).
BAKE FOR 15-20 MINUTES.
THUNK
REMOVE FROM THE OVEN ONCE YOU CAN STICK A SKEWER IN AND JUST A BIT OF MOIST BATTER STICKS TO IT. LET THE RESIDUAL HEAT COOK THE BROWNIES THE REST OF THE WAY, THEN COOL THEM OFF TO FINISH!
You want to take them out once a little batter sticks to a skewer. If it gets covered in batter, it needs to be cooked more. If there's nothing on the skewer, you overcooked it.

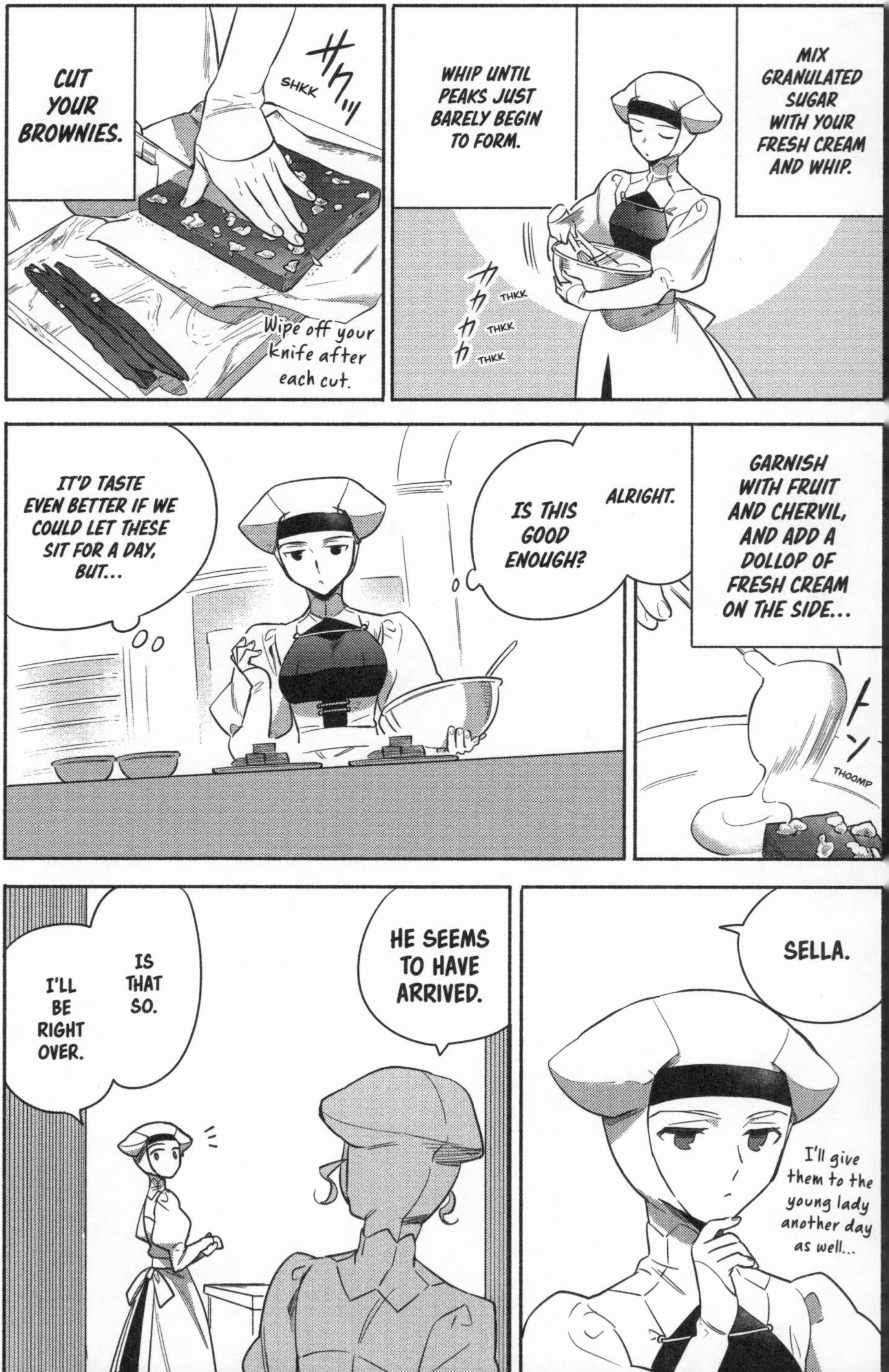
MIX GRANULATED SUGAR WITH YOUR FRESH CREAM AND WHIP.
WHIP UNTIL PEAKS JUST BARELY BEGIN TO FORM.
カカカ
THKK THKK THKK
CUT YOUR BROWNIES.
サク
SHKK
Wipe off your knife after each cut.
GARNISH WITH FRUIT AND CHERVIL, AND ADD A DOLLOP OF FRESH CREAM ON THE SIDE...
トン
THOOMP
IS THIS GOOD ENOUGH? ALRIGHT.
IT'D TASTE EVEN BETTER IF WE COULD LET THESE SIT FOR A DAY, BUT...
SELLA.
I'll give them to the young lady another day as well...
HE SEEMS TO HAVE ARRIVED.
IS THAT SO.
I'LL BE RIGHT OVER.

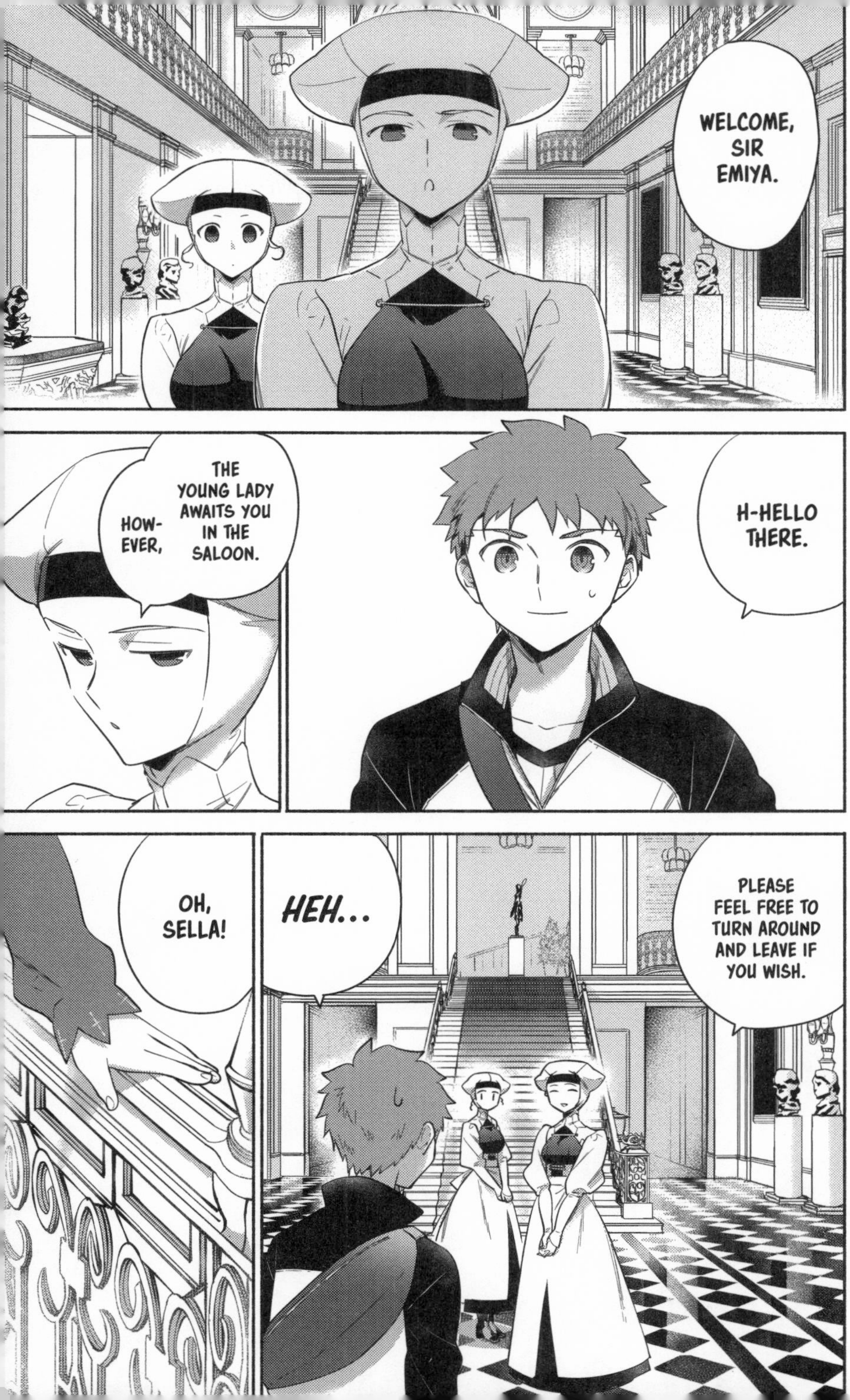
WELCOME, SIR EMIYA.
H-HELLO THERE.
HOW-EVER, THE YOUNG LADY AWAITS YOU IN THE SALOON.
PLEASE FEEL FREE TO TURN AROUND AND LEAVE IF YOU WISH.
HEH...
OH, SELLA!

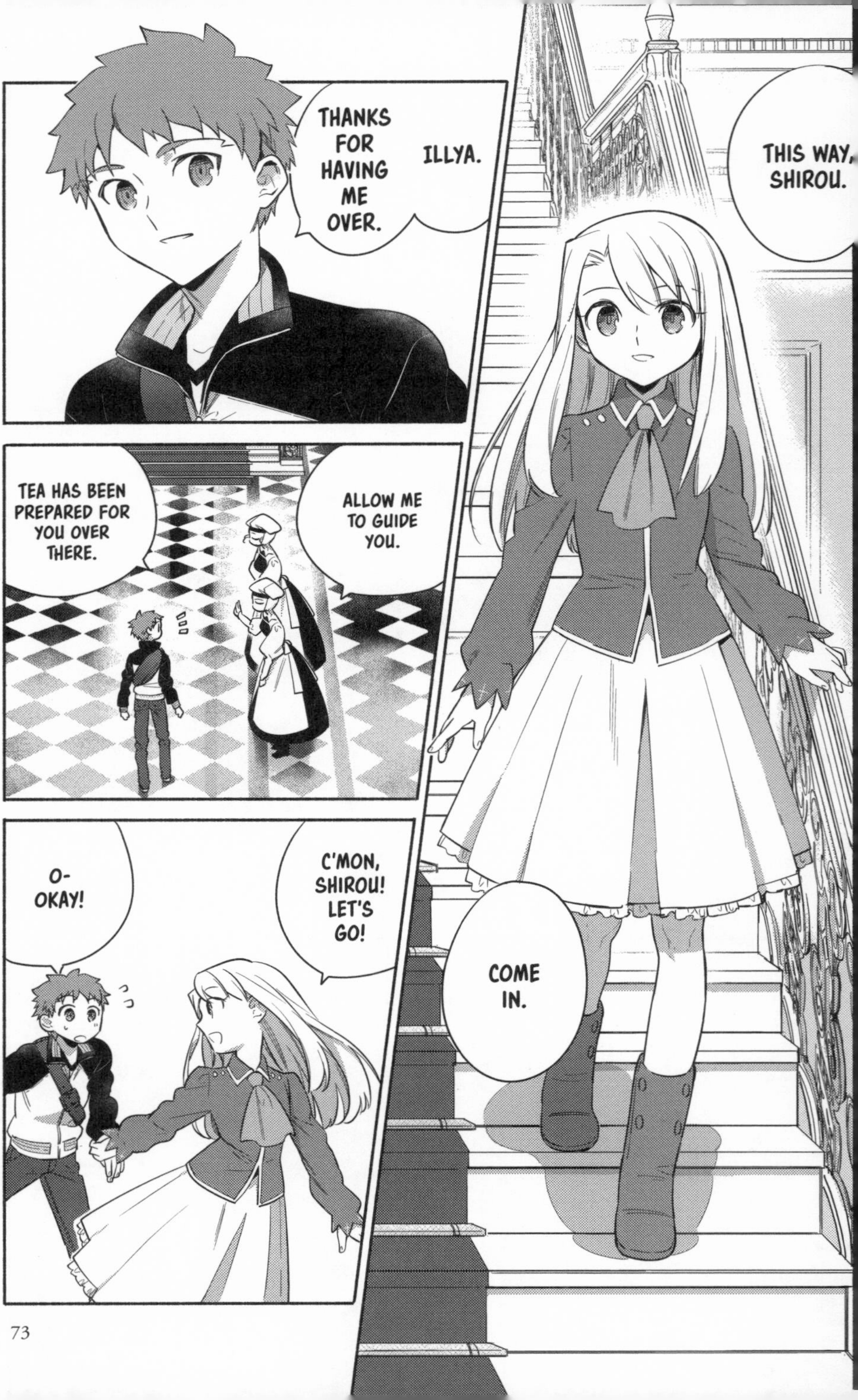
THIS WAY, SHIROU.
COME IN.
THANKS FOR HAVING ME OVER.
ILLYA.
ALLOW ME TO GUIDE YOU.
TEA HAS BEEN PREPARED FOR YOU OVER THERE.
C'MON, SHIROU! LET'S GO!
O-OKAY!

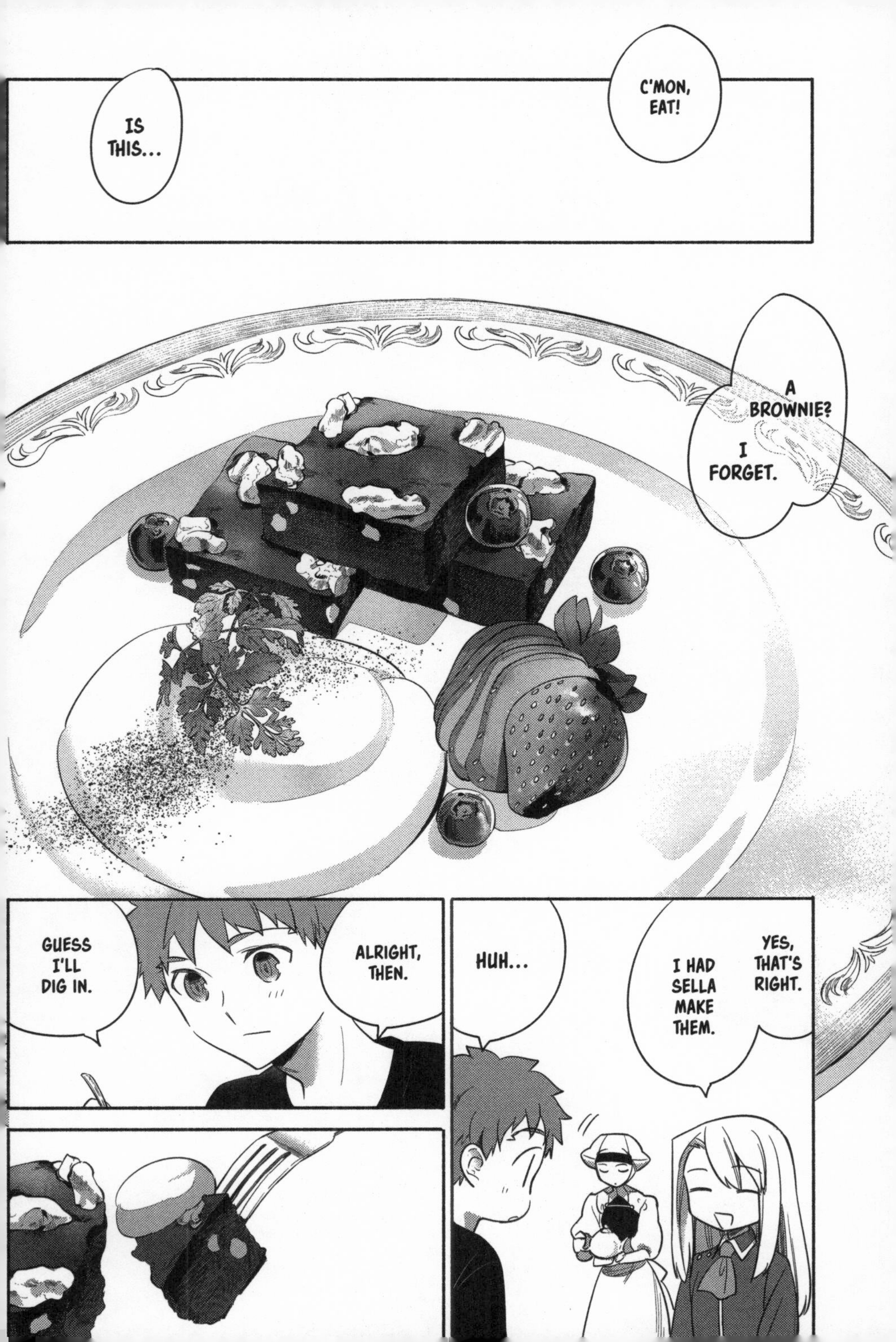
C'MON, EAT!
IS THIS...
A BROWNIE?
I FORGET.
YES, THAT'S RIGHT.
I HAD SELLA MAKE THEM.
HUH...
ALRIGHT, THEN.
GUESS I'LL DIG IN.

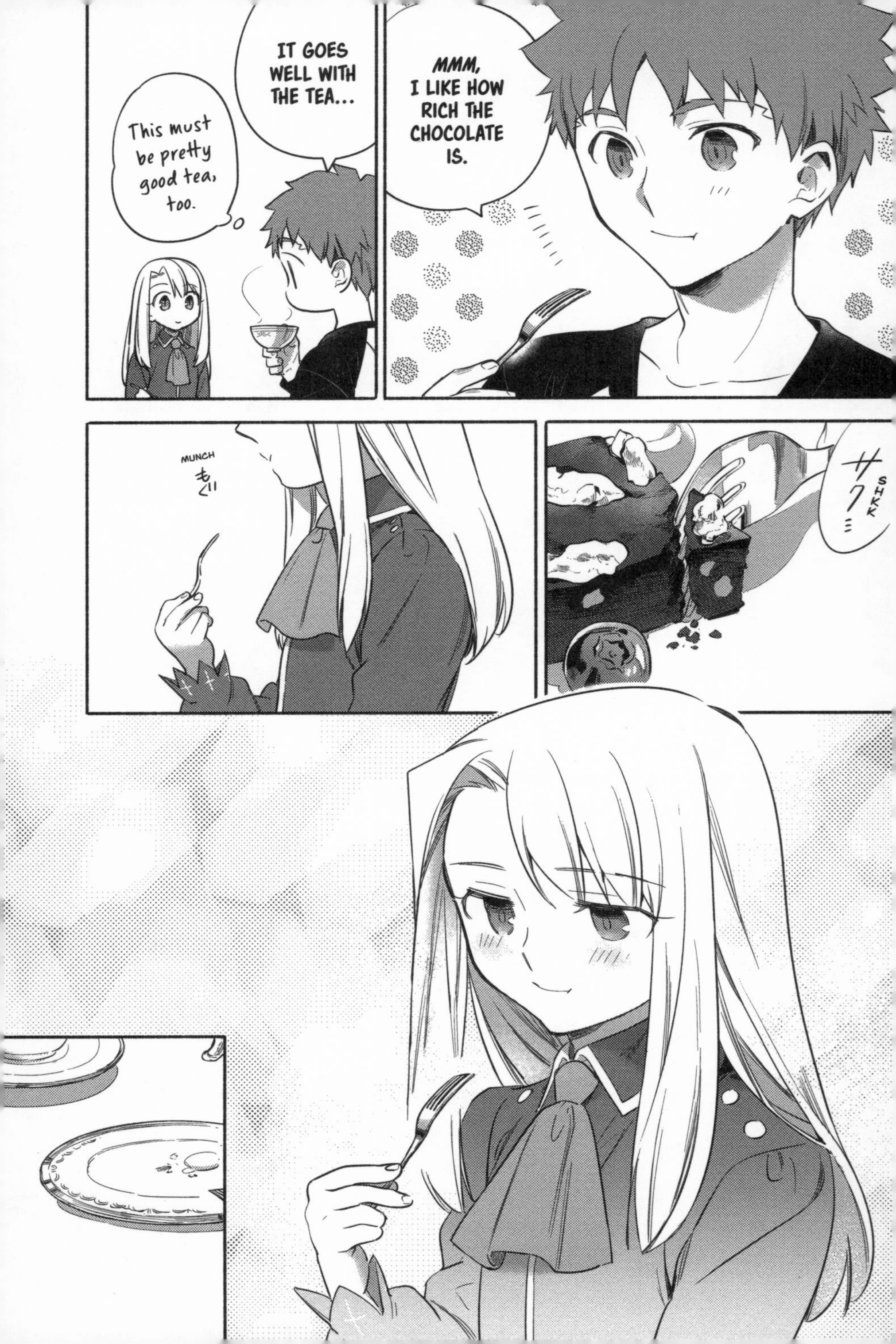
MMM, I LIKE HOW RICH THE CHOCOLATE IS.
IT GOES WELL WITH THE TEA...
This must be pretty good tea, too.
サク
SHKK
MUNCH
もぐ

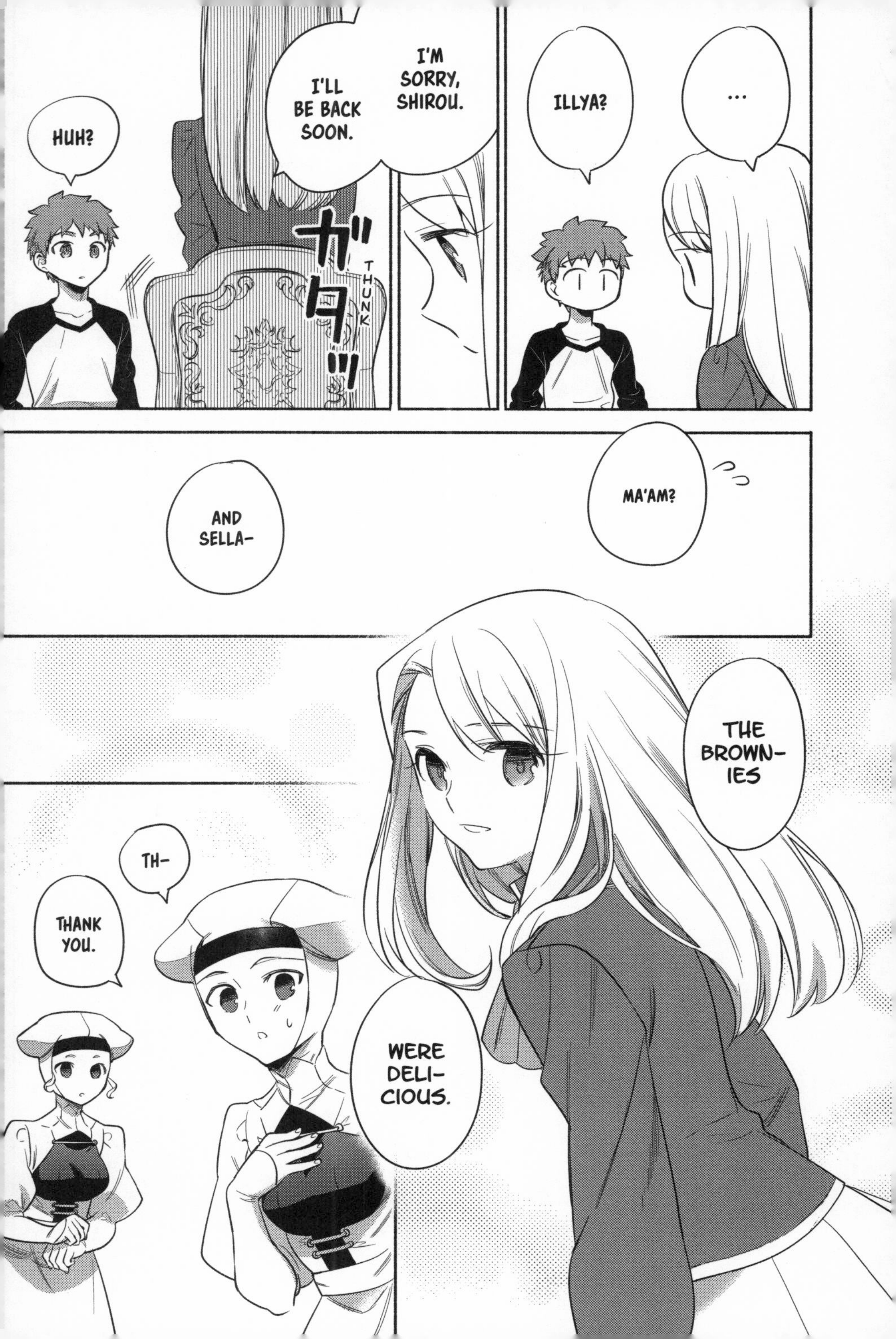
...
ILLYA?
I'M SORRY, SHIROU.
I'LL BE BACK SOON.
ガタッ
THUNK
HUH?
MA'AM?
AND SELLA-
THE BROWN-IES
WERE DELI-CIOUS.
TH-
THANK YOU.

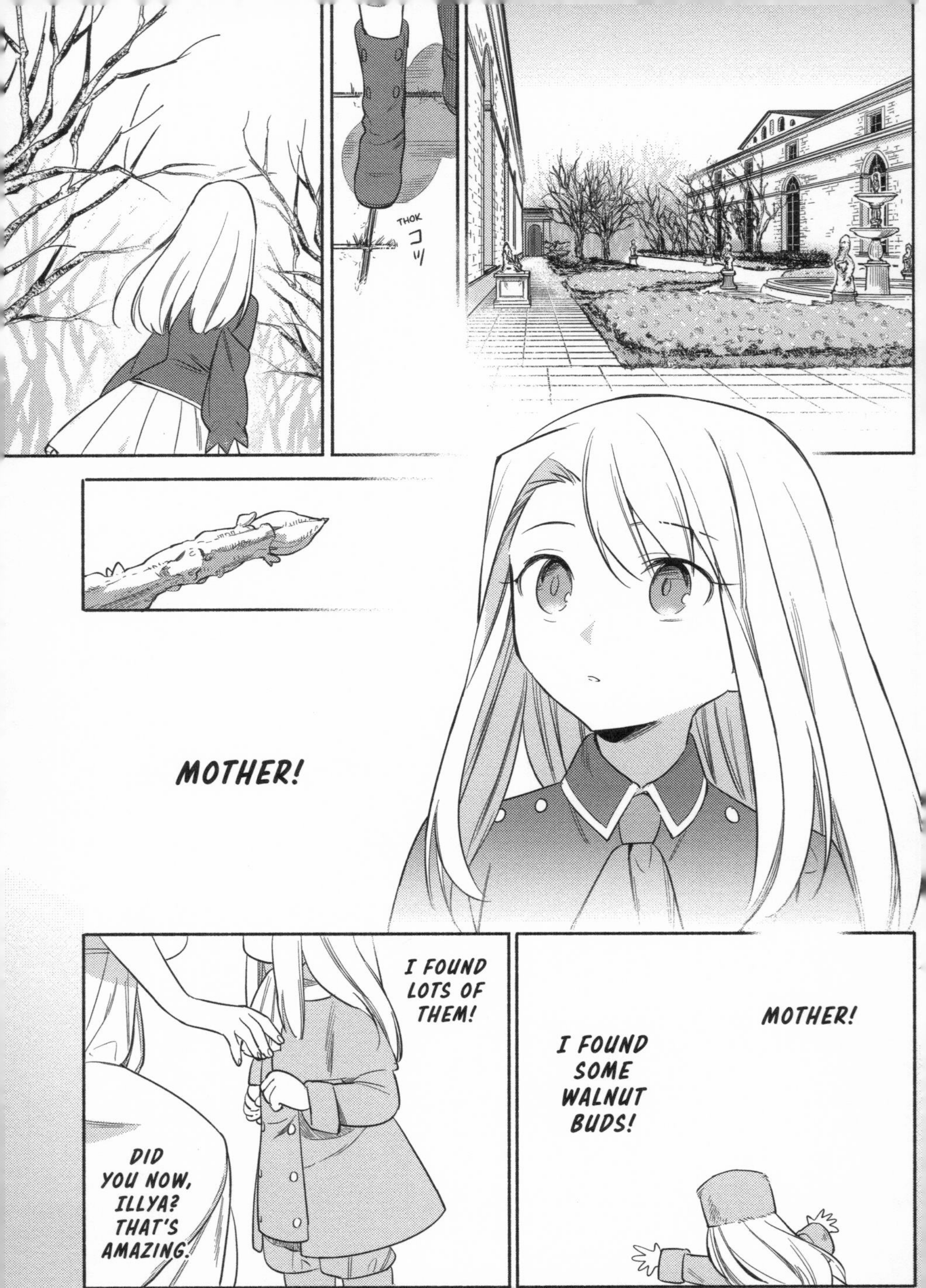
THOK
コッ
MOTHER!
MOTHER!
I FOUND SOME WALNUT BUDS!
I FOUND LOTS OF THEM!
DID YOU NOW, ILLYA? THAT'S AMAZING.

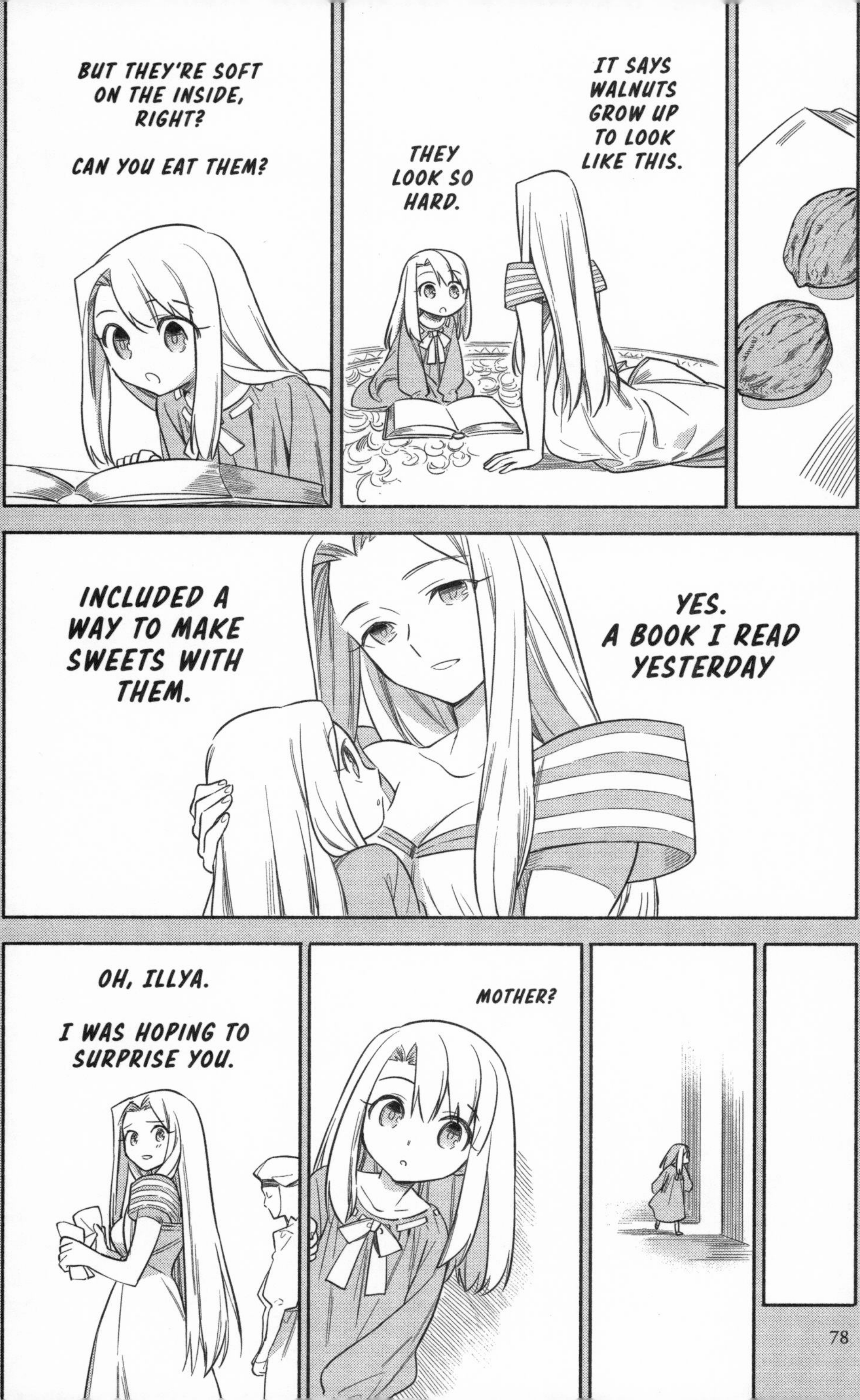
IT SAYS WALNUTS GROW UP TO LOOK LIKE THIS.
THEY LOOK SO HARD.
BUT THEY'RE SOFT ON THE INSIDE, RIGHT?
CAN YOU EAT THEM?
YES. A BOOK I READ YESTERDAY
INCLUDED A WAY TO MAKE SWEETS WITH THEM.
MOTHER?
OH, ILLYA.
I WAS HOPING TO SURPRISE YOU.

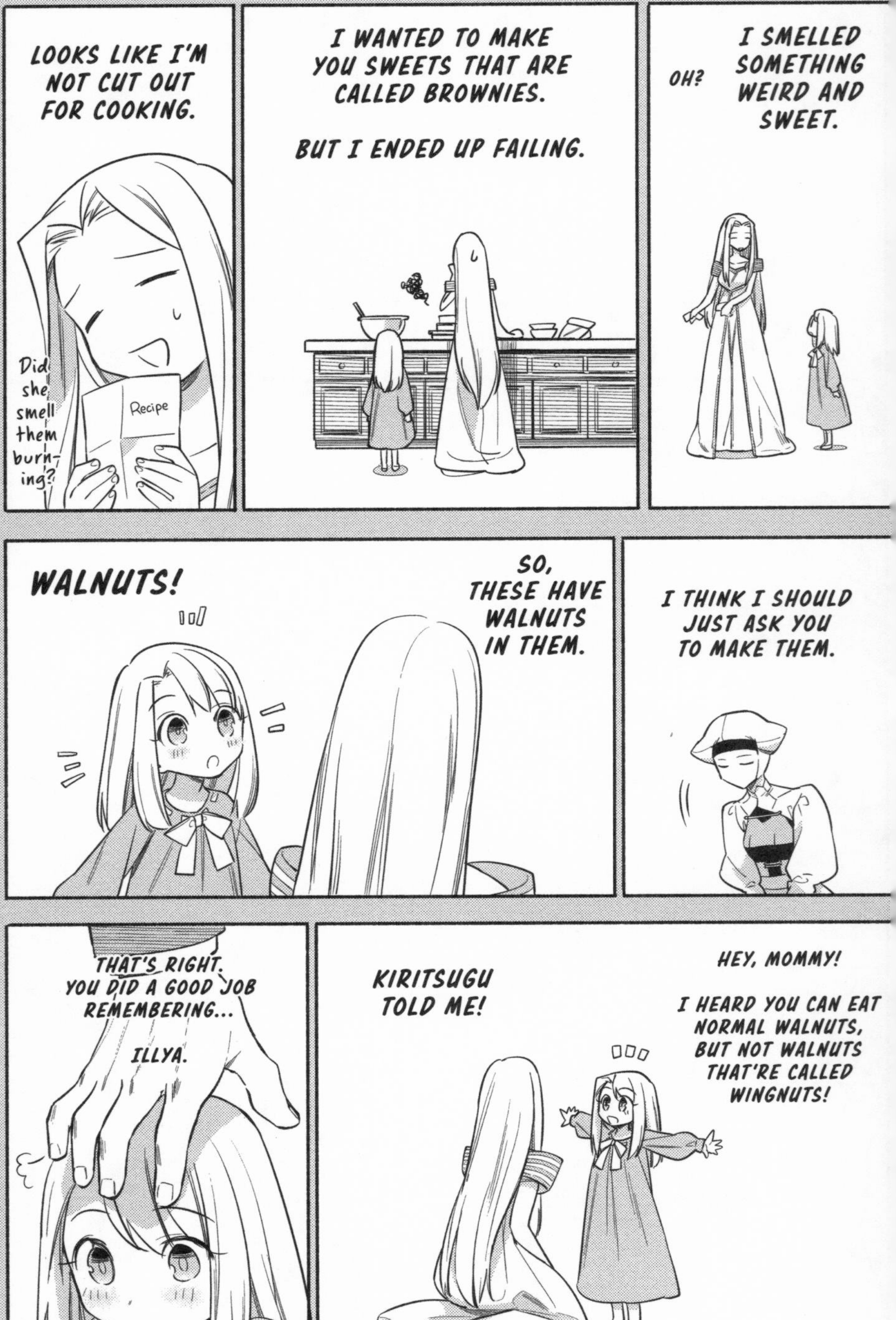
I SMELLED SOMETHING WEIRD AND SWEET.
OH?
I WANTED TO MAKE YOU SWEETS THAT ARE CALLED BROWNIES.
BUT I ENDED UP FAILING.
LOOKS LIKE I'M NOT CUT OUT FOR COOKING.
Recipe
Did she smell them burning?
I THINK I SHOULD JUST ASK YOU TO MAKE THEM.
SO, THESE HAVE WALNUTS IN THEM.
WALNUTS!
HEY, MOMMY!
I HEARD YOU CAN EAT NORMAL WALNUTS, BUT NOT WALNUTS THAT'RE CALLED WINGNUTS!
KIRITSUGU TOLD ME!
THAT'S RIGHT. YOU DID A GOOD JOB REMEMBERING...
ILLYA.

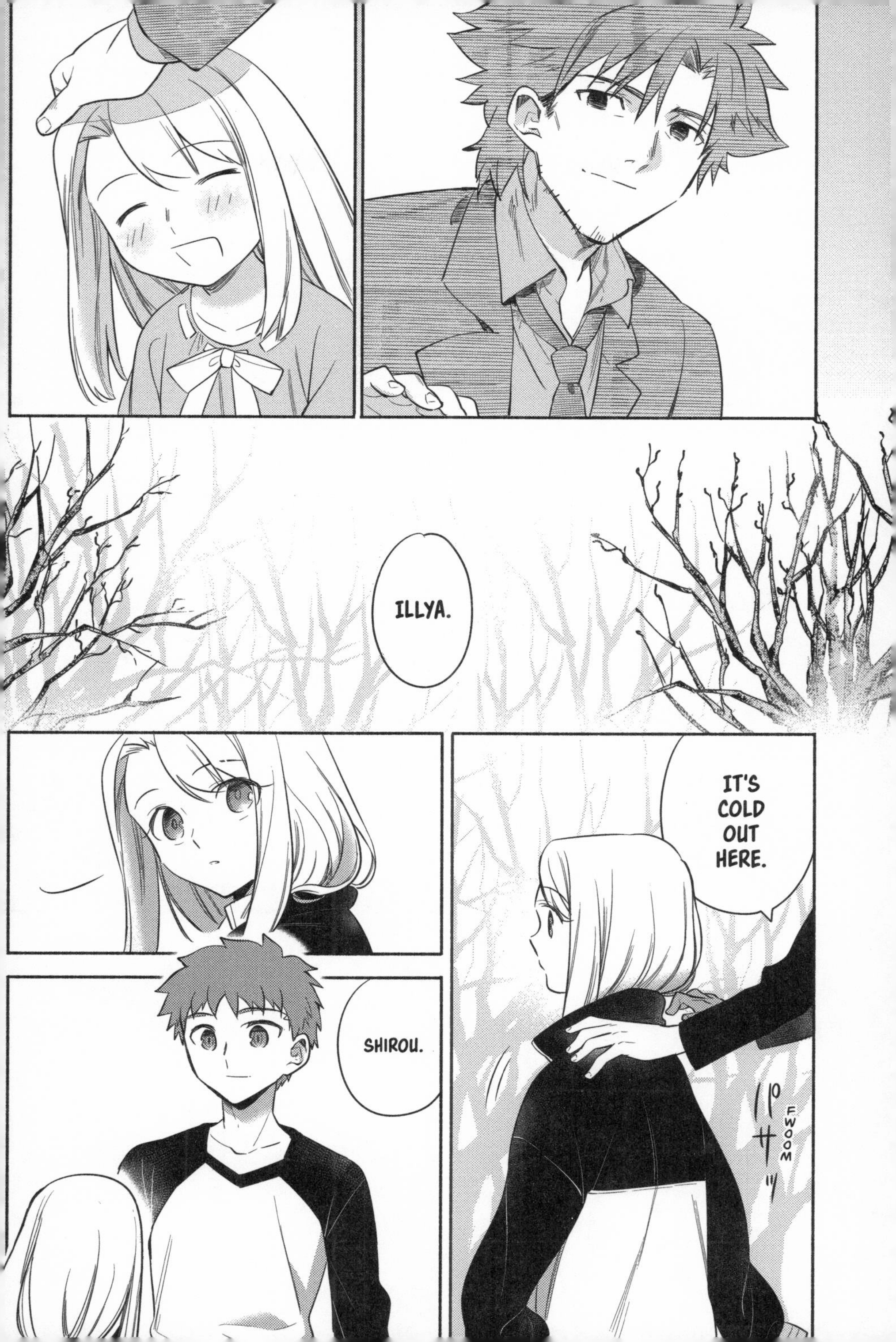
ILLYA.
IT'S COLD OUT HERE.
パサッ
FWOOM
SHIROU.

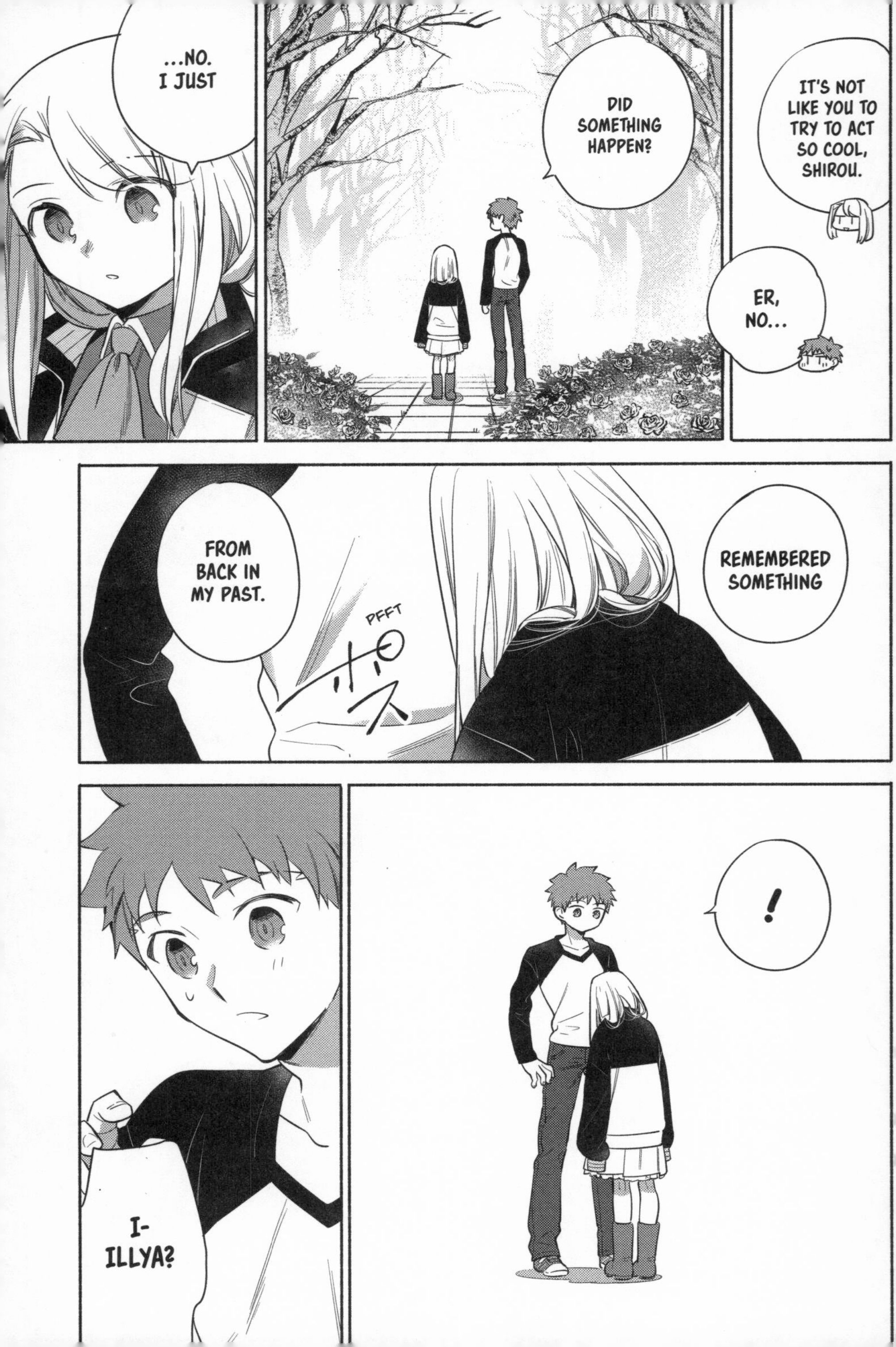
IT'S NOT LIKE YOU TO TRY TO ACT SO COOL, SHIROU.
ER, NO...
DID SOMETHING HAPPEN?
...NO. I JUST
REMEMBERED SOMETHING
PFFT
FROM BACK IN MY PAST.
!
I- ILLYA?

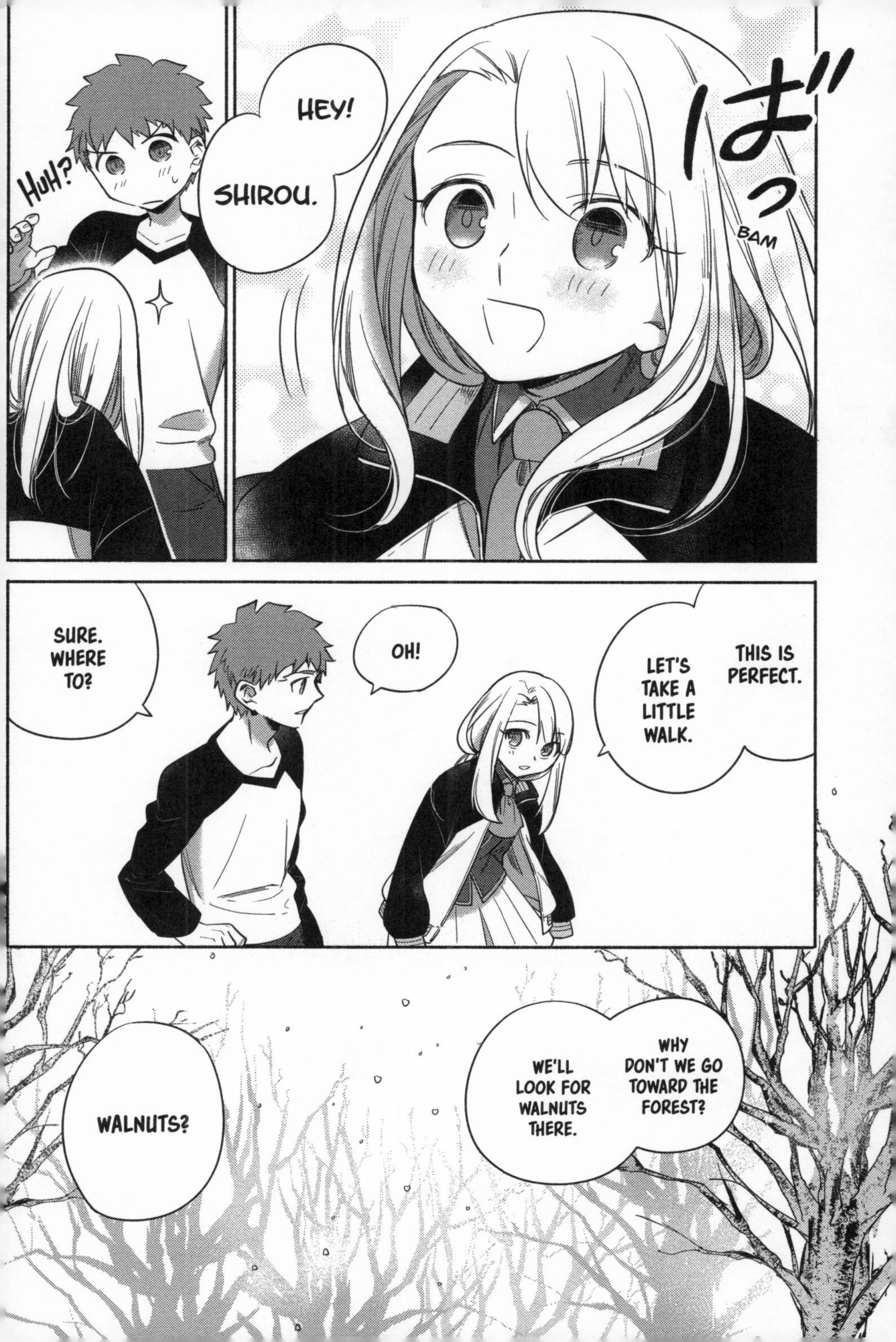
ばっ
BAM
HEY!
SHIROU.
HUH?
THIS IS PERFECT.
LET'S TAKE A LITTLE WALK.
OH!
SURE. WHERE TO?
WHY DON'T WE GO TOWARD THE FOREST?
WE'LL LOOK FOR WALNUTS THERE.
WALNUTS?

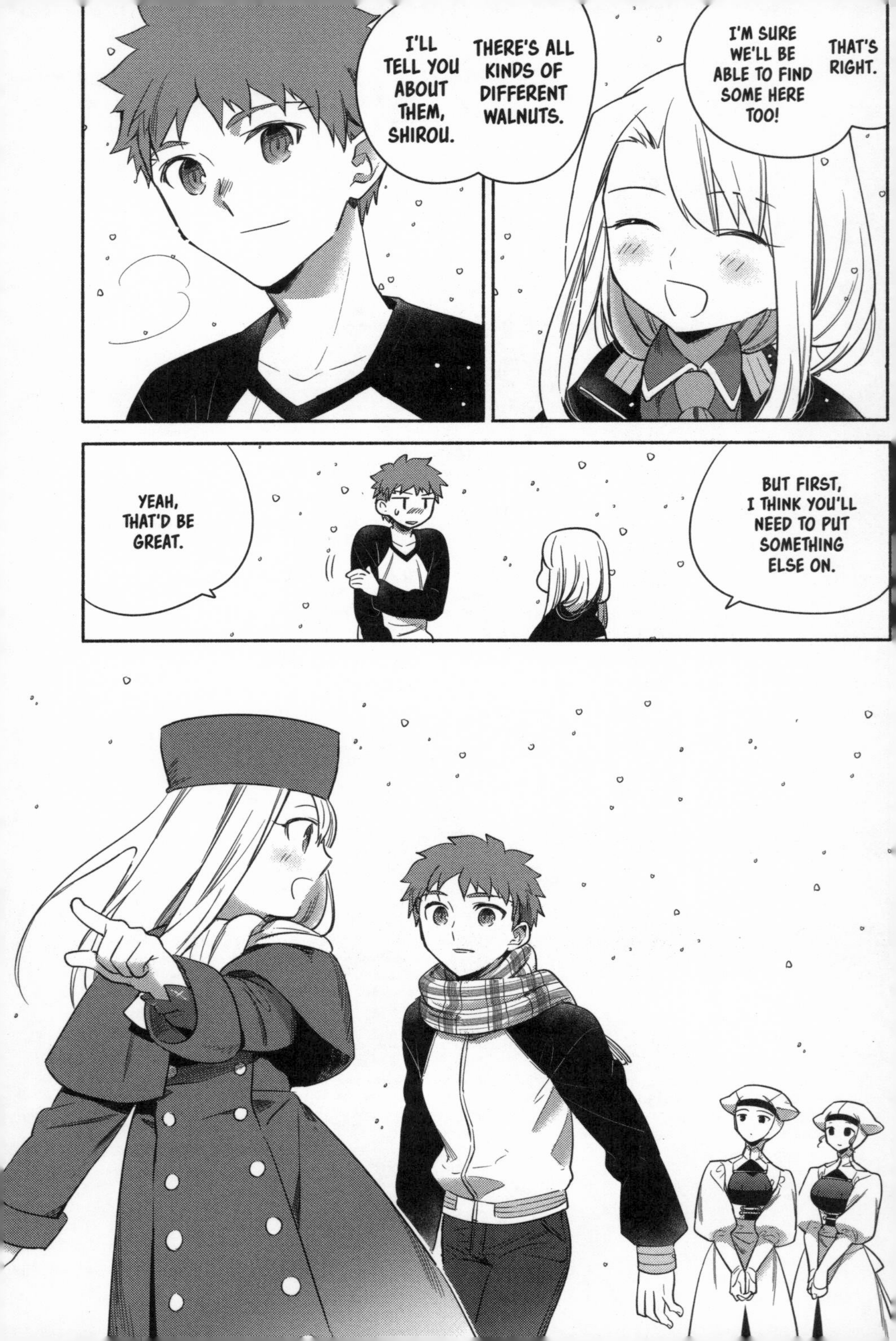
THAT'S RIGHT.
I'M SURE WE'LL BE ABLE TO FIND SOME HERE TOO!
THERE'S ALL KINDS OF DIFFERENT WALNUTS.
I'LL TELL YOU ABOUT THEM, SHIROU.
BUT FIRST, I THINK YOU'LL NEED TO PUT SOMETHING ELSE ON.
YEAH, THAT'D BE GREAT.

Walnut Brownies

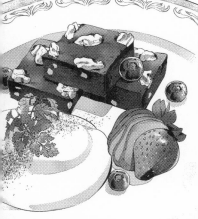

Preparation

1. Let your butter come up to room temperature.

2. Toast your walnuts in an oven at 160°C (320°F).
   *Removing excess moisture will improve the texture of your walnuts.

3. Pre-heat your oven to 170°C (338°F).

4. Place a sheet of parchment paper over your mold.

Ingredients - Makes 1 20 x 20 centimeter square

- 150 g (5.3 oz) chocolate
- A [70 g (2.5 oz) cake flour
      30 g (1.06 oz) pure cocoa powder
- 100 g (3.5 oz) unsalted butter
- 70 g (2.5 oz) granulated sugar
- 2 medium eggs (whole)
- 10-15 ml (2-3 tsp) rum
- 30 g (1.06 oz) walnuts (for mixing)
- 50 g (1.8 oz) walnuts (for decoration)

Garnish
- (100 g (3.5 oz) fresh cream
- (8 g (.3 oz) granulated sugar
- 4-8 strawberries
- 12-16 blueberries
- Chervil or mint as needed

*Feel free to use whatever (dark) chocolate you prefer, whether sweet or bitter.

*In addition to walnuts, you can also add almonds, peanuts, cashews, pumpkin seeds, and more.

*Try using different kinds of sugar with your fresh cream according to your tastes.
Powdered sugar: Highly sweet and rich.
Granulated sugar: A clean and refreshing sweetness.

Instructions

1. Use a knife to lightly chop up the walnuts that will be mixed into the batter. Mix A together. Chop up the chocolate and melt it in a bowl placed in a hot water bath.

2. Add the butter to the bowl and whisk until the mixture is the consistency of cream. Add your granulated sugar and mix well until the butter turns whiteish. The butter turns white as the granulated sugar melts and causes small amounts of air to be incorporated into the butter.
   *You need to make sure to do this or else the eggs may separate when added later, or the batter may not expand properly when cooked.

3. Break your beaten eggs up into two to three portions and add them one at a time, mixing well. Once you do, add the melted chocolate (and rum) and mix.

4. Sift A into the mixture, then add the chopped walnuts and mix quickly with a cutting motion using a rubber spatula. Don't knead them in! it'll make the walnuts hard.

5. Pour 4 into the mold lined with parchment paper, even out the surface, then sprinkle the decorative walnuts on top.

6. Bake for 15-20 minutes at 170°C.
   *You may encounter discrepancies in heat or uneven cooking depending on your oven. If your oven doesn't rotate, turn the pan 180 degrees once it's halfway cooked. Check once at the 12-13 minute mark, then adjust from there. If things go according to the recipe, they should be done at around 15 minutes.

7. Stick a skewer in, and if just a little bit of moist batter sticks to it, take the brownies out of the oven and let the residual heat finish cooking them. Once they cool off, you're done!
   *It's easy for the brownies to lose their shape at this point, so keep them in the mold as they cool. You can eat them as soon as they're cool, but putting them in the refrigerator for a day is recommended. This will cause the flavor to come together, and the texture will be more moist.

8. Mix granulated sugar with fresh cream and whip until peaks just barely begin to form. Garnish the cut brownies with fruit, chervil, and more. And dollop some fresh cream on the side.

Today's Menu for the Emiya Family

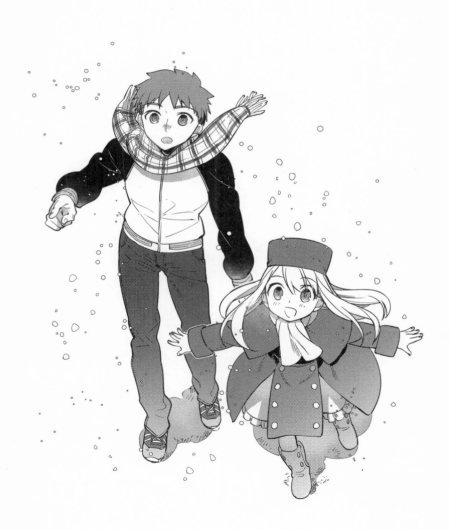

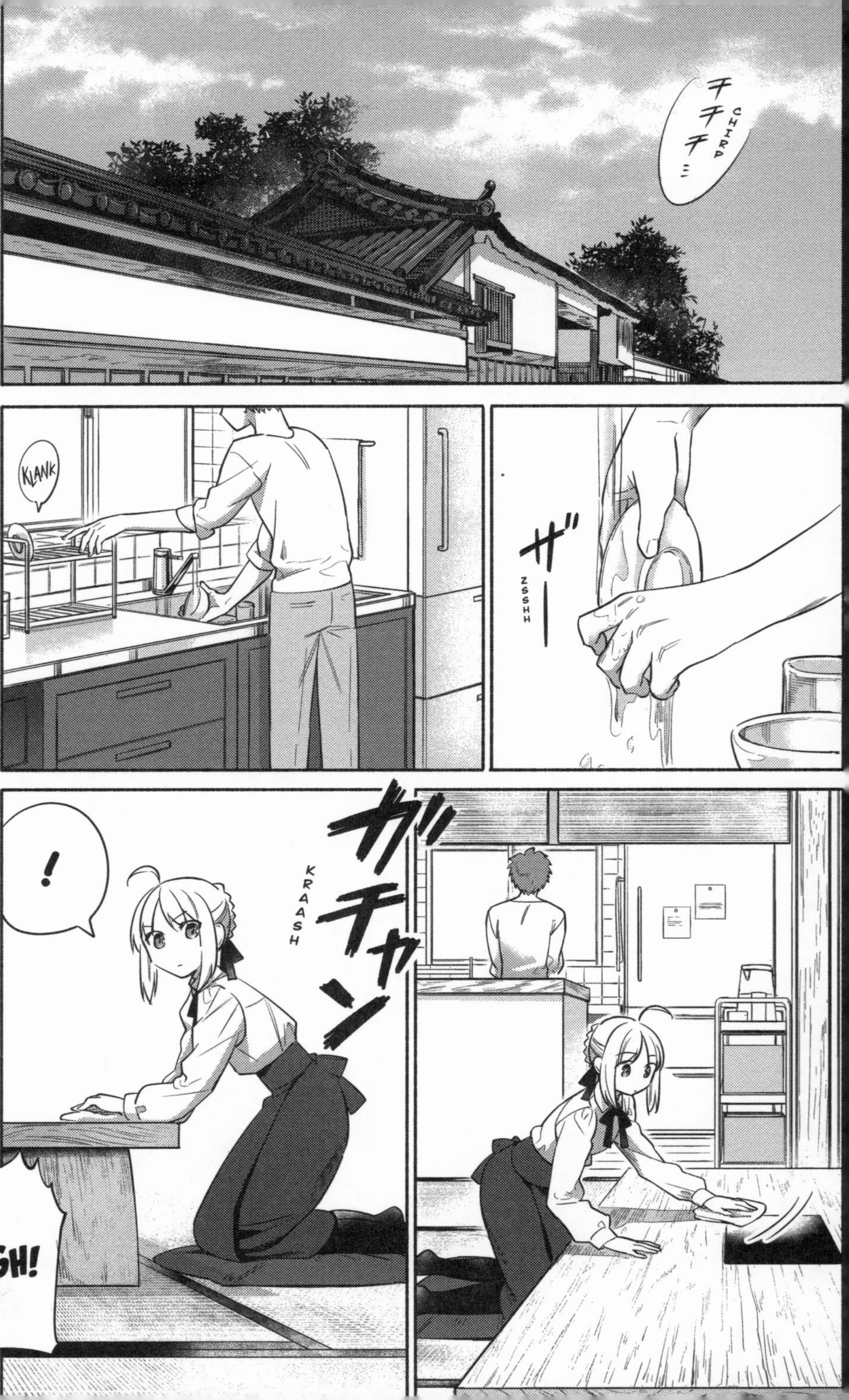
チチチ
CHIRP
ザー
ZSSHH
KLANK
ガチャン
KRAASH
!
AGH!

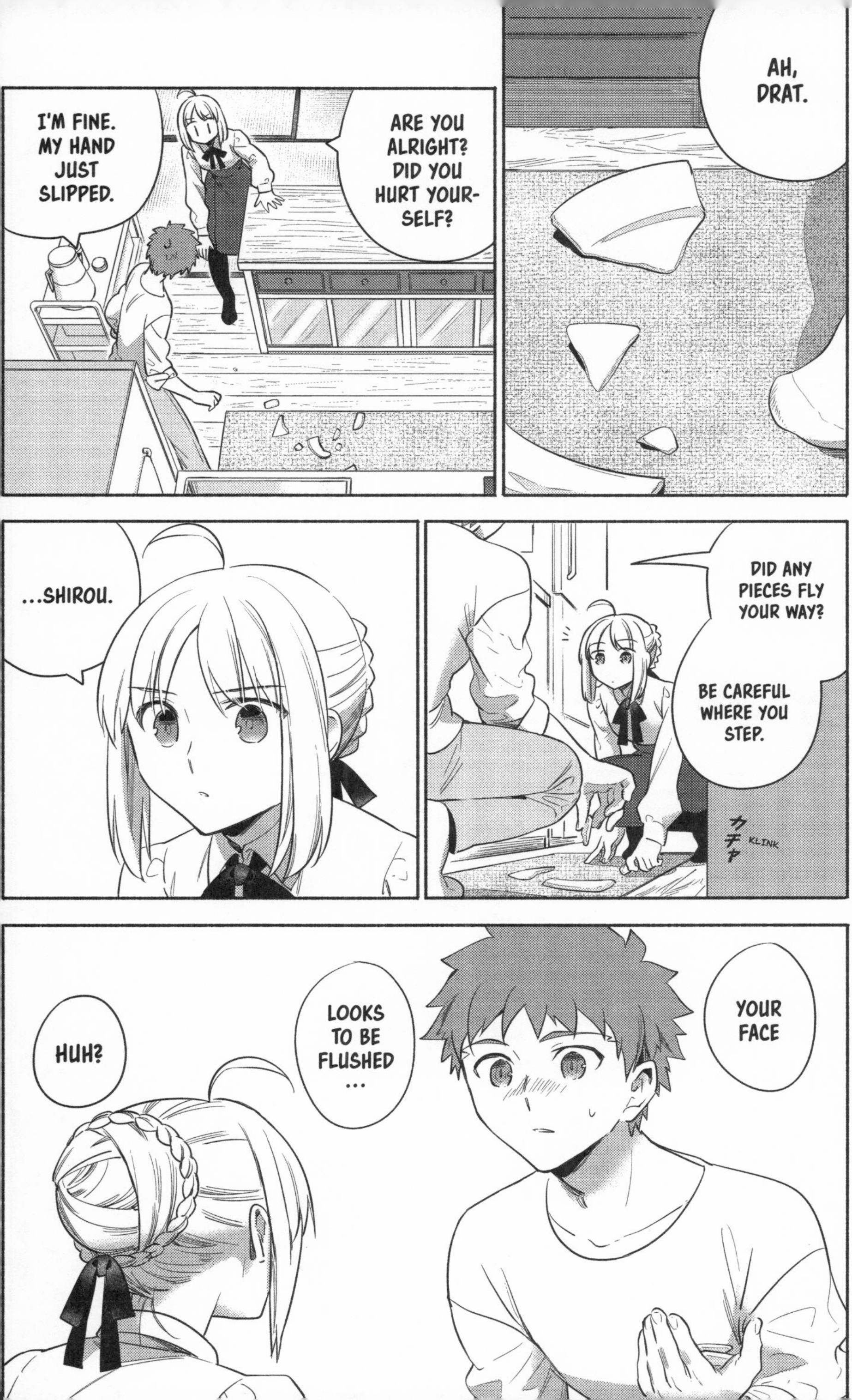
AH, DRAT.
ARE YOU ALRIGHT? DID YOU HURT YOUR-SELF?
I'M FINE. MY HAND JUST SLIPPED.
DID ANY PIECES FLY YOUR WAY?
BE CAREFUL WHERE YOU STEP.
カチャ
KLINK
...SHIROU.
YOUR FACE
LOOKS TO BE FLUSHED ...
HUH?

Chapter 29: Comforting Hot Pot Udon

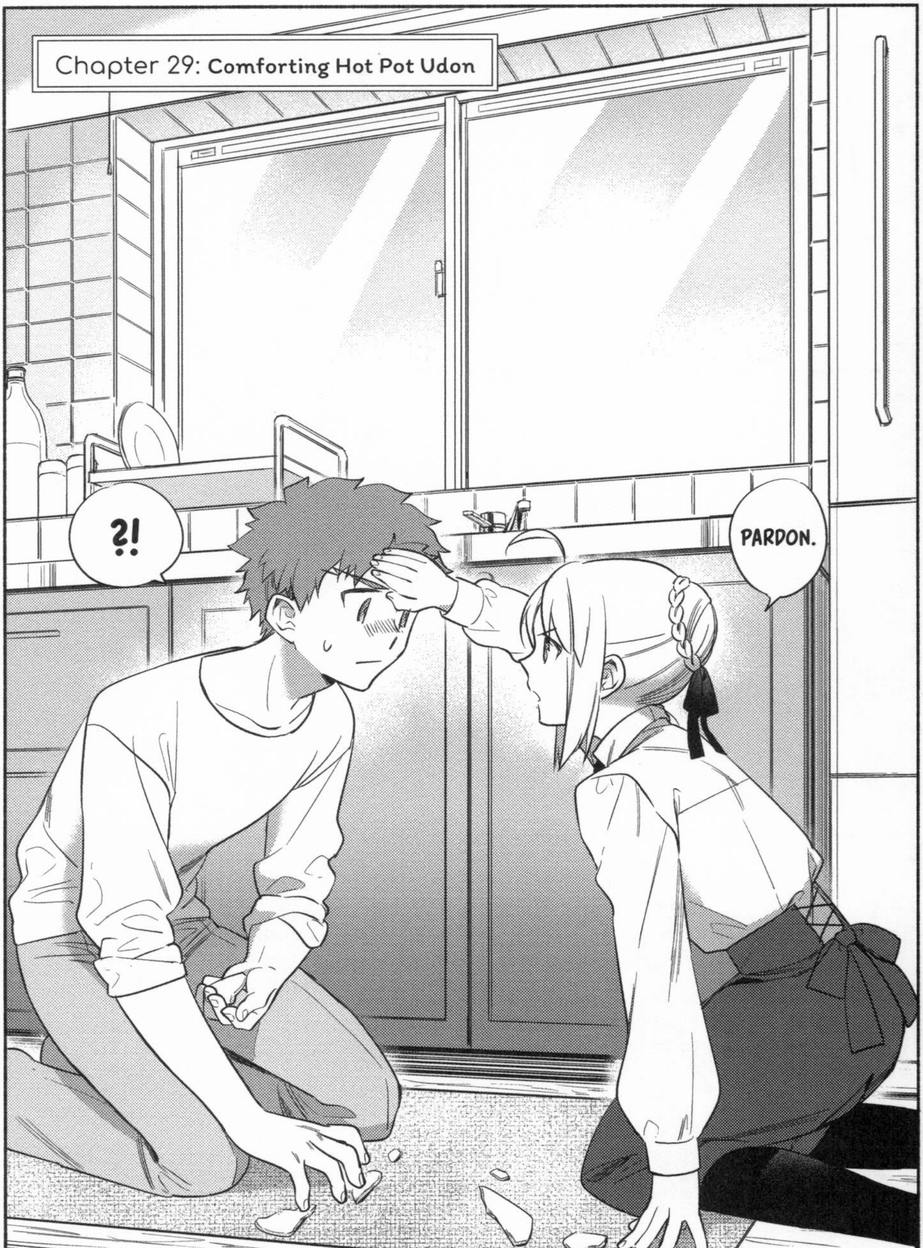
PARDON.
?!

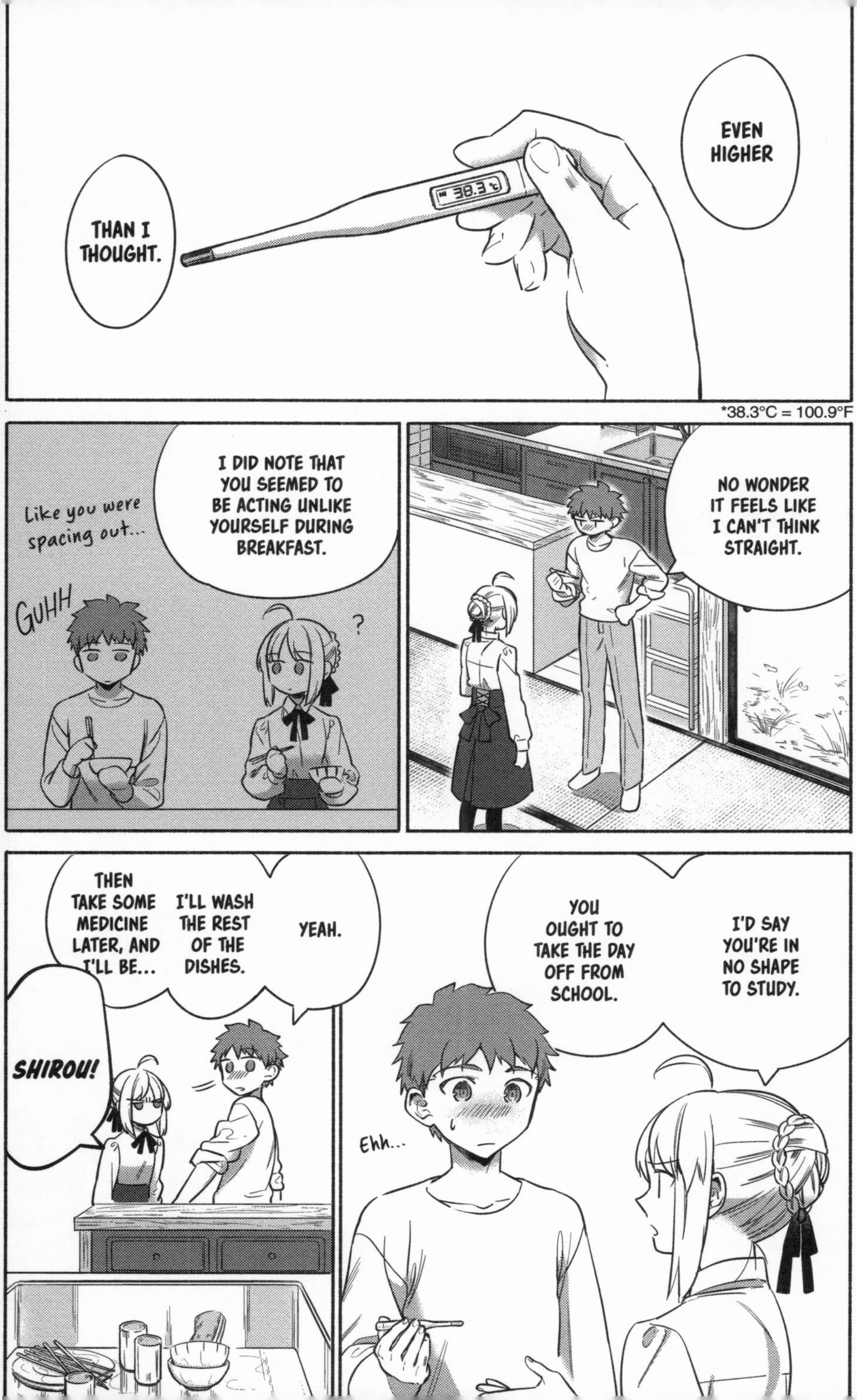
EVEN HIGHER
38.3°C
THAN I THOUGHT.
NO WONDER IT FEELS LIKE I CAN'T THINK STRAIGHT.
I DID NOTE THAT YOU SEEMED TO BE ACTING UNLIKE YOURSELF DURING BREAKFAST.
Like you were spacing out...
GUHH
?
I'D SAY YOU'RE IN NO SHAPE TO STUDY.
YOU OUGHT TO TAKE THE DAY OFF FROM SCHOOL.
Ehh...
YEAH.
I'LL WASH THE REST OF THE DISHES.
THEN TAKE SOME MEDICINE LATER, AND I'LL BE...
SHIROU!

*38.3°C = 100.9°F

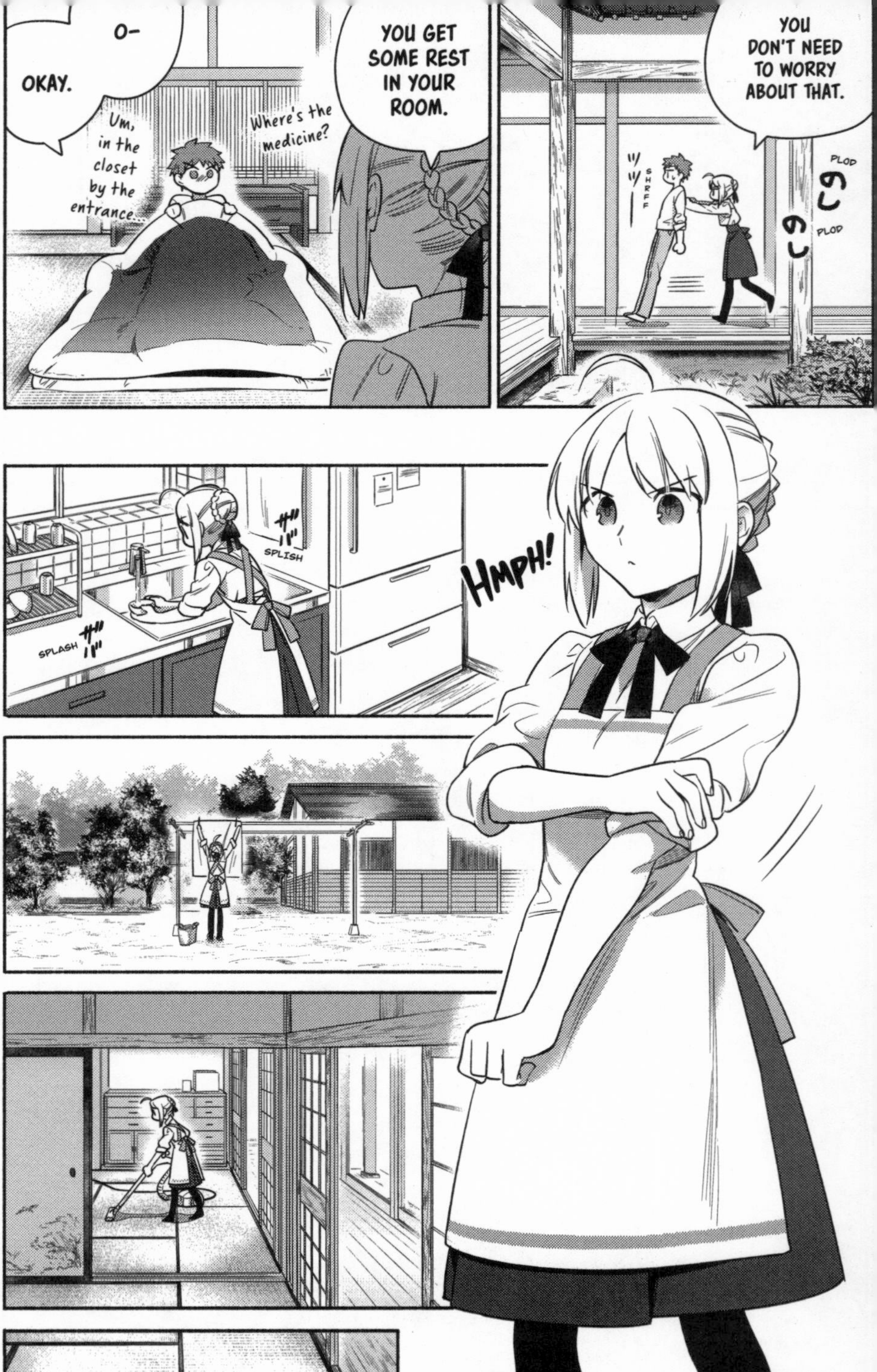
YOU GET SOME REST IN YOUR ROOM.
O-
OKAY.
Where's the medicine?
Um, in the closet by the entrance...
YOU DON'T NEED TO WORRY ABOUT THAT.
ツツー SHRFF
のし PLOD
のし PLOD
HMPH!
SPLASH
SPLASH

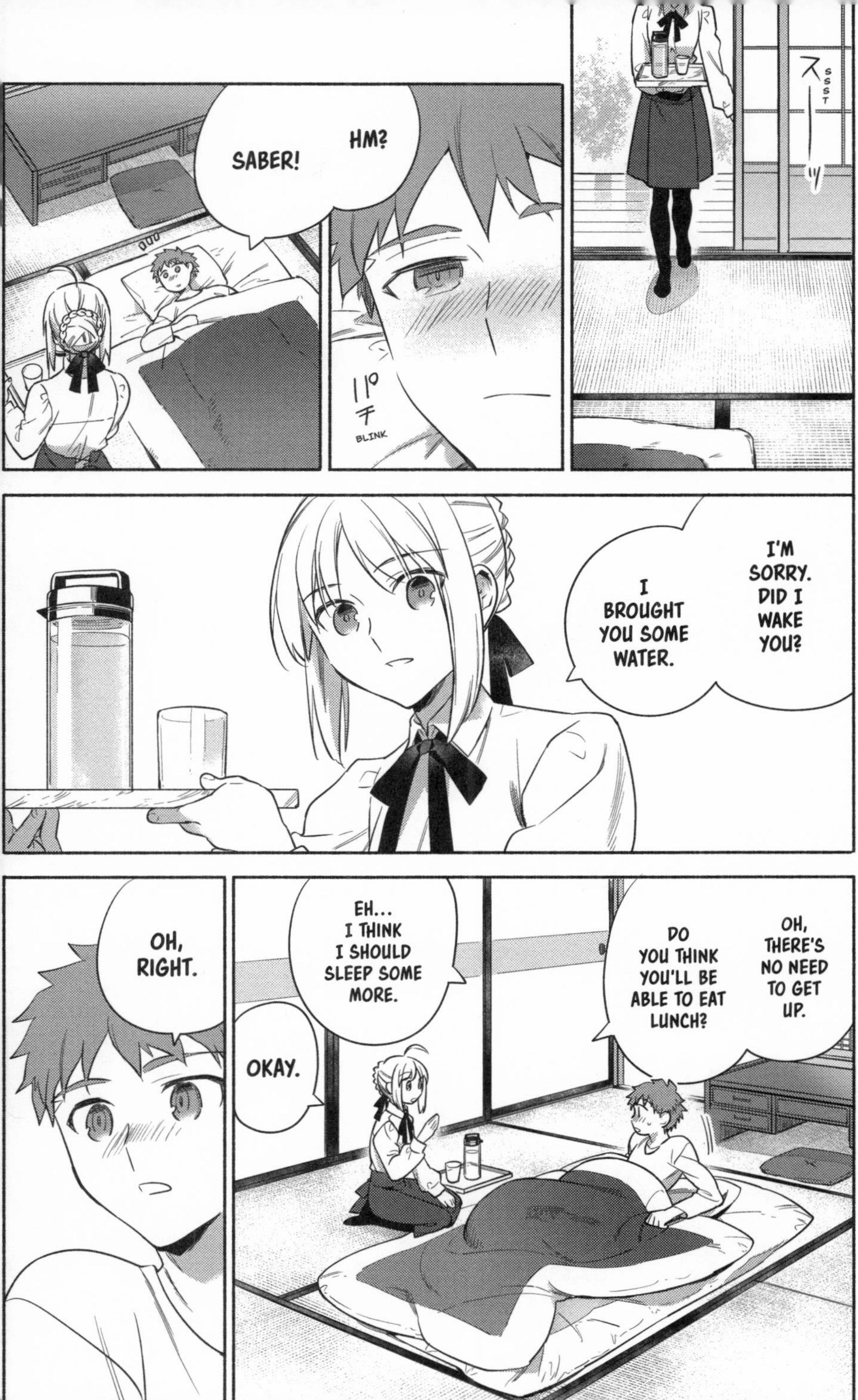

スーッ
SSST
HM?
SABER!
パチ
BLINK
I'M SORRY. DID I WAKE YOU?
I BROUGHT YOU SOME WATER.
OH, THERE'S NO NEED TO GET UP.
DO YOU THINK YOU'LL BE ABLE TO EAT LUNCH?
EH... I THINK I SHOULD SLEEP SOME MORE.
OKAY.
OH, RIGHT.

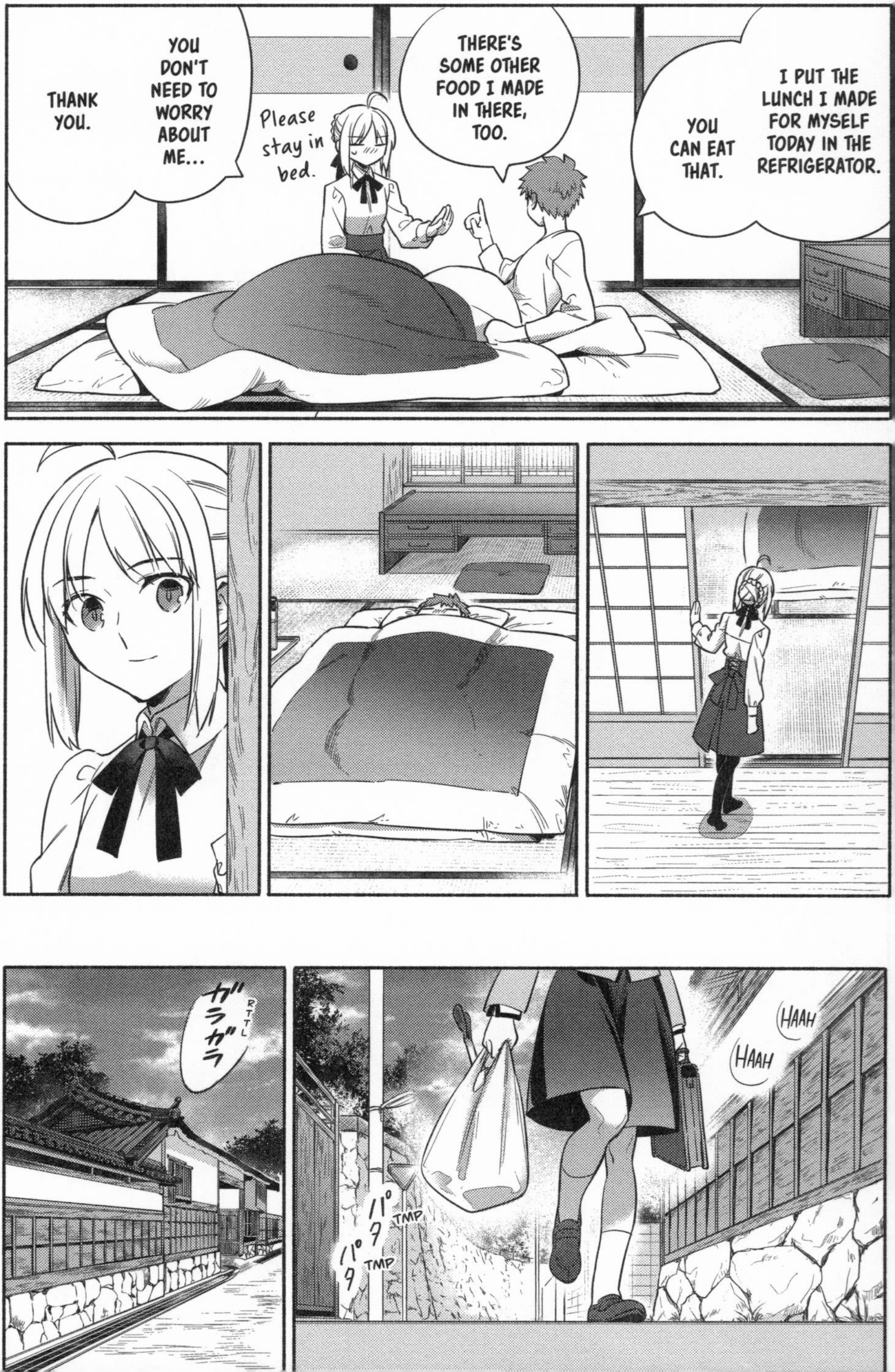
I PUT THE LUNCH I MADE FOR MYSELF TODAY IN THE REFRIGERATOR.
YOU CAN EAT THAT.
THERE'S SOME OTHER FOOD I MADE IN THERE, TOO.
Please stay in bed.
YOU DON'T NEED TO WORRY ABOUT ME...
THANK YOU.
HAAH
HAAH
パタ TMP
パタ TMP
ガラガラ RTTL

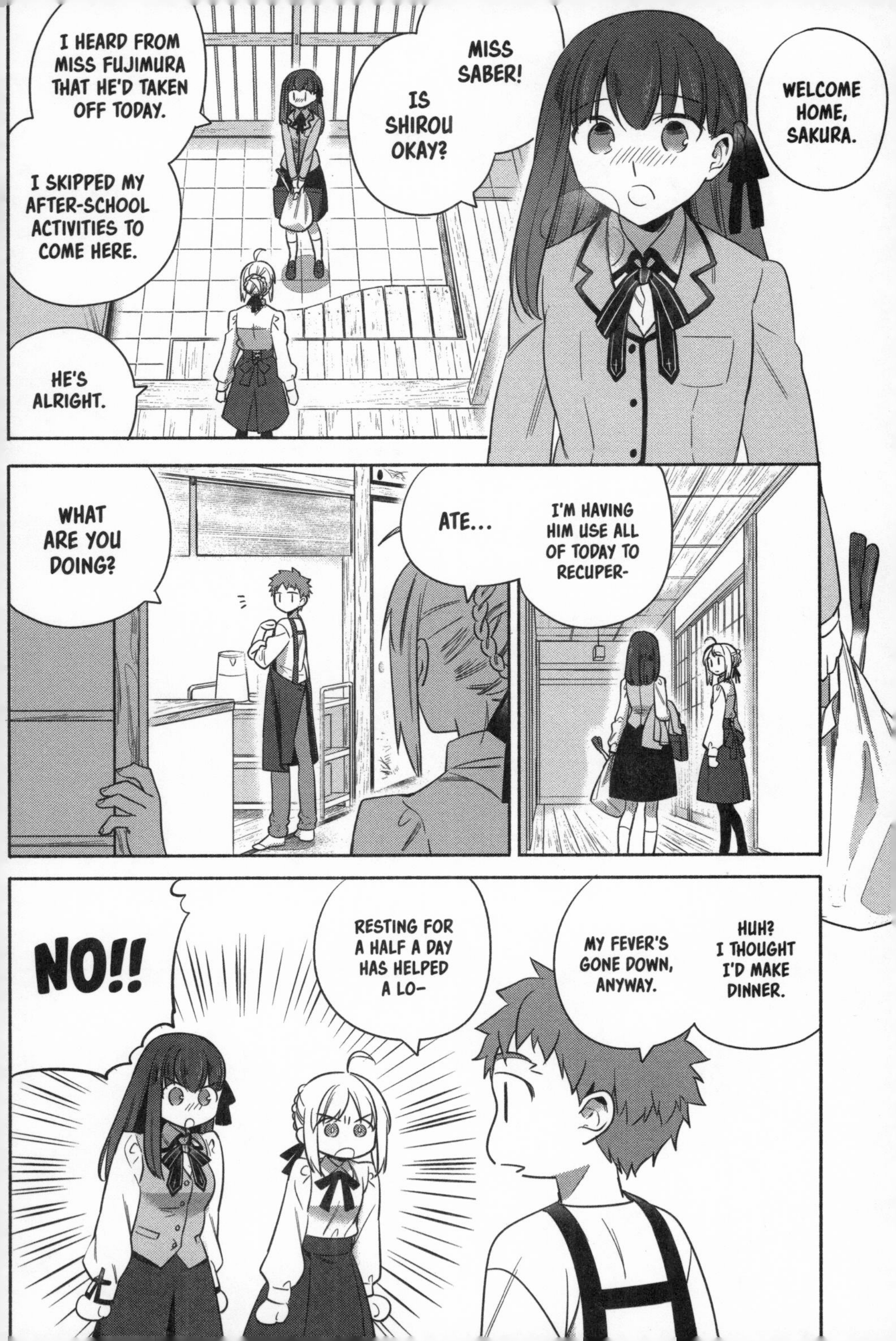
WELCOME HOME, SAKURA.
MISS SABER!
IS SHIROU OKAY?
I HEARD FROM MISS FUJIMURA THAT HE'D TAKEN OFF TODAY.
I SKIPPED MY AFTER-SCHOOL ACTIVITIES TO COME HERE.
HE'S ALRIGHT.
I'M HAVING HIM USE ALL OF TODAY TO RECUPER-
ATE...
WHAT ARE YOU DOING?
HUH? I THOUGHT I'D MAKE DINNER.
MY FEVER'S GONE DOWN, ANYWAY.
RESTING FOR A HALF A DAY HAS HELPED A LO-
NO!!

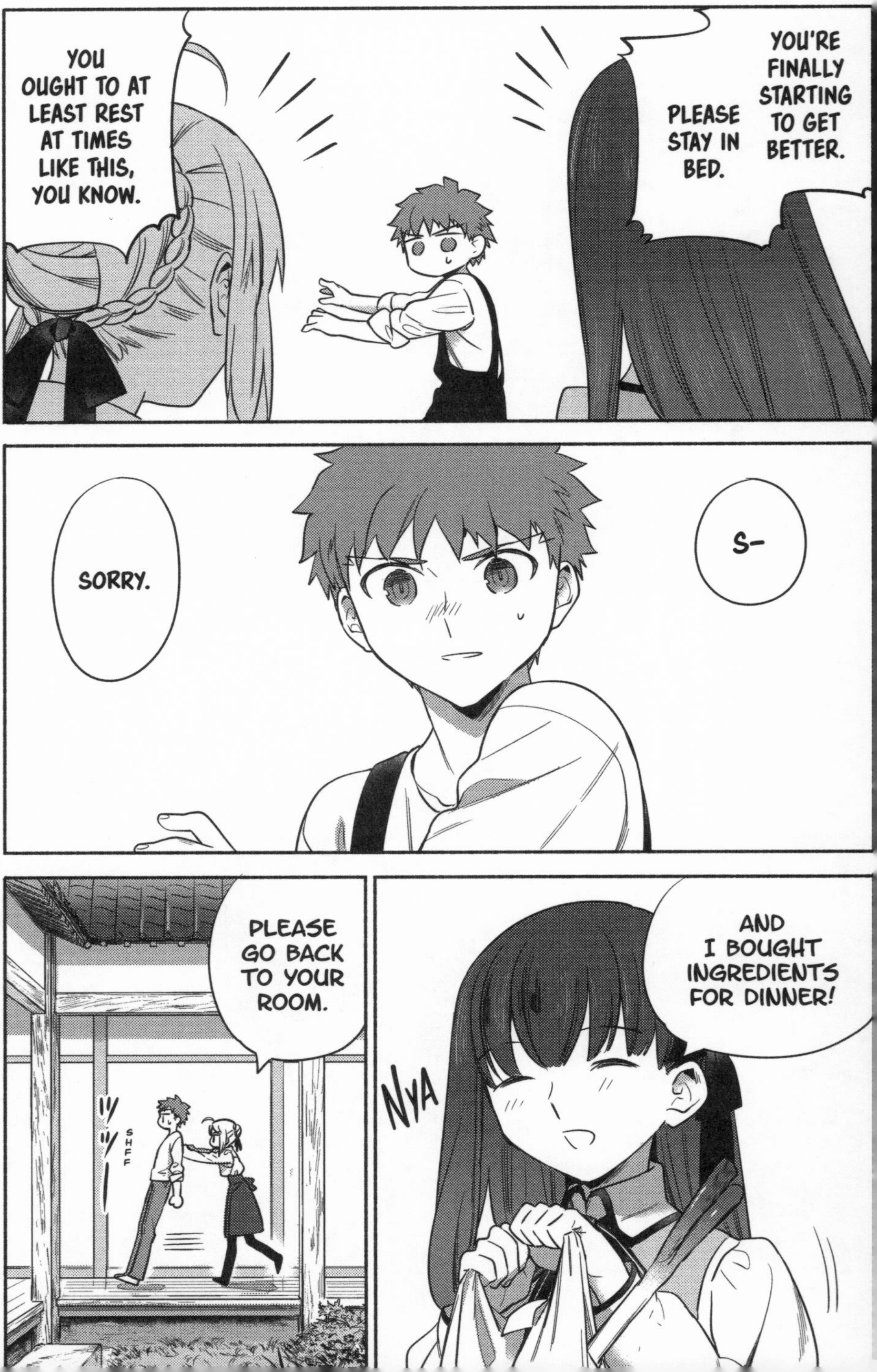
YOU'RE FINALLY STARTING TO GET BETTER.
PLEASE STAY IN BED.
YOU OUGHT TO AT LEAST REST AT TIMES LIKE THIS, YOU KNOW.
S-
SORRY.
AND I BOUGHT INGREDIENTS FOR DINNER!
NYA
PLEASE GO BACK TO YOUR ROOM.
SHFF

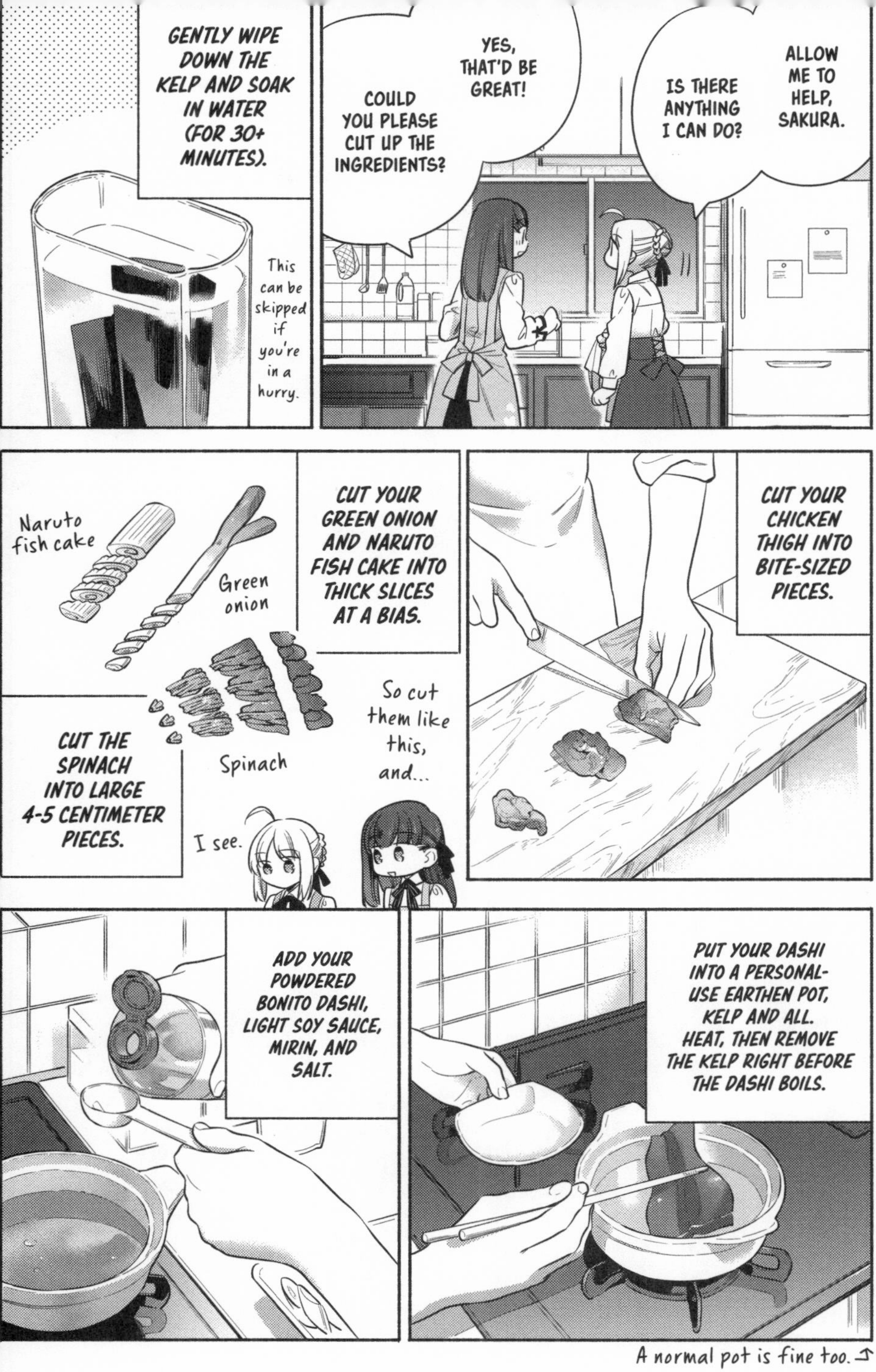
ALLOW ME TO HELP, SAKURA.
IS THERE ANYTHING I CAN DO?
YES, THAT'D BE GREAT!
COULD YOU PLEASE CUT UP THE INGREDIENTS?
GENTLY WIPE DOWN THE KELP AND SOAK IN WATER (FOR 30+ MINUTES).
This can be skipped if you're in a hurry.
CUT YOUR CHICKEN THIGH INTO BITE-SIZED PIECES.
CUT YOUR GREEN ONION AND NARUTO FISH CAKE INTO THICK SLICES AT A BIAS.
Naruto fish cake
Green onion
Spinach
CUT THE SPINACH INTO LARGE 4-5 CENTIMETER PIECES.
So cut them like this, and...
I see.
PUT YOUR DASHI INTO A PERSONAL-USE EARTHEN POT, KELP AND ALL. HEAT, THEN REMOVE THE KELP RIGHT BEFORE THE DASHI BOILS.
A normal pot is fine too.
ADD YOUR POWDERED BONITO DASHI, LIGHT SOY SAUCE, MIRIN, AND SALT.

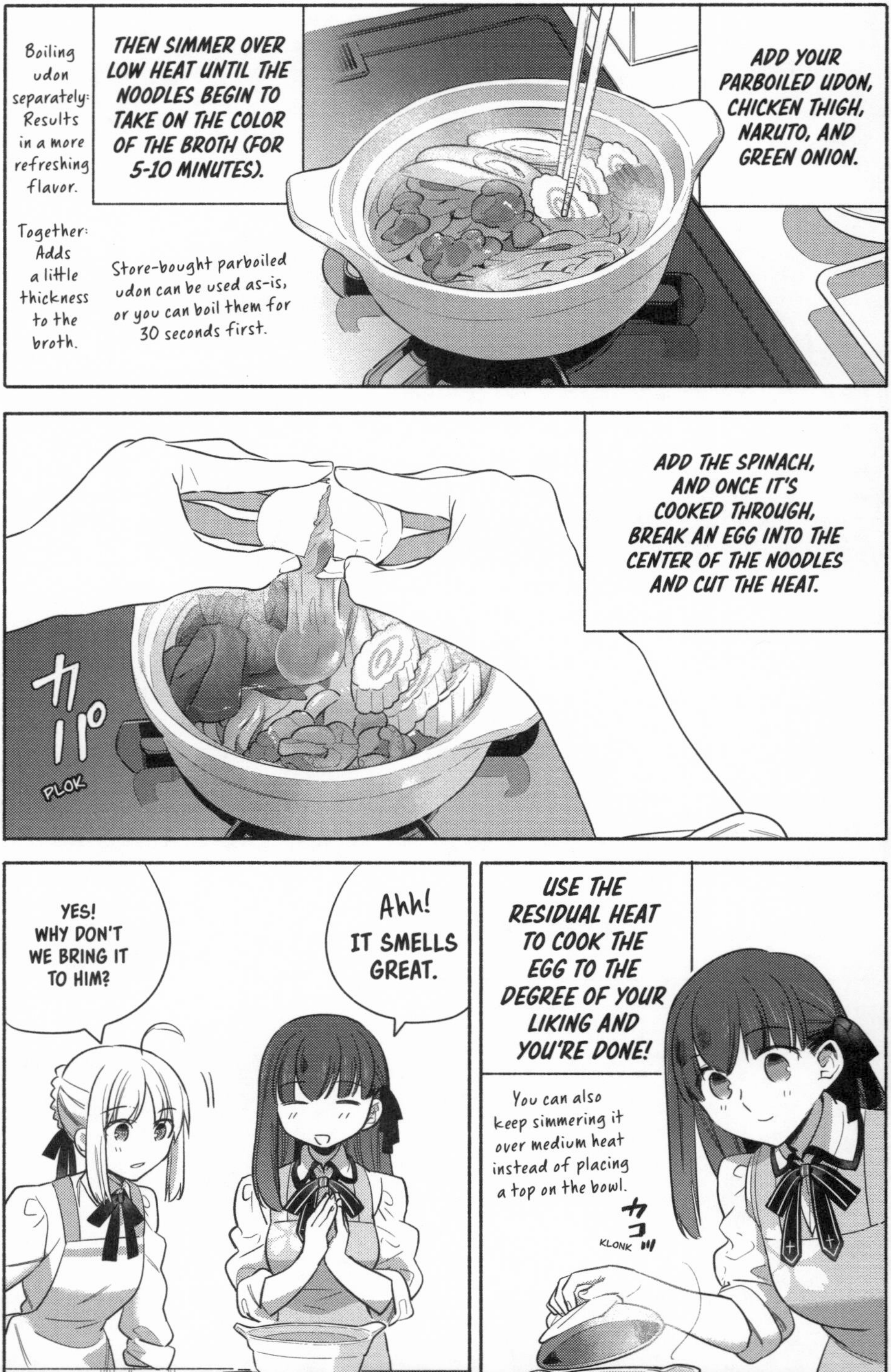
ADD YOUR PARBOILED UDON, CHICKEN THIGH, NARUTO, AND GREEN ONION.
THEN SIMMER OVER LOW HEAT UNTIL THE NOODLES BEGIN TO TAKE ON THE COLOR OF THE BROTH (FOR 5-10 MINUTES).
Store-bought parboiled udon can be used as-is, or you can boil them for 30 seconds first.
Boiling udon separately: Results in a more refreshing flavor.
Together: Adds a little thickness to the broth.
ADD THE SPINACH, AND ONCE IT'S COOKED THROUGH, BREAK AN EGG INTO THE CENTER OF THE NOODLES AND CUT THE HEAT.
カパ
PLOK
USE THE RESIDUAL HEAT TO COOK THE EGG TO THE DEGREE OF YOUR LIKING AND YOU'RE DONE!
You can also keep simmering it over medium heat instead of placing a top on the bowl.
カコ
KLONK
Ahh! IT SMELLS GREAT.
YES! WHY DON'T WE BRING IT TO HIM?

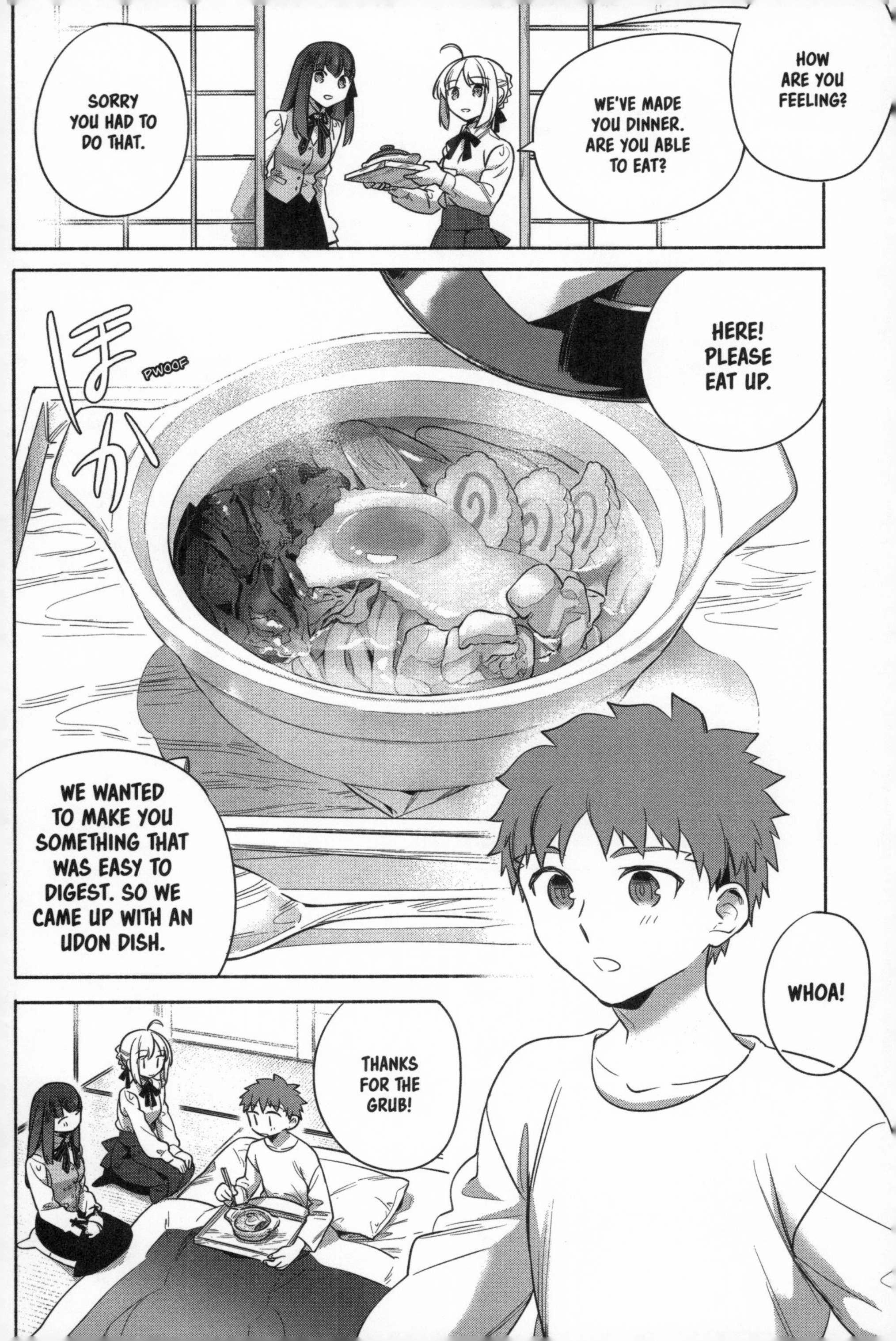
HOW ARE YOU FEELING?
WE'VE MADE YOU DINNER. ARE YOU ABLE TO EAT?
SORRY YOU HAD TO DO THAT.
HERE! PLEASE EAT UP.
ほか
PWOOF
WHOA!
WE WANTED TO MAKE YOU SOMETHING THAT WAS EASY TO DIGEST. SO WE CAME UP WITH AN UDON DISH.
THANKS FOR THE GRUB!

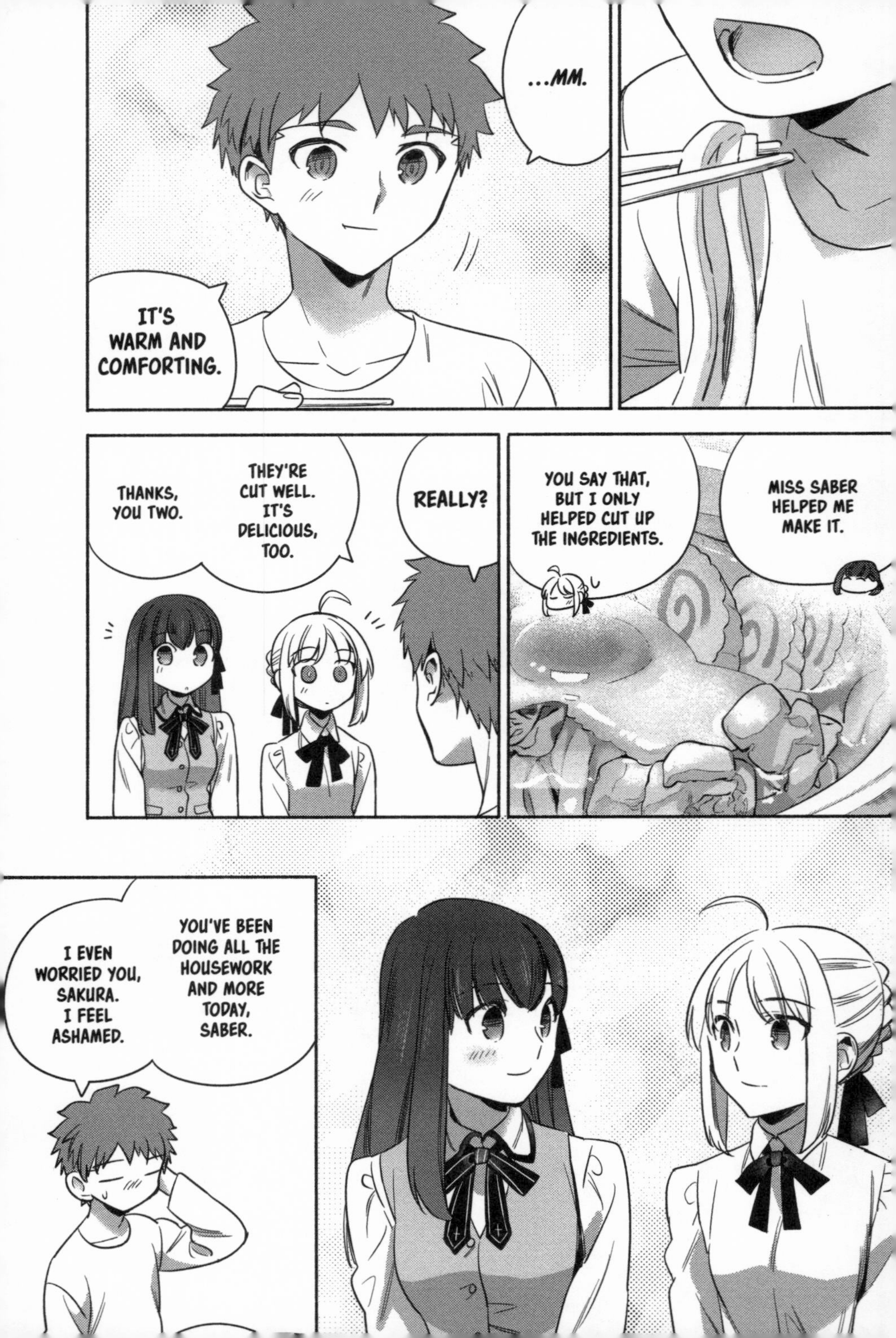
...MM.
IT'S WARM AND COMFORTING.
MISS SABER HELPED ME MAKE IT.
YOU SAY THAT, BUT I ONLY HELPED CUT UP THE INGREDIENTS.
REALLY?
THEY'RE CUT WELL. IT'S DELICIOUS, TOO.
THANKS, YOU TWO.
YOU'VE BEEN DOING ALL THE HOUSEWORK AND MORE TODAY, SABER.
I EVEN WORRIED YOU, SAKURA. I FEEL ASHAMED.

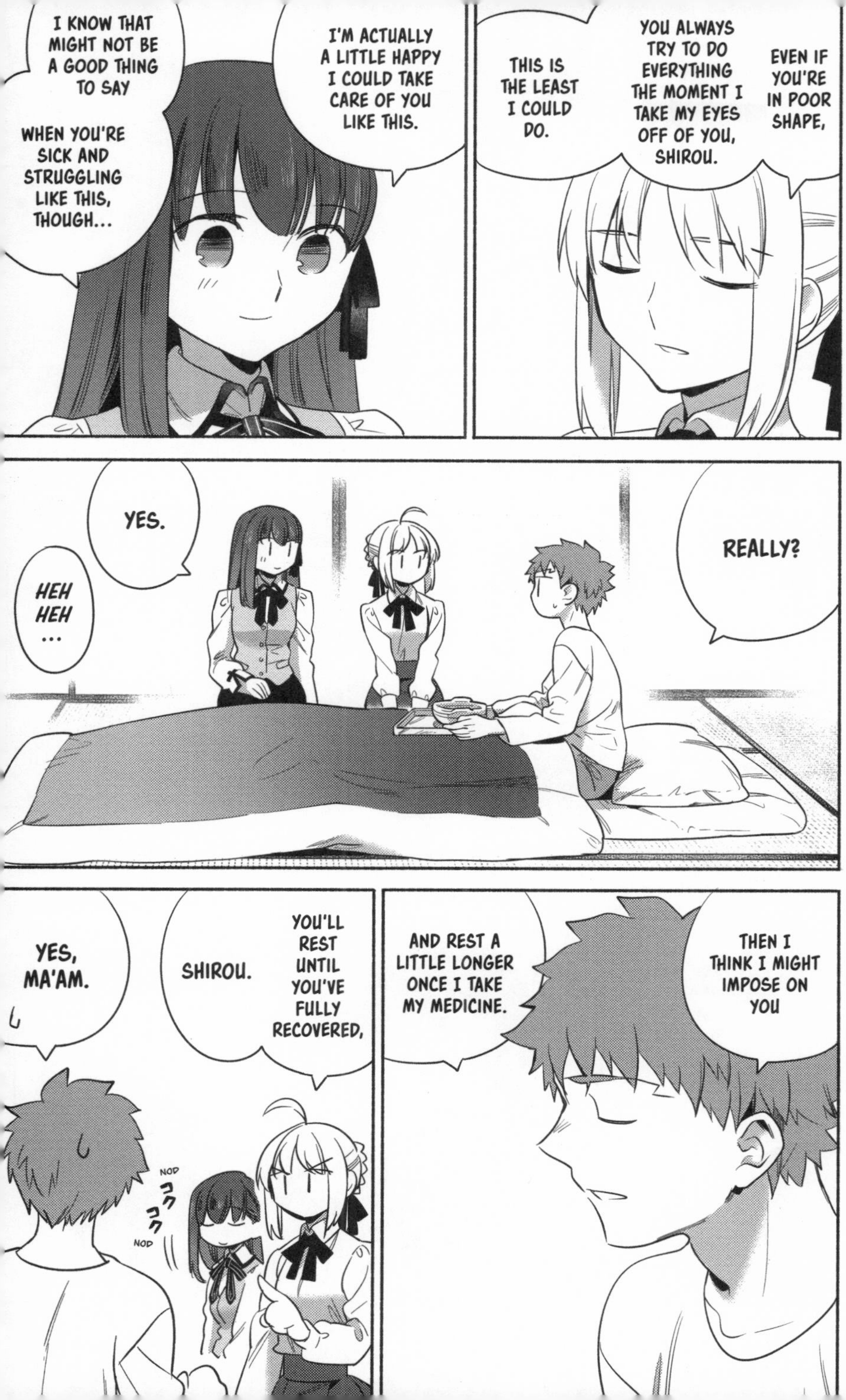
EVEN IF YOU'RE IN POOR SHAPE,
YOU ALWAYS TRY TO DO EVERYTHING THE MOMENT I TAKE MY EYES OFF OF YOU, SHIROU.
THIS IS THE LEAST I COULD DO.
I'M ACTUALLY A LITTLE HAPPY I COULD TAKE CARE OF YOU LIKE THIS.
I KNOW THAT MIGHT NOT BE A GOOD THING TO SAY
WHEN YOU'RE SICK AND STRUGGLING LIKE THIS, THOUGH...
REALLY?
YES.
HEH HEH ...
THEN I THINK I MIGHT IMPOSE ON YOU
AND REST A LITTLE LONGER ONCE I TAKE MY MEDICINE.
YOU'LL REST UNTIL YOU'VE FULLY RECOVERED,
SHIROU.
YES, MA'AM.
NOD
コク
コク
NOD

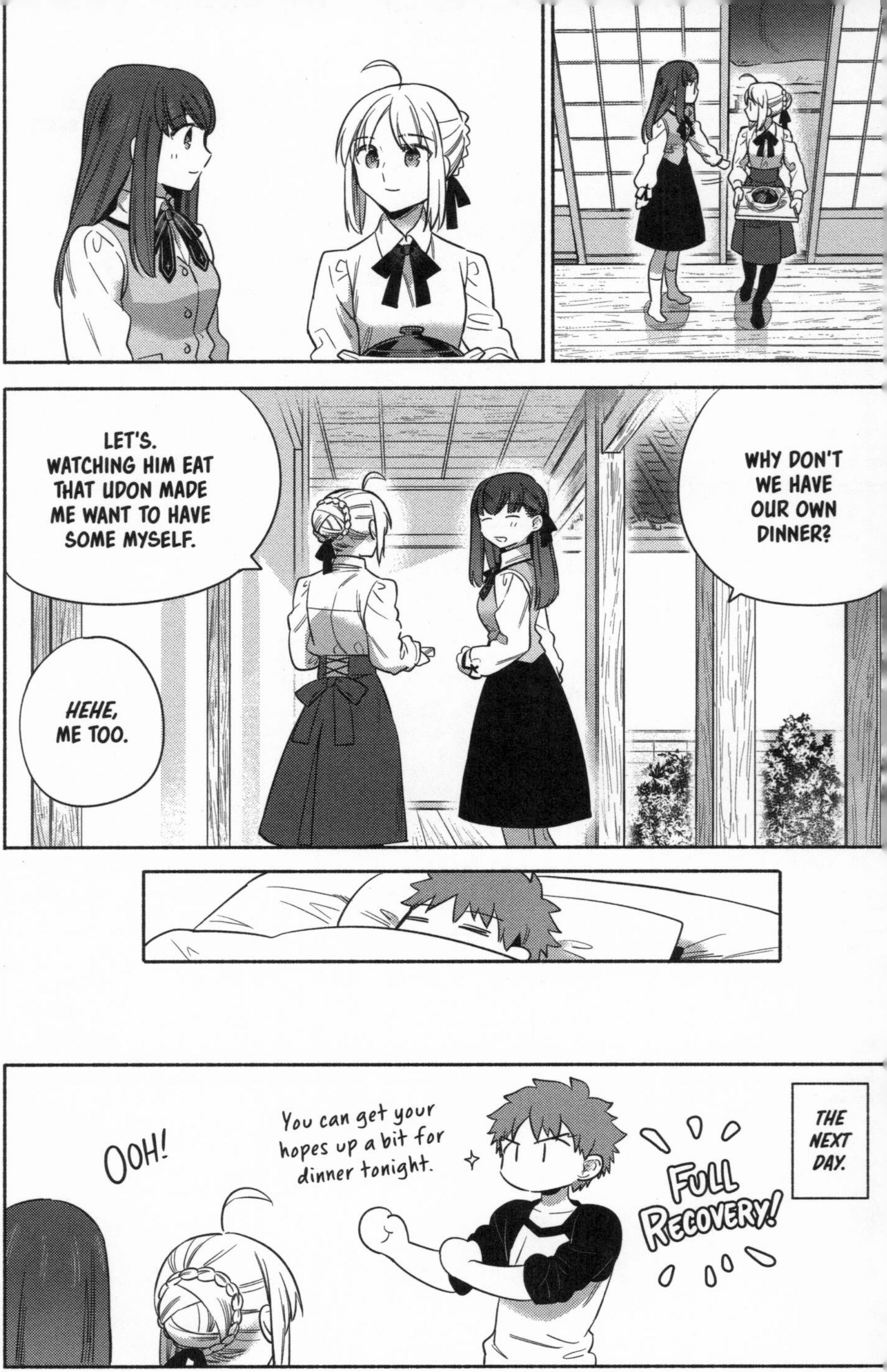
WHY DON'T WE HAVE OUR OWN DINNER?
LET'S. WATCHING HIM EAT THAT UDON MADE ME WANT TO HAVE SOME MYSELF.
HEHE, ME TOO.
THE NEXT DAY.
FULL RECOVERY!
You can get your hopes up a bit for dinner tonight.
OOH!

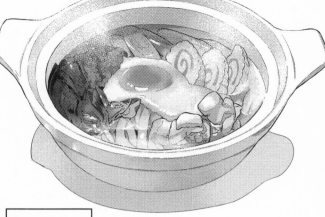

Comforting Hot Pot Udon

Ingredients - Serves 1

1 serving (about 10 oz) parboiled udon

80 g (2.8 oz) chicken thigh

1/4 stick (40 g / 1.4 oz) naruto fish cake

1/4 green onion (50 g / 1.8 oz)

1-2 stalks spinach (20 g / .7 oz)

1 egg

Udon Broth

10 cm (3.9 in) kelp

500 ml (16.9 oz) water

A ⎡ 1 tsp powdered bonito dashi
  ⎢ 2 tsp light soy sauce
  ⎢ 2 Tbsp mirin
  ⎣ 1 pinch salt

As desired:

Shichimi pepper mix

Yuzu kosho

Etc

Feel free to add abura-age or tempura fish cakes, tempura flakes and more to your udon.

Frozen noodles are okay as well. If you have dry udon, boil them once before using.

Preparation

① Gently wipe down the kelp and soak in water (for 30+ minutes).
   *You can also make this the night before and let it sit overnight in the refrigerator. This can be skipped if you're in a hurry.

② While you can use store-bought parboiled udon as-is, you can also boil them for 30 seconds first. This will result in different final products, so use the method you like best.

| Boil udon separately: | Doesn't cloud the broth, resulting in a more refreshing flavor. |
| Boil udon in the pot: | Adds a little thickness to the broth. |

Instructions

❶ Cut your chicken thigh into bite-sized pieces, cut your green onion and naruto fish cake into thick slices at a bias, and cut the spinach into large 4-5 centimeter pieces.

❷ Pour your dashi into a personal-use earthen pot (or a regular pot), kelp and all. Heat, then remove the kelp right before it boils. Add A, then add the parboiled udon, chicken thigh, naruto, and green onion, then simmer over low heat until the noodles begin to take on the color of the broth (for 5-10 minutes).
   *Skim any scum and add water if it boils down.

❸ Add the spinach, and once it's cooked through, break an egg into the center of the noodles and cut the heat.

❹ Let the pot's residual heat cook the egg to your desired level of firmness and you're done!
   *You can also keep simmering it over medium heat instead of placing a lid on the bowl.

Today's Menu for the Emiya Family

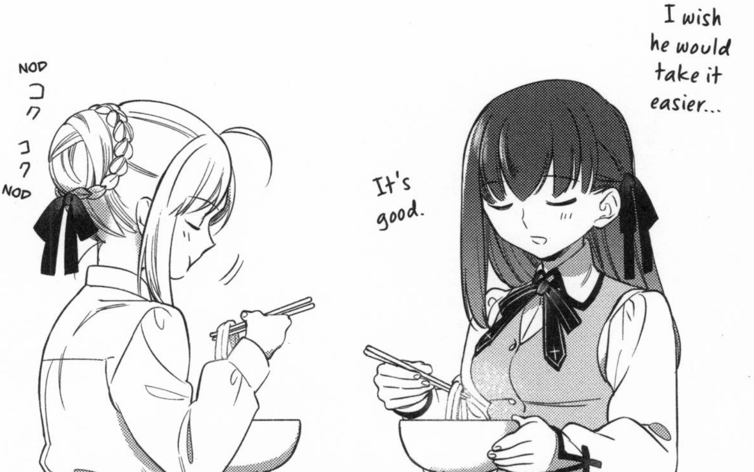
I wish he would take it easier...
It's good.
NOD コク
コク NOD

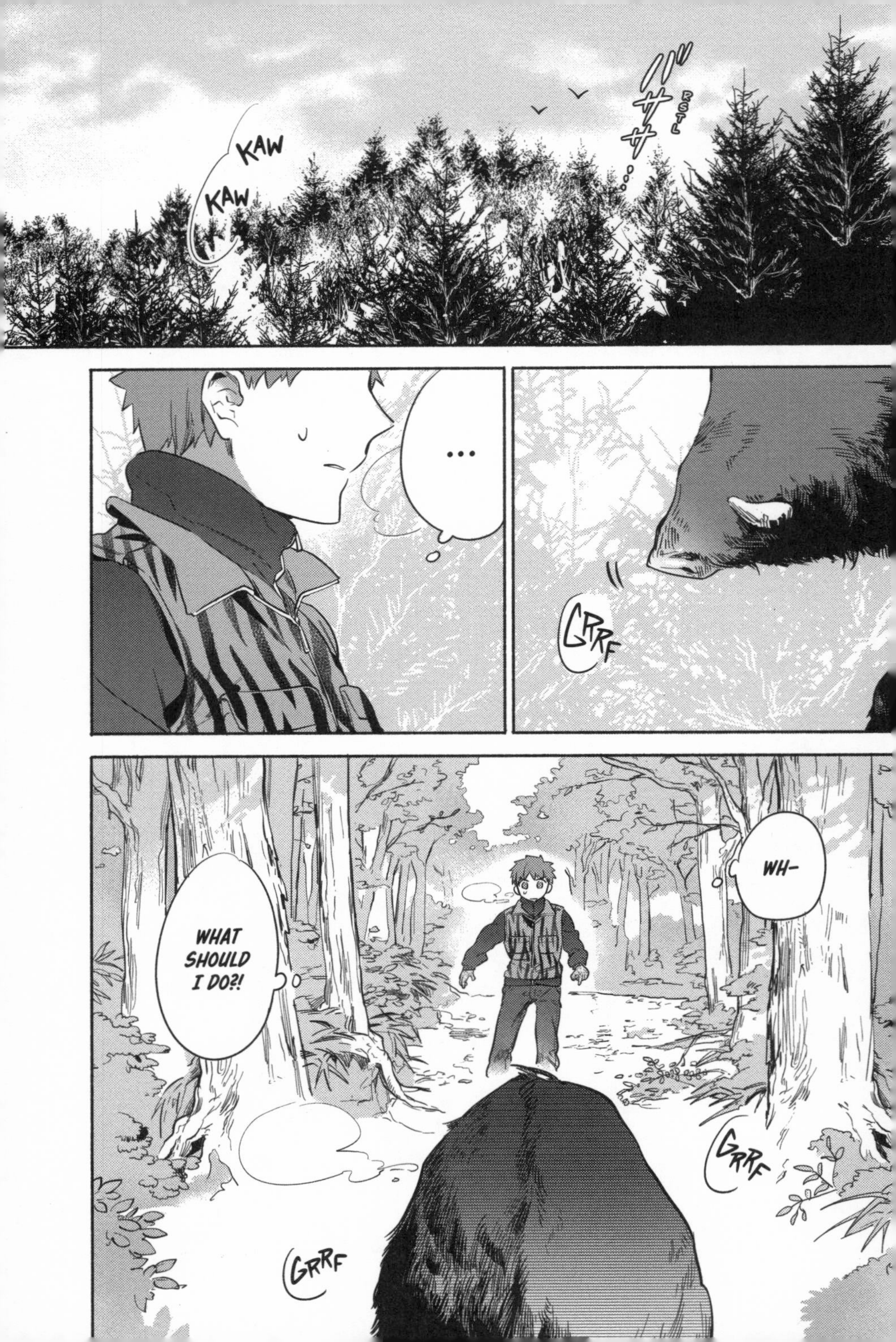
バササ…
RSTL
KAW
KAW
GRRF
...
WH-
WHAT SHOULD I DO?!
GRRF
GRRF

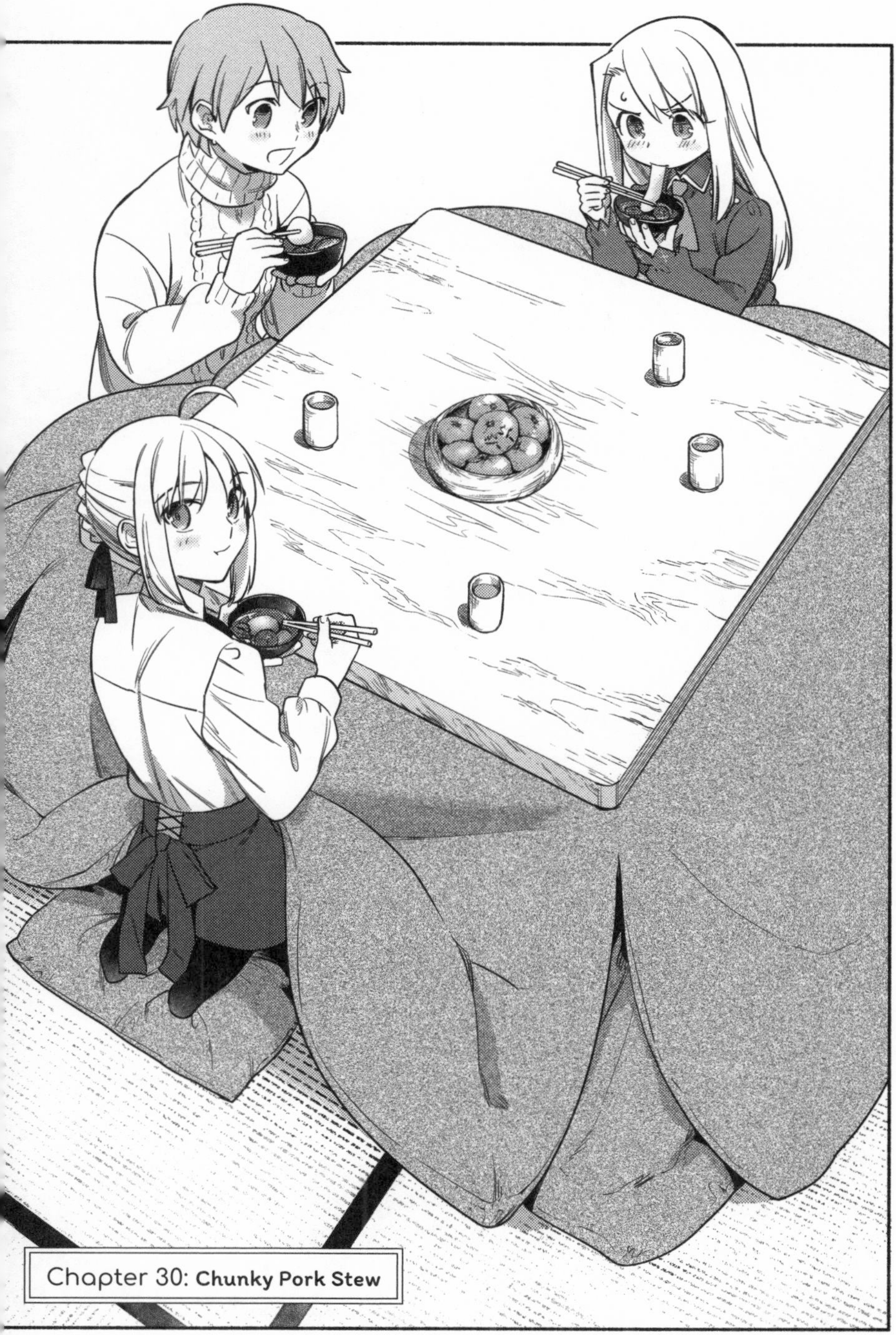
Chapter 30: Chunky Pork Stew

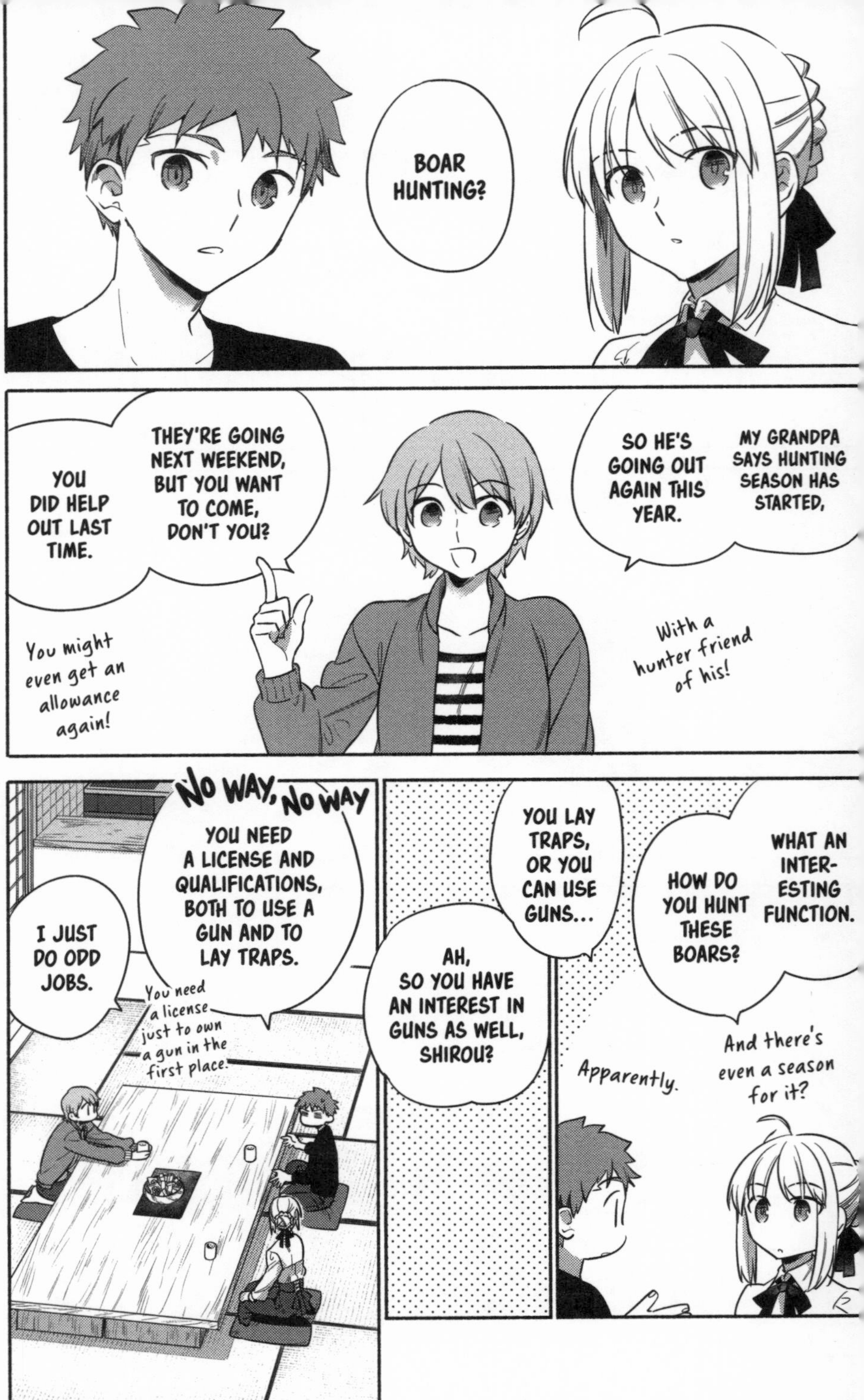
BOAR HUNTING?
MY GRANDPA SAYS HUNTING SEASON HAS STARTED,
SO HE'S GOING OUT AGAIN THIS YEAR.
With a hunter friend of his!
THEY'RE GOING NEXT WEEKEND, BUT YOU WANT TO COME, DON'T YOU?
YOU DID HELP OUT LAST TIME.
You might even get an allowance again!
WHAT AN INTER-ESTING FUNCTION.
HOW DO YOU HUNT THESE BOARS?
And there's even a season for it?
YOU LAY TRAPS, OR YOU CAN USE GUNS...
Apparently.
AH, SO YOU HAVE AN INTEREST IN GUNS AS WELL, SHIROU?
NO WAY, NO WAY
YOU NEED A LICENSE AND QUALIFICATIONS, BOTH TO USE A GUN AND TO LAY TRAPS.
You need a license just to own a gun in the first place.
I JUST DO ODD JOBS.

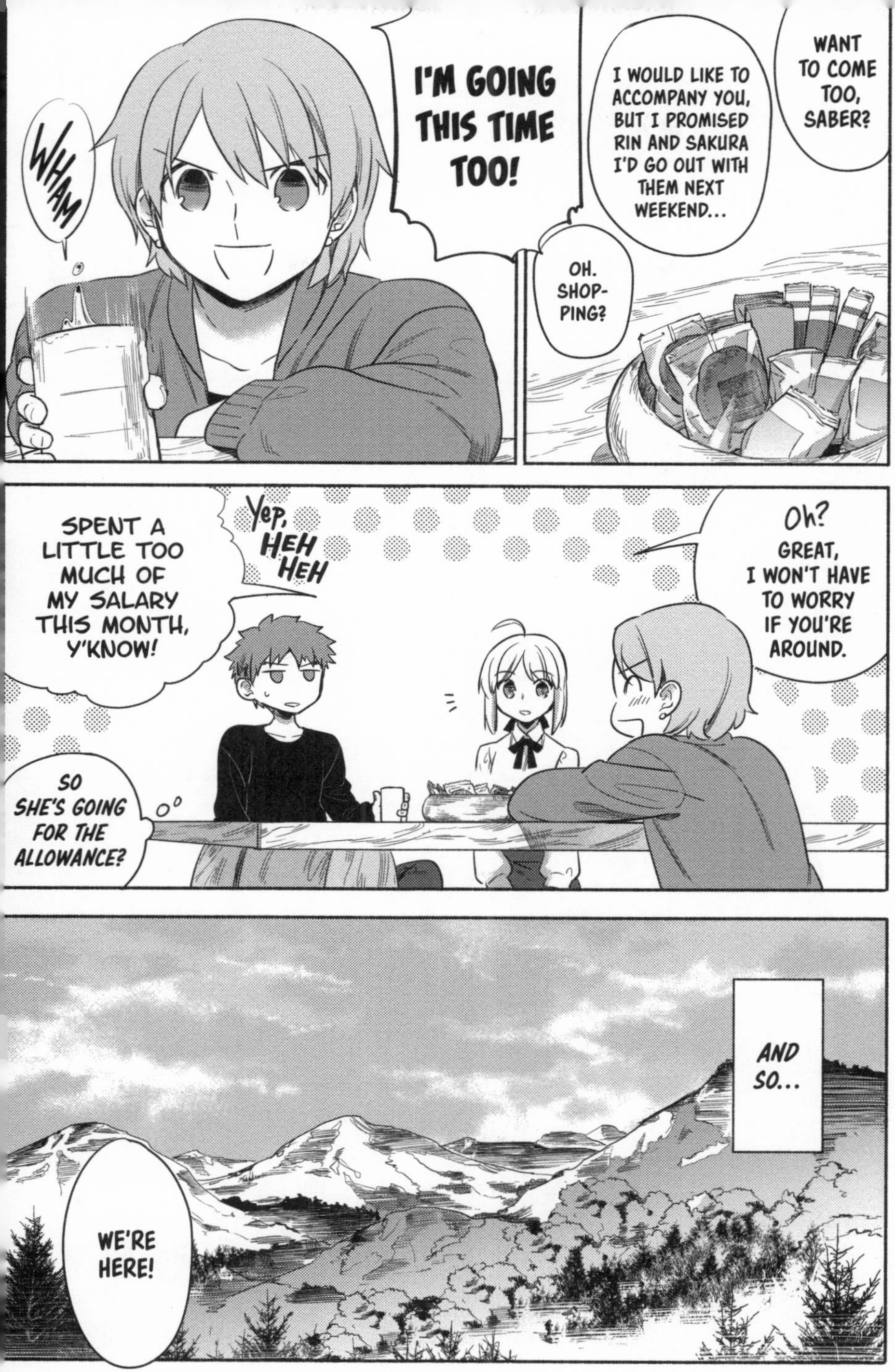
WANT TO COME TOO, SABER?
I WOULD LIKE TO ACCOMPANY YOU, BUT I PROMISED RIN AND SAKURA I'D GO OUT WITH THEM NEXT WEEKEND...
OH. SHOP-PING?
I'M GOING THIS TIME TOO!
WHAM
Oh? GREAT, I WON'T HAVE TO WORRY IF YOU'RE AROUND.
Yep, HEH HEH
SPENT A LITTLE TOO MUCH OF MY SALARY THIS MONTH, Y'KNOW!
SO SHE'S GOING FOR THE ALLOWANCE?
AND SO...
WE'RE HERE!

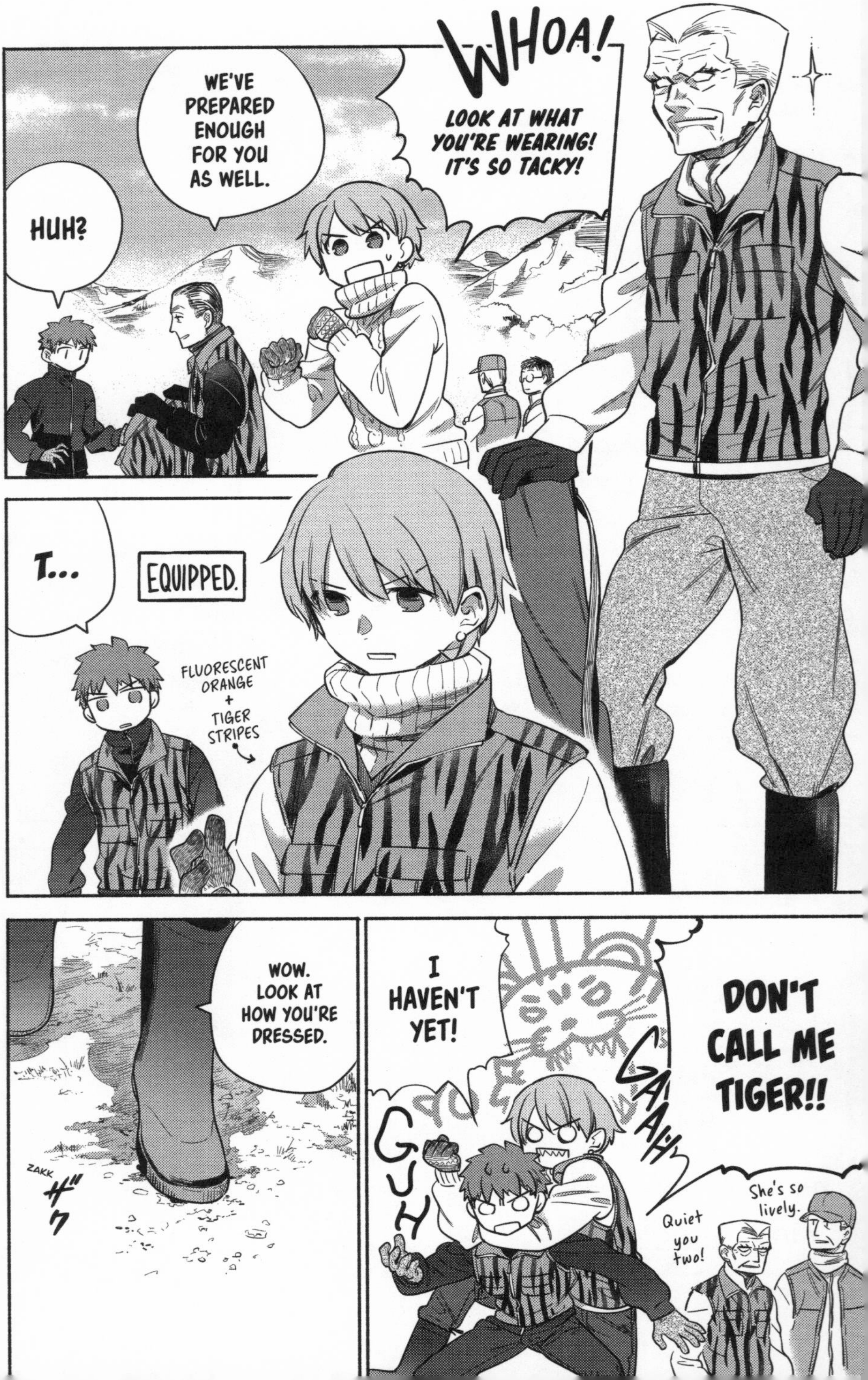

WHOA!
LOOK AT WHAT YOU'RE WEARING! IT'S SO TACKY!
WE'VE PREPARED ENOUGH FOR YOU AS WELL.
HUH?
EQUIPPED.
T...
FLUORESCENT ORANGE + TIGER STRIPES
DON'T CALL ME TIGER!!
GAAAH
I HAVEN'T YET!
GUH
She's so lively.
Quiet you two!
WOW. LOOK AT HOW YOU'RE DRESSED.
ZAKK
ザッ

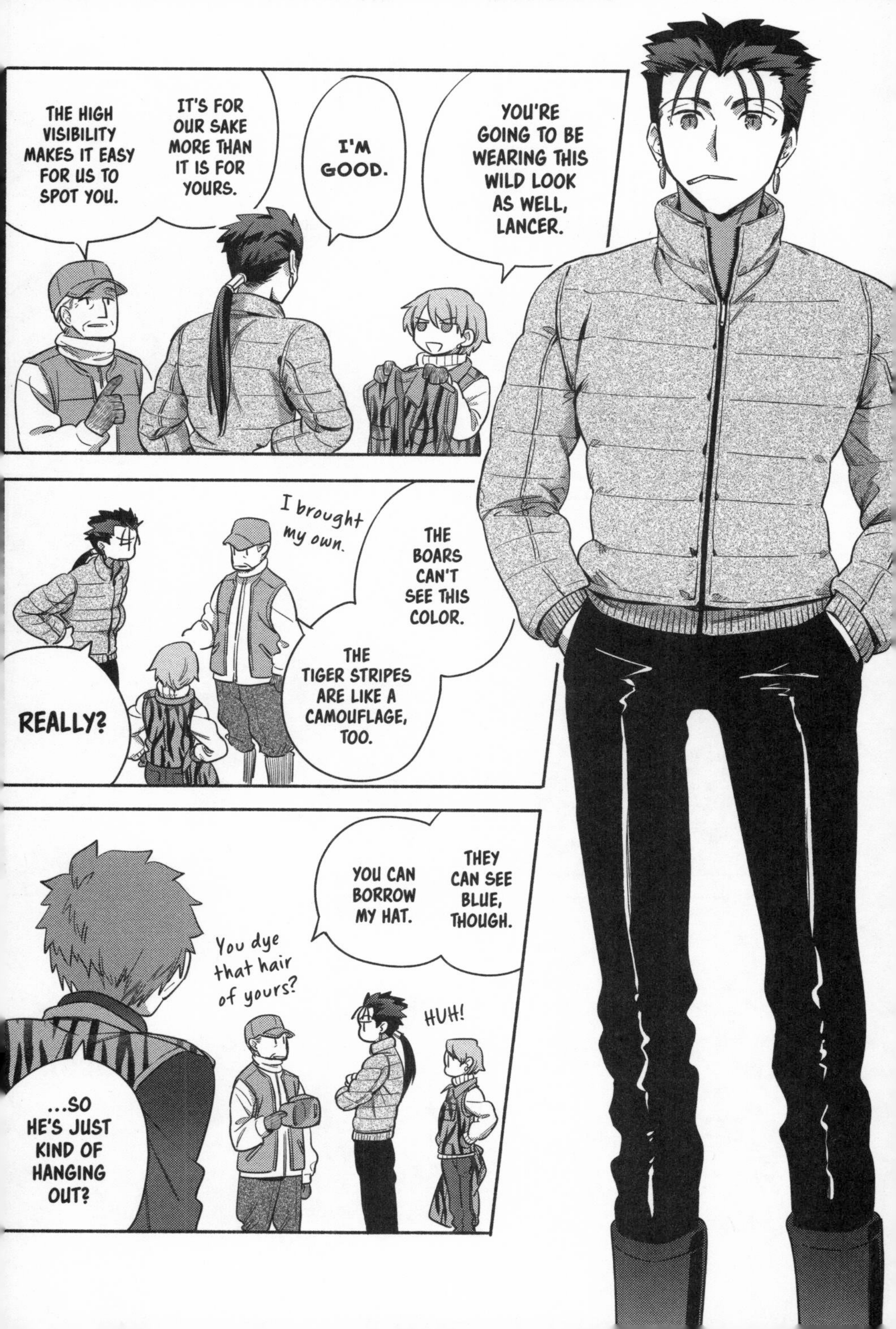
YOU'RE GOING TO BE WEARING THIS WILD LOOK AS WELL, LANCER.
I'M GOOD.
IT'S FOR OUR SAKE MORE THAN IT IS FOR YOURS.
THE HIGH VISIBILITY MAKES IT EASY FOR US TO SPOT YOU.
THE BOARS CAN'T SEE THIS COLOR.
I brought my own.
THE TIGER STRIPES ARE LIKE A CAMOUFLAGE, TOO.
REALLY?
THEY CAN SEE BLUE, THOUGH.
YOU CAN BORROW MY HAT.
HUH!
You dye that hair of yours?
...SO HE'S JUST KIND OF HANGING OUT?

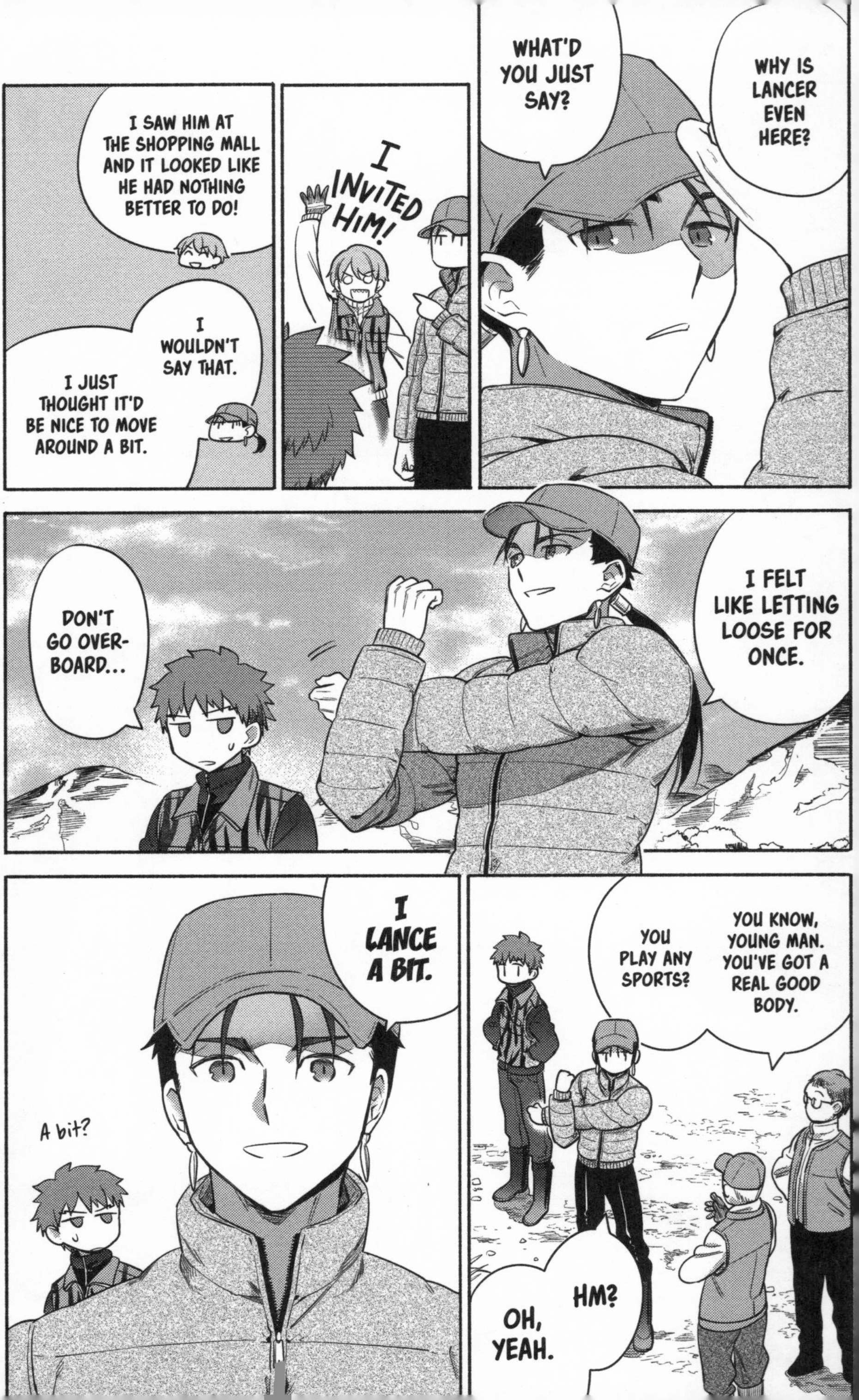
WHY IS LANCER EVEN HERE?
WHAT'D YOU JUST SAY?
I INVITED HIM!
I SAW HIM AT THE SHOPPING MALL AND IT LOOKED LIKE HE HAD NOTHING BETTER TO DO!
I WOULDN'T SAY THAT.
I JUST THOUGHT IT'D BE NICE TO MOVE AROUND A BIT.
I FELT LIKE LETTING LOOSE FOR ONCE.
DON'T GO OVER-BOARD...
YOU KNOW, YOUNG MAN. YOU'VE GOT A REAL GOOD BODY.
YOU PLAY ANY SPORTS?
HM?
OH, YEAH.
I LANCE A BIT.
A bit?

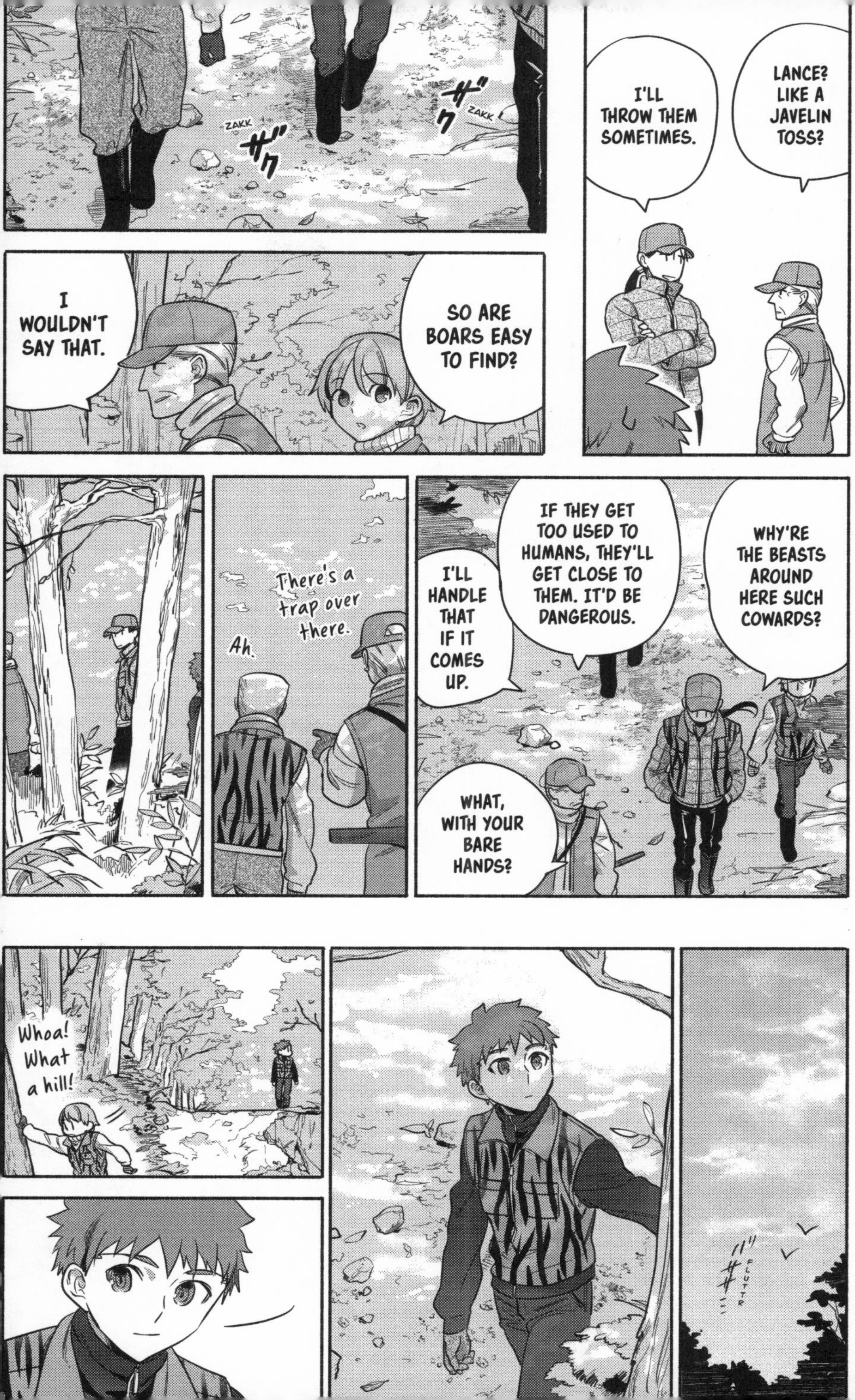
LANCE? LIKE A JAVELIN TOSS?
I'LL THROW THEM SOMETIMES.
ZAKK
ザク
ZAKK
ザク
SO ARE BOARS EASY TO FIND?
I WOULDN'T SAY THAT.
WHY'RE THE BEASTS AROUND HERE SUCH COWARDS?
IF THEY GET TOO USED TO HUMANS, THEY'LL GET CLOSE TO THEM. IT'D BE DANGEROUS.
I'LL HANDLE THAT IF IT COMES UP.
WHAT, WITH YOUR BARE HANDS?
There's a trap over there.
Ah.
FLUTTR
Whoa! What a hill!

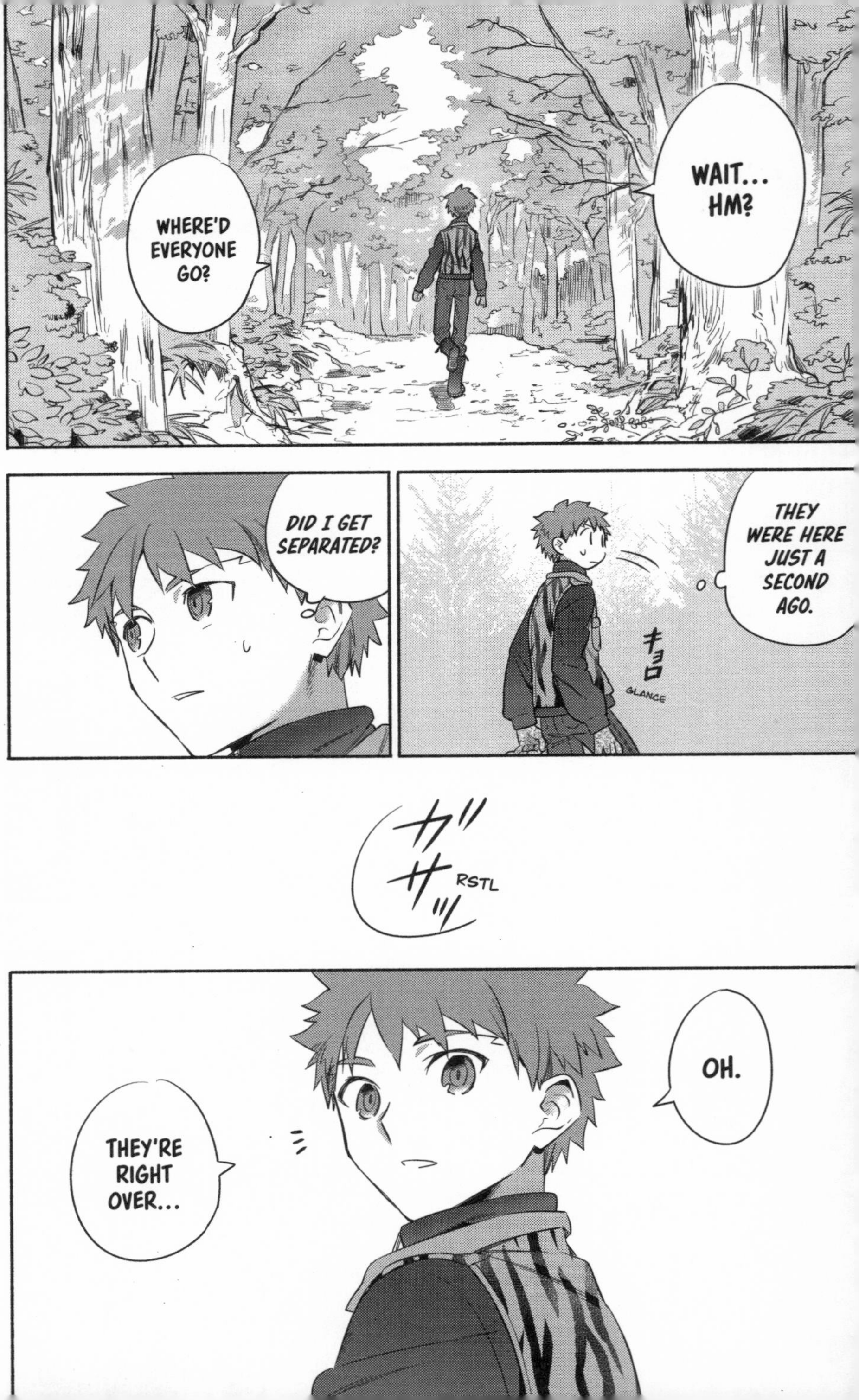
WAIT... HM?
WHERE'D EVERYONE GO?
THEY WERE HERE JUST A SECOND AGO.
キョロ
GLANCE
DID I GET SEPARATED?
ガサッ
RSTL
OH.
THEY'RE RIGHT OVER...

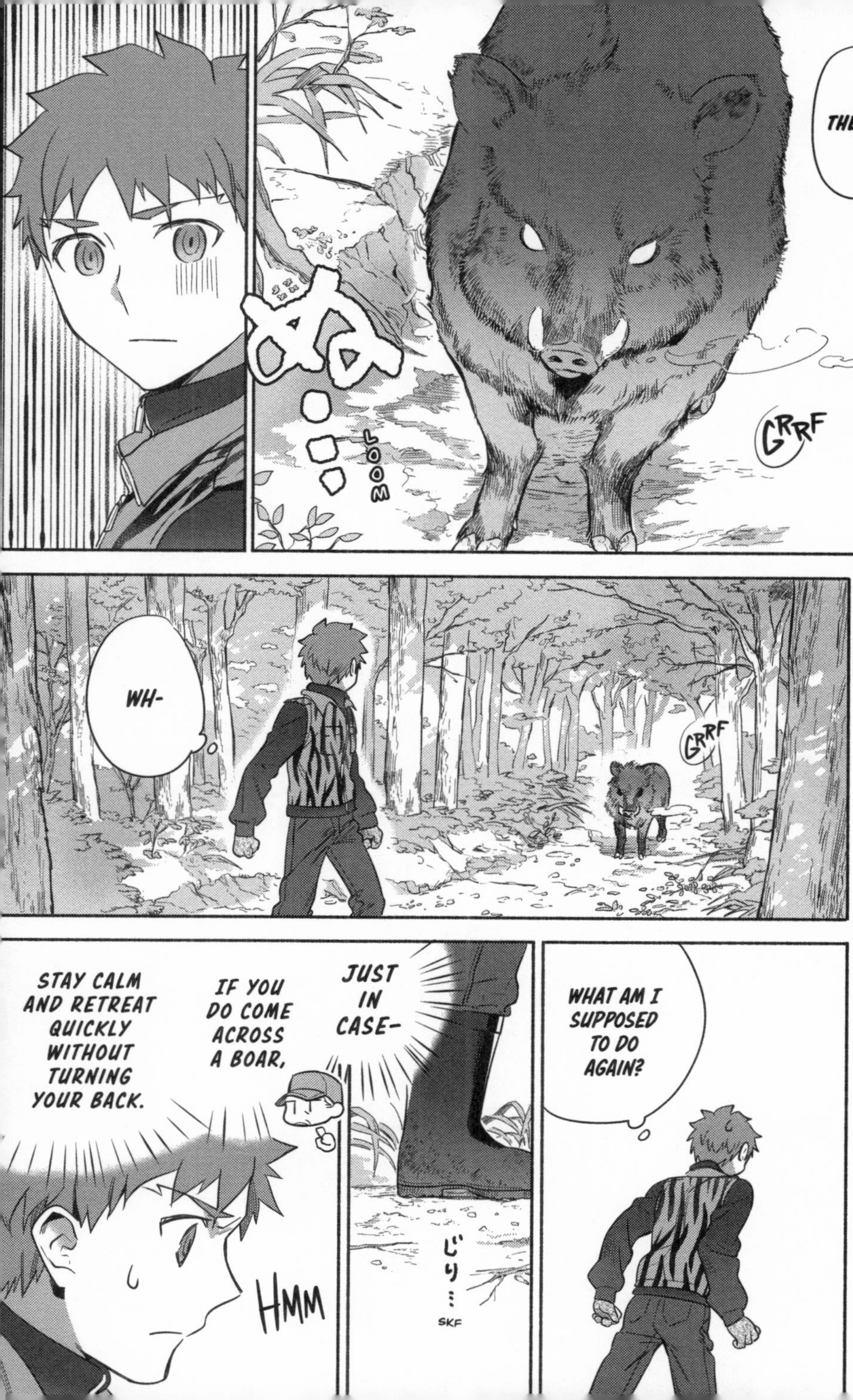
THERE...
ぬ…
LOOM
GRRF
WH-
GRRF
WHAT AM I SUPPOSED TO DO AGAIN?
JUST IN CASE-
IF YOU DO COME ACROSS A BOAR,
STAY CALM AND RETREAT QUICKLY WITHOUT TURNING YOUR BACK.
HMM
じり…
SKF

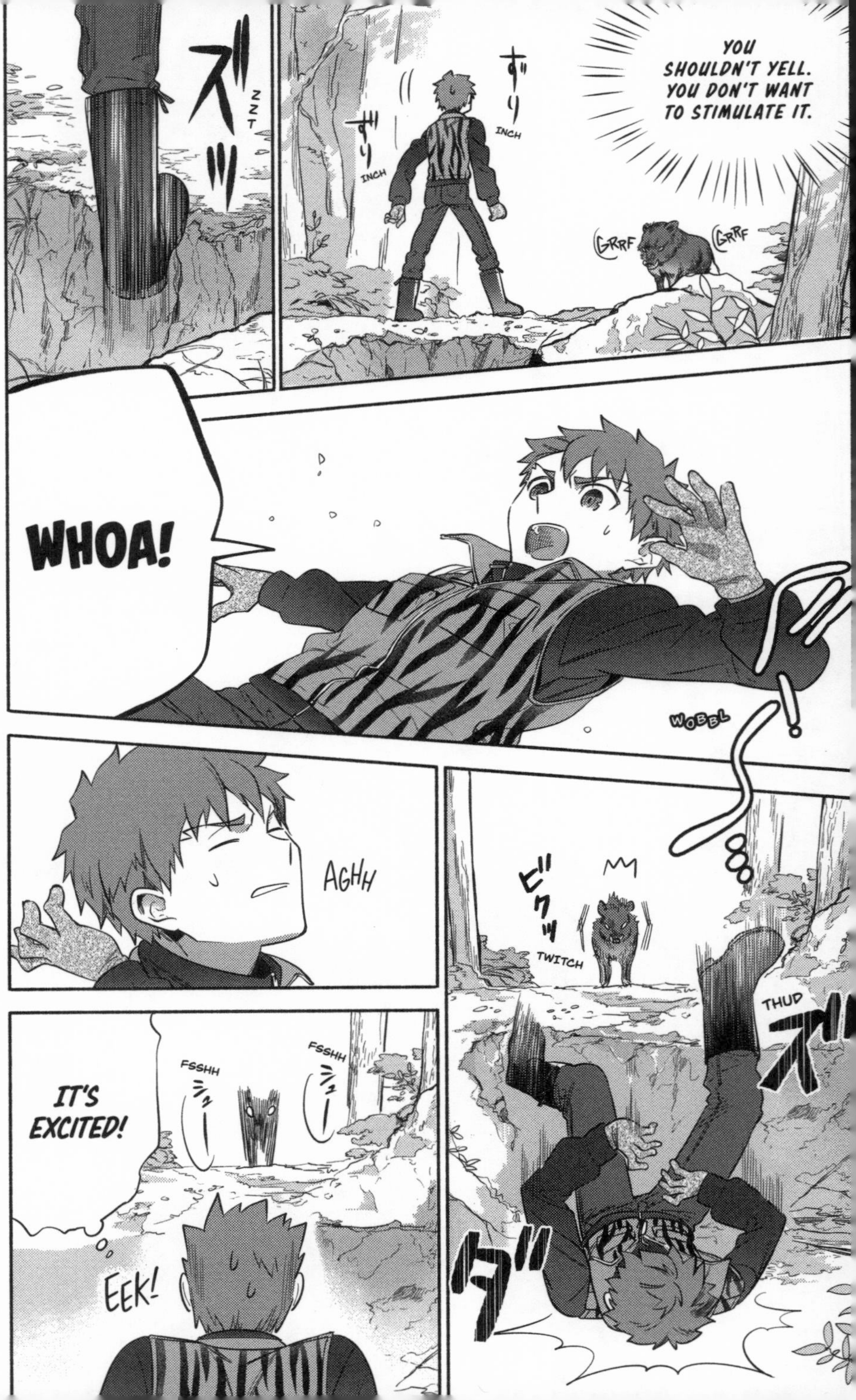
YOU SHOULDN'T YELL. YOU DON'T WANT TO STIMULATE IT.
ずり
INCH
ずり
INCH
GRRF
GRRF
ズ
ZZT
WHOA!
WOBBL
ビクッ
TWITCH
THUD
ダ
AGHH
IT'S EXCITED!
FSSHH
FSSHH
EEK!

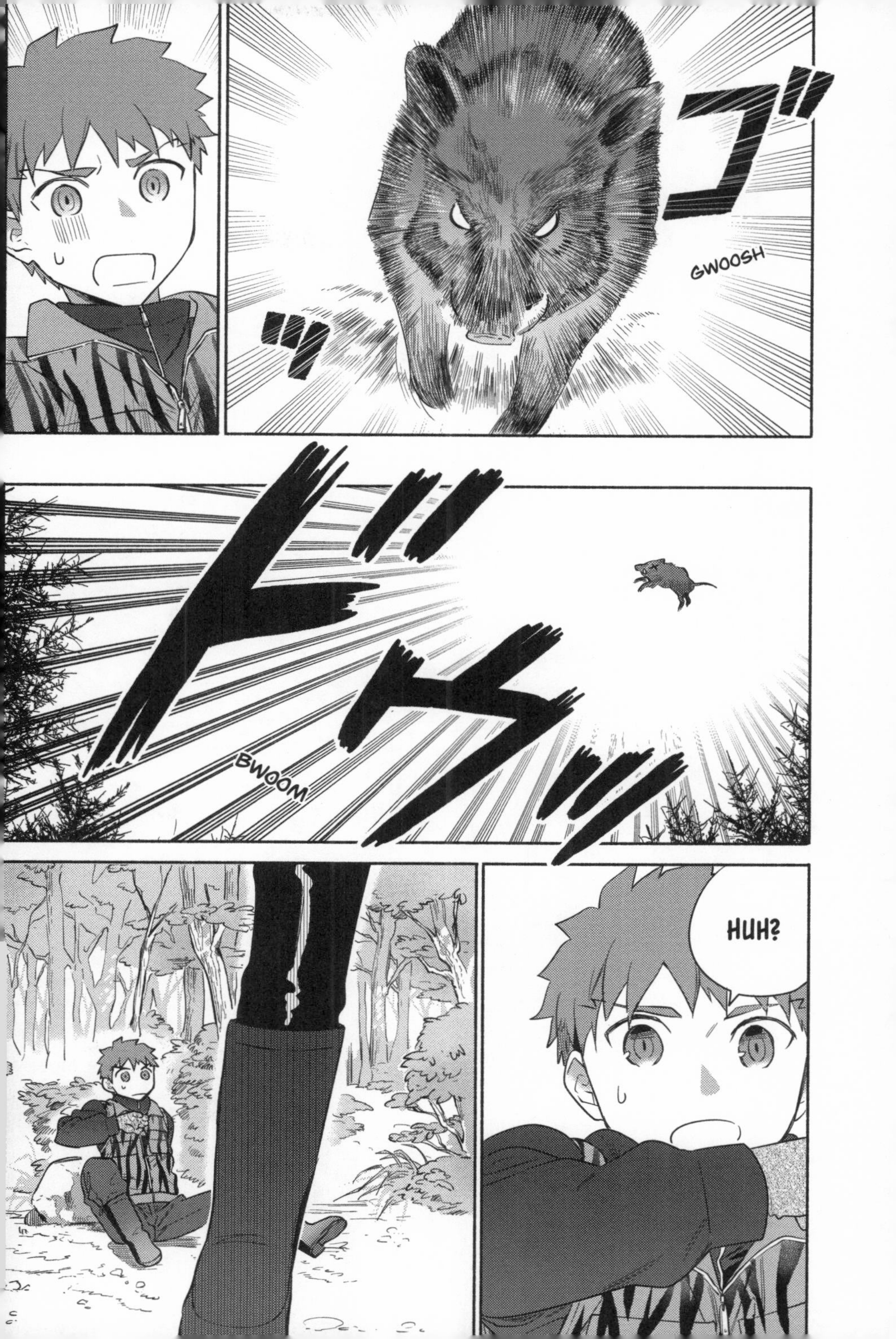
GWOOSH
BWOOM
HUH?

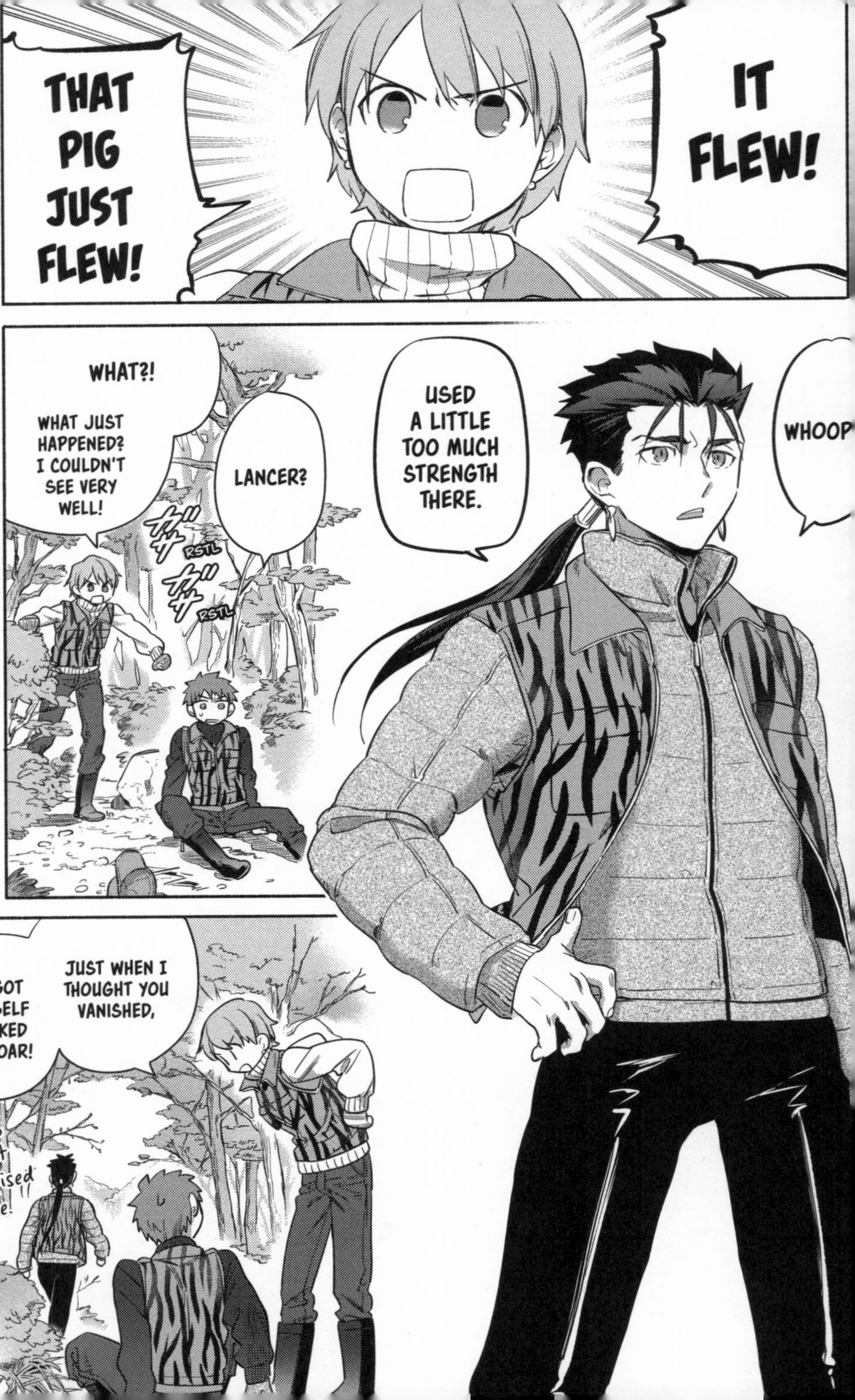
IT FLEW!
THAT PIG JUST FLEW!
WHOOP
USED A LITTLE TOO MUCH STRENGTH THERE.
LANCER?
WHAT?!
WHAT JUST HAPPENED? I COULDN'T SEE VERY WELL!
RSTL
RSTL
JUST WHEN I THOUGHT YOU VANISHED,
YOU GOT YOURSELF ATTACKED BY A BOAR!
Wow, that surprised me!

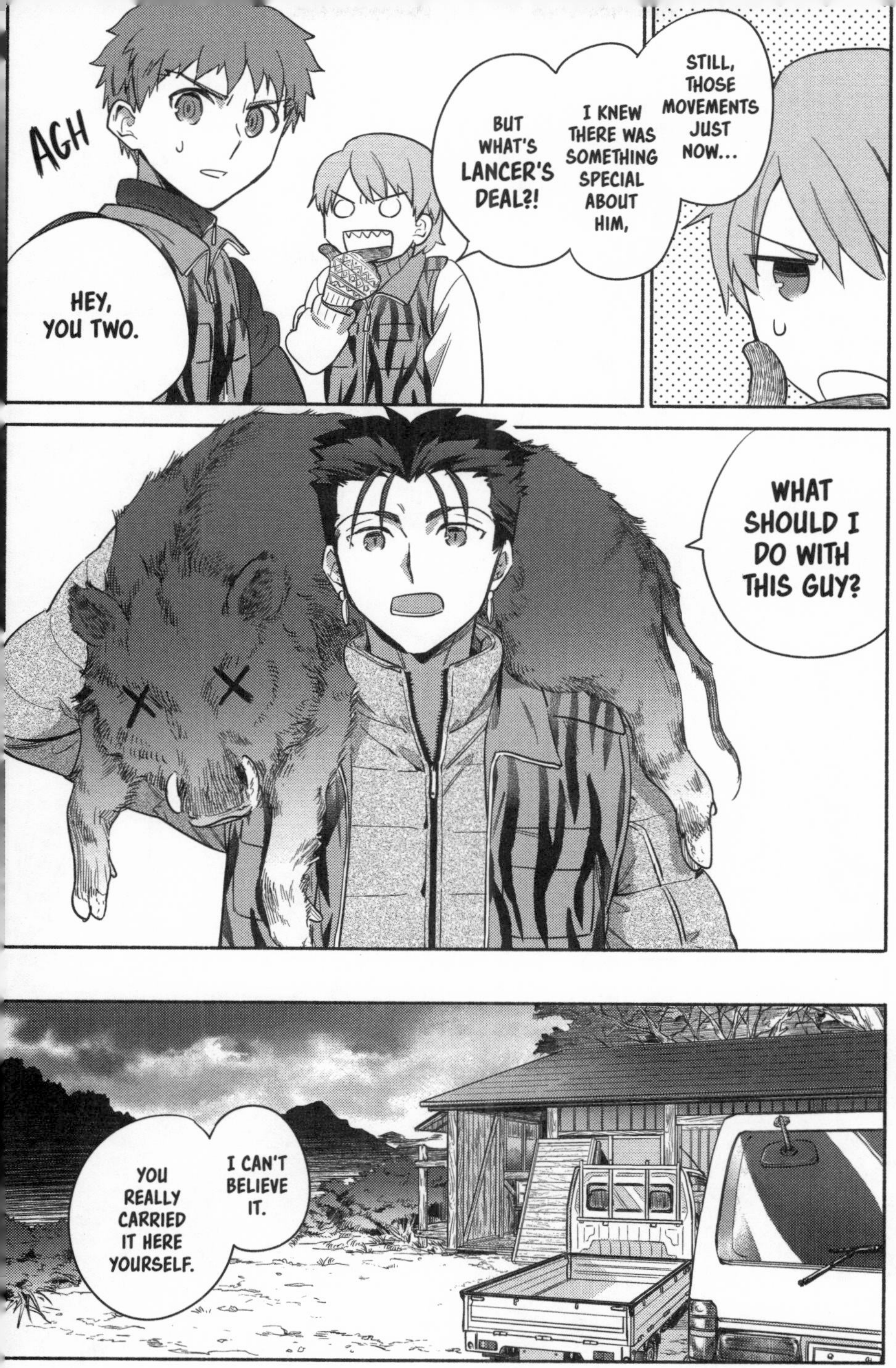
STILL, THOSE MOVEMENTS JUST NOW...
I KNEW THERE WAS SOMETHING SPECIAL ABOUT HIM,
BUT WHAT'S LANCER'S DEAL?!
AGH
HEY, YOU TWO.
WHAT SHOULD I DO WITH THIS GUY?
I CAN'T BELIEVE IT.
YOU REALLY CARRIED IT HERE YOURSELF.

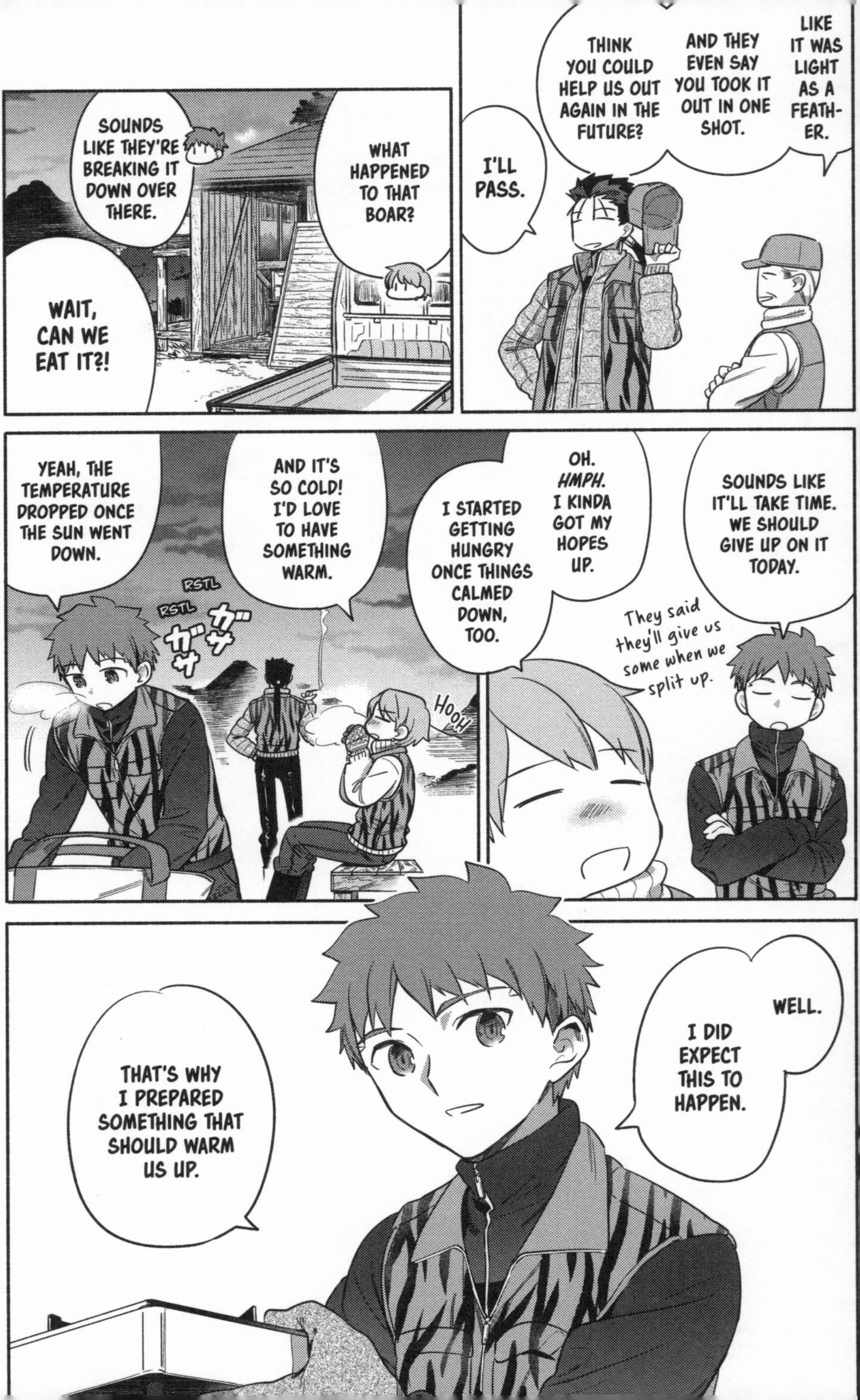
LIKE IT WAS LIGHT AS A FEATHER.
AND THEY EVEN SAY YOU TOOK IT OUT IN ONE SHOT.
THINK YOU COULD HELP US OUT AGAIN IN THE FUTURE?
I'LL PASS.
WHAT HAPPENED TO THAT BOAR?
SOUNDS LIKE THEY'RE BREAKING IT DOWN OVER THERE.
WAIT, CAN WE EAT IT?!
SOUNDS LIKE IT'LL TAKE TIME. WE SHOULD GIVE UP ON IT TODAY.
OH. *HMPH.* I KINDA GOT MY HOPES UP.
I STARTED GETTING HUNGRY ONCE THINGS CALMED DOWN, TOO.
They said they'll give us some when we split up.
AND IT'S SO COLD! I'D LOVE TO HAVE SOMETHING WARM.
YEAH, THE TEMPERATURE DROPPED ONCE THE SUN WENT DOWN.
RSTL
RSTL
ガサ
ガサ
HOOH
WELL.
I DID EXPECT THIS TO HAPPEN.
THAT'S WHY I PREPARED SOMETHING THAT SHOULD WARM US UP.

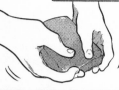

PEEL YOUR DAIKON, CARROTS, AND TAROS.
LEAVE THE SKIN ON YOUR BURDOCK ROOT, ONLY WASHING ANY DIRT OFF. IF THE SKIN BOTHERS YOU, USE THE BACK EDGE OF A KNIFE TO SCRAPE IT AWAY, OR RUB IT OFF WITH ALUMINUM FOIL TO GET RID OF A THIN LAYER OF SKIN.
PREP YOUR KONJAC JELLY BY RUBBING IT IN SALT TO REMOVE HARSH FLAVORS. RINSE THE SALT OFF WITH WARM WATER BEFORE CUTTING.
Wash it with water afterwards if you use salt.
Rubbing it also makes it softer.
CUT THE TAROS INTO BITE-SIZED PIECES, THE DAIKON INTO QUARTER-CIRCLES, AND THE CARROTS INTO HALF-CIRCLES.
Daikon
Taro
Carrots
SHAVE THE BURDOCK ROOT INTO SLIVERS AND SOAK.
SHKK
SHKK
Making an incision first will make this easier.
CUT THE KONJAC INTO THIN RECTANGLES ABOUT 4.5 CENTIMETERS WIDE. TO PREPARE YOUR SHIMEJI MUSHROOMS, CUT OFF THE VERY END AND SPLIT INTO SMALL TUFTS. CUT YOUR GREEN ONION INTO PIECES ON A BIAS.
Konjac jelly
Shimeji
Green onion
SEPARATE THE WHITE AND GREEN PORTIONS OF YOUR GREEN ONION.
I'LL BRING ALL OF THIS
AND DO THE REST THERE.

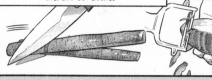

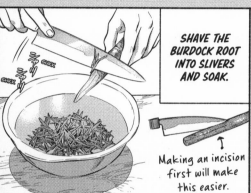

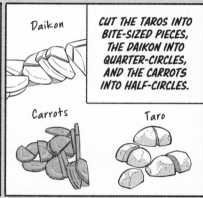

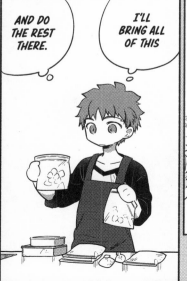

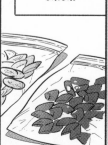

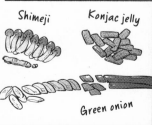

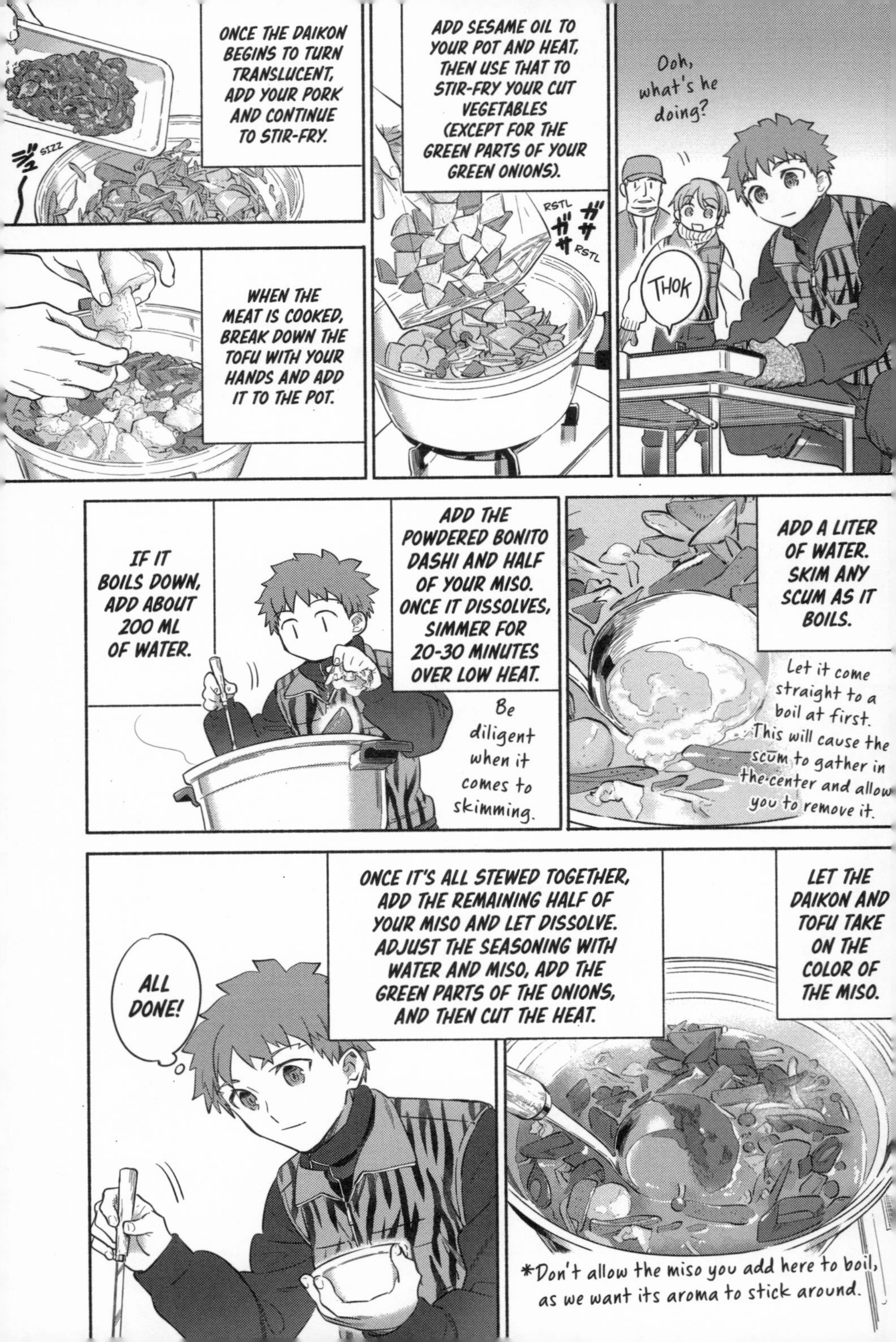
Ooh, what's he doing?
THOK
ADD SESAME OIL TO YOUR POT AND HEAT, THEN USE THAT TO STIR-FRY YOUR CUT VEGETABLES (EXCEPT FOR THE GREEN PARTS OF YOUR GREEN ONIONS).
RSTL
RSTL
ONCE THE DAIKON BEGINS TO TURN TRANSLUCENT, ADD YOUR PORK AND CONTINUE TO STIR-FRY.
SIZZ
WHEN THE MEAT IS COOKED, BREAK DOWN THE TOFU WITH YOUR HANDS AND ADD IT TO THE POT.
ADD A LITER OF WATER. SKIM ANY SCUM AS IT BOILS.
Let it come straight to a boil at first. This will cause the scum to gather in the center and allow you to remove it.
ADD THE POWDERED BONITO DASHI AND HALF OF YOUR MISO. ONCE IT DISSOLVES, SIMMER FOR 20-30 MINUTES OVER LOW HEAT.
IF IT BOILS DOWN, ADD ABOUT 200 ML OF WATER.
Be diligent when it comes to skimming.
LET THE DAIKON AND TOFU TAKE ON THE COLOR OF THE MISO.
ONCE IT'S ALL STEWED TOGETHER, ADD THE REMAINING HALF OF YOUR MISO AND LET DISSOLVE. ADJUST THE SEASONING WITH WATER AND MISO, ADD THE GREEN PARTS OF THE ONIONS, AND THEN CUT THE HEAT.
ALL DONE!
*Don't allow the miso you add here to boil, as we want its aroma to stick around.

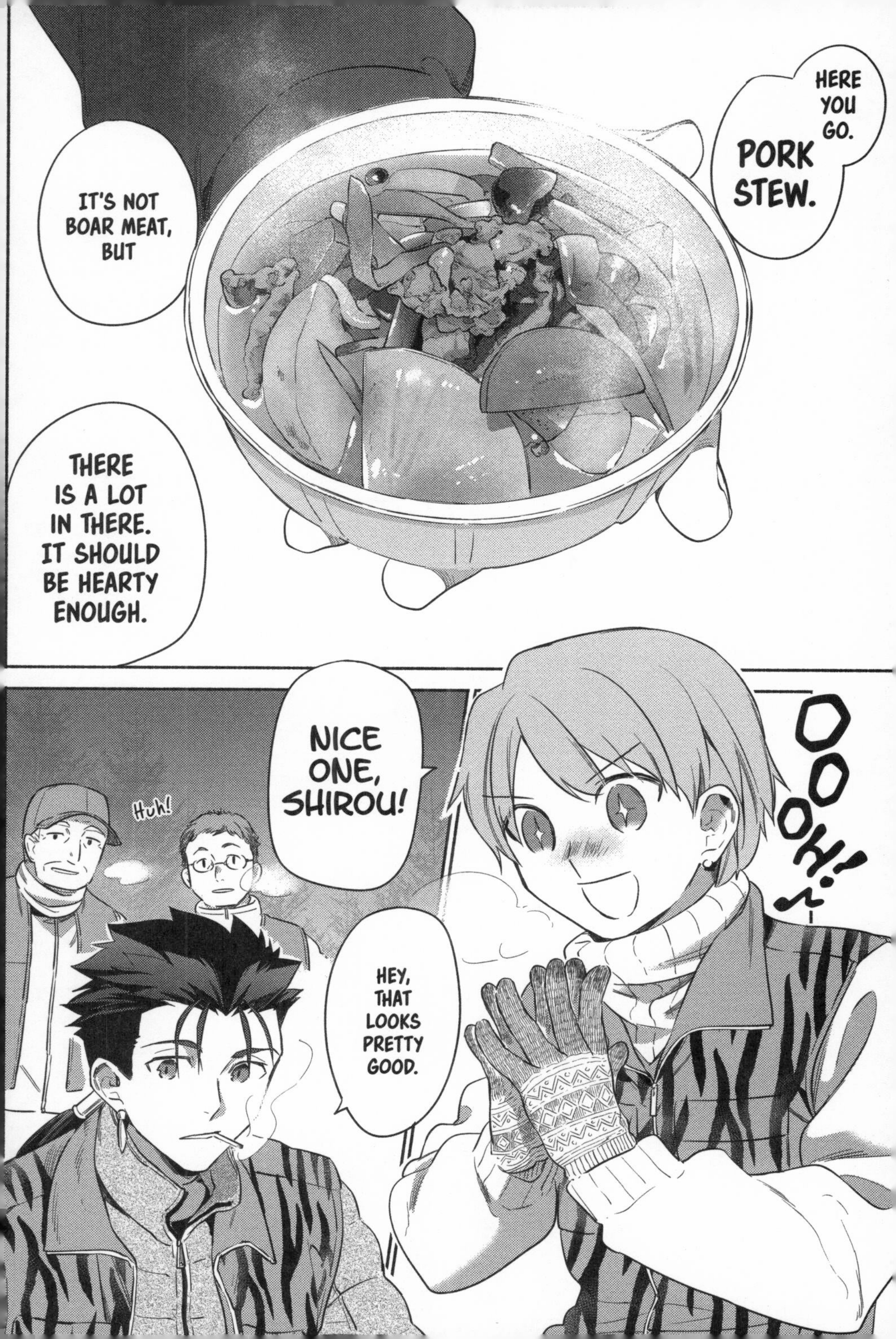
HERE YOU GO.
PORK STEW.
IT'S NOT BOAR MEAT, BUT
THERE IS A LOT IN THERE. IT SHOULD BE HEARTY ENOUGH.
OOOOH!
NICE ONE, SHIROU!
HEY, THAT LOOKS PRETTY GOOD.
Huh!

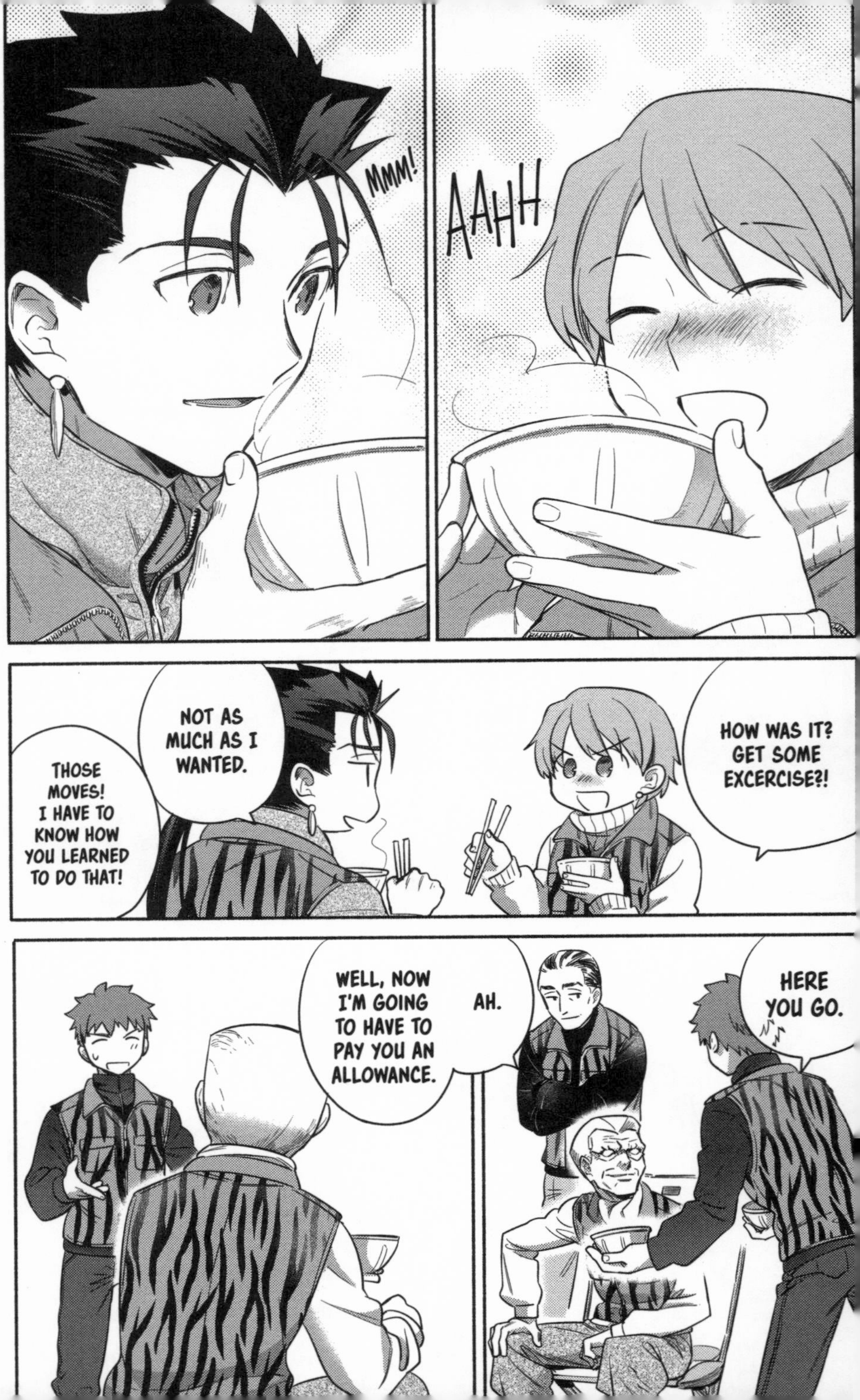
AAHH
MMM!
HOW WAS IT? GET SOME EXCERCISE?!
NOT AS MUCH AS I WANTED.
THOSE MOVES! I HAVE TO KNOW HOW YOU LEARNED TO DO THAT!
HERE YOU GO.
AH.
WELL, NOW I'M GOING TO HAVE TO PAY YOU AN ALLOWANCE.

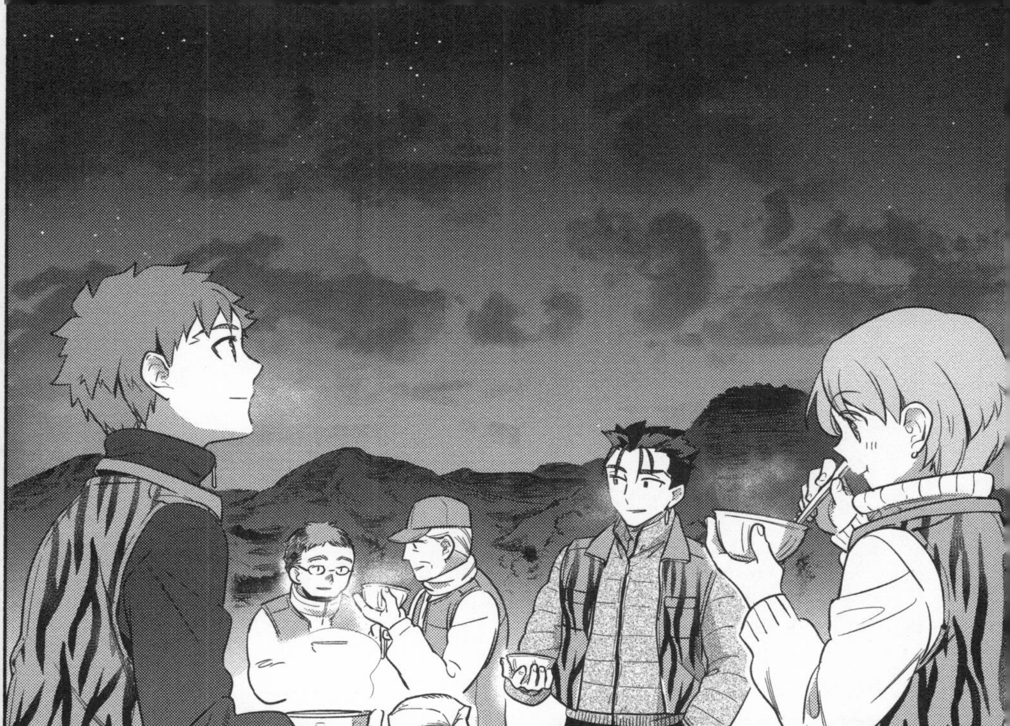

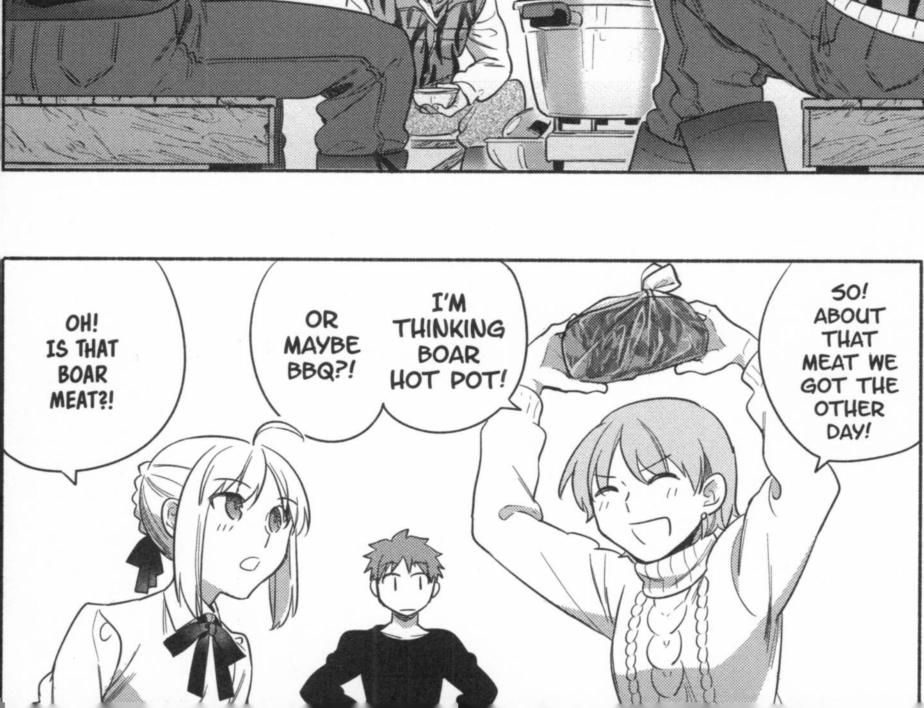
SO! ABOUT THAT MEAT WE GOT THE OTHER DAY!
I'M THINKING BOAR HOT POT!
OR MAYBE BBQ?!
OH! IS THAT BOAR MEAT?!

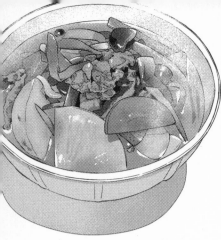

Chunky Pork Stew

Ingredients - Serves 8-10

200 g (7 oz) pork scraps

400 g (14.1 oz) taros

1/4 (200 g / 7 oz) daikon

1 carrot

1/2 (150 g / 5.3 oz) burdock root

1 block konjac jelly

1 pack shimeji mushrooms

1-2 green onions

1 block coarse tofu

About 90-100 g (3.2-3.5 oz) miso

1 l (33.8 oz) water

2 tsp powdered bonito dashi

Sesame or vegetable oil as needed

Shichimi pepper mix if desired

🔥 Letting the stew sit for a day allows the flavor to seep into the vegetables even more, making them taste even better, which is why this recipe makes a somewhat larger amount (enough for 8-10).

*If you want to finish this in one sitting, use about half of each ingredient.

*It's often said that you should stir-fry your meat before your vegetables, that you shouldn't let your miso boil, and that you shouldn't add your sesame oil until the end to maintain the aroma, but we're intentionally making this pork stew the other way around.

Preparation

1. Peel your daikon, carrots, and taros. Leave the skin on your burdock root, making sure to wash before prep. If the skin irritates you, use the back edge of a knife to scrape it away, or rub it off with aluminum foil to get rid of a thin layer of skin.

2. To get rid of harsh flavors from your konjac, either knead salt into it or parboil it.

Instructions

1. Cut the taros into bite-sized pieces, the daikon into quarter-circles, and the carrots into half-circles. Shave the burdock root into slivers and soak. Cut the konjac into thin rectangles about 4.5 centimeters wide. To prepare your shimeji mushrooms, cut off the very end and split into small tufts. Cut your green onion into pieces on a bias. Separate the white and green portions of your green onion.

   •For a thicker stew: Go to 2.
   •For a more refreshing stew: Parboil the taros, then wash with water to reduce sliminess.
   → Add first to maintain just the body of the sesame oil.

2. Add sesame oil to your pot and heat, then use that to stir-fry what you cut in step 1 (except for the green parts of the green onions). This will help the tofu absorb other flavors.

3. Add a liter of water and skim off any scum once it boils. Add the powdered bonito dashi and half of your miso. Once it dissolves, simmer for 20-30 minutes over low heat (be diligent when it comes to skimming). If it boils down, add about 200 ml of water.

4. Let the daikon and tofu take on the color of the miso. Once it's all stewed together, add the remaining half of your miso and let dissolve.
   *You can let it come to a weak boil up until step 3, but don't let it come to a boil after adding this final amount of miso, because we want to preserve its aroma.

5. Adjust the seasoning with water and miso, then add the green parts of your green onions. Once they're cooked, you're done!

   *The miso added in step 3 is meant to add flavor to the vegetables. The miso added in step 4 is meant to add aroma.

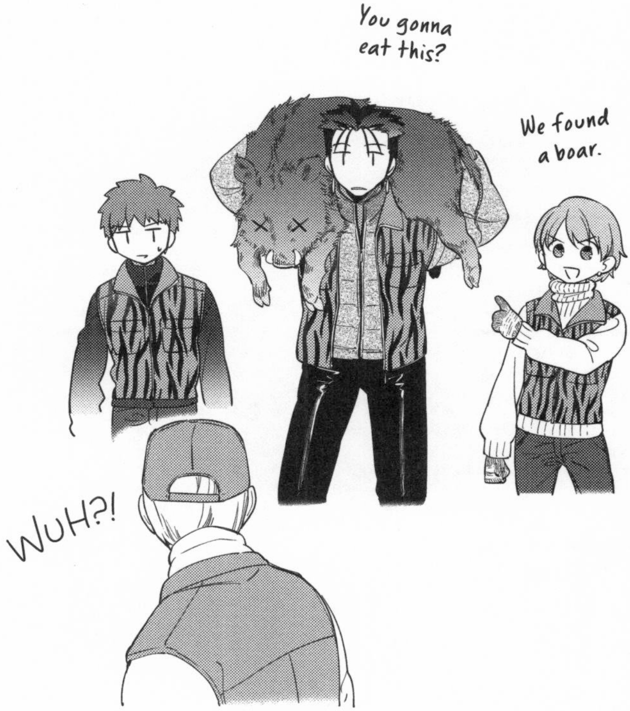
We found a boar.
You gonna eat this?
WUH?!

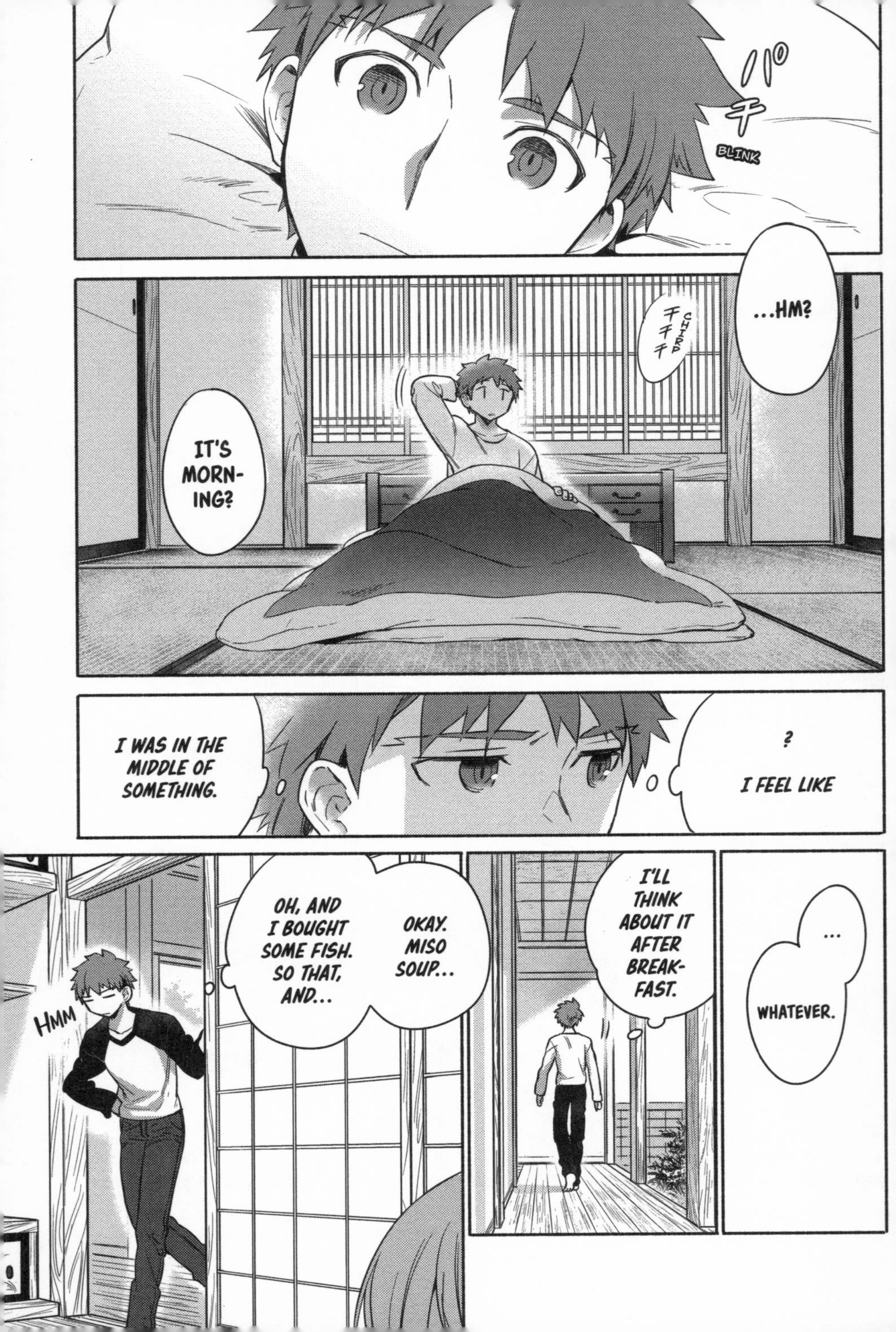
パチ
BLINK
...HM?
チチチ
CHIRP
IT'S MORNING?
? I FEEL LIKE
I WAS IN THE MIDDLE OF SOMETHING.
... WHATEVER.
I'LL THINK ABOUT IT AFTER BREAKFAST.
OKAY. MISO SOUP...
OH, AND I BOUGHT SOME FISH. SO THAT, AND...
HMM

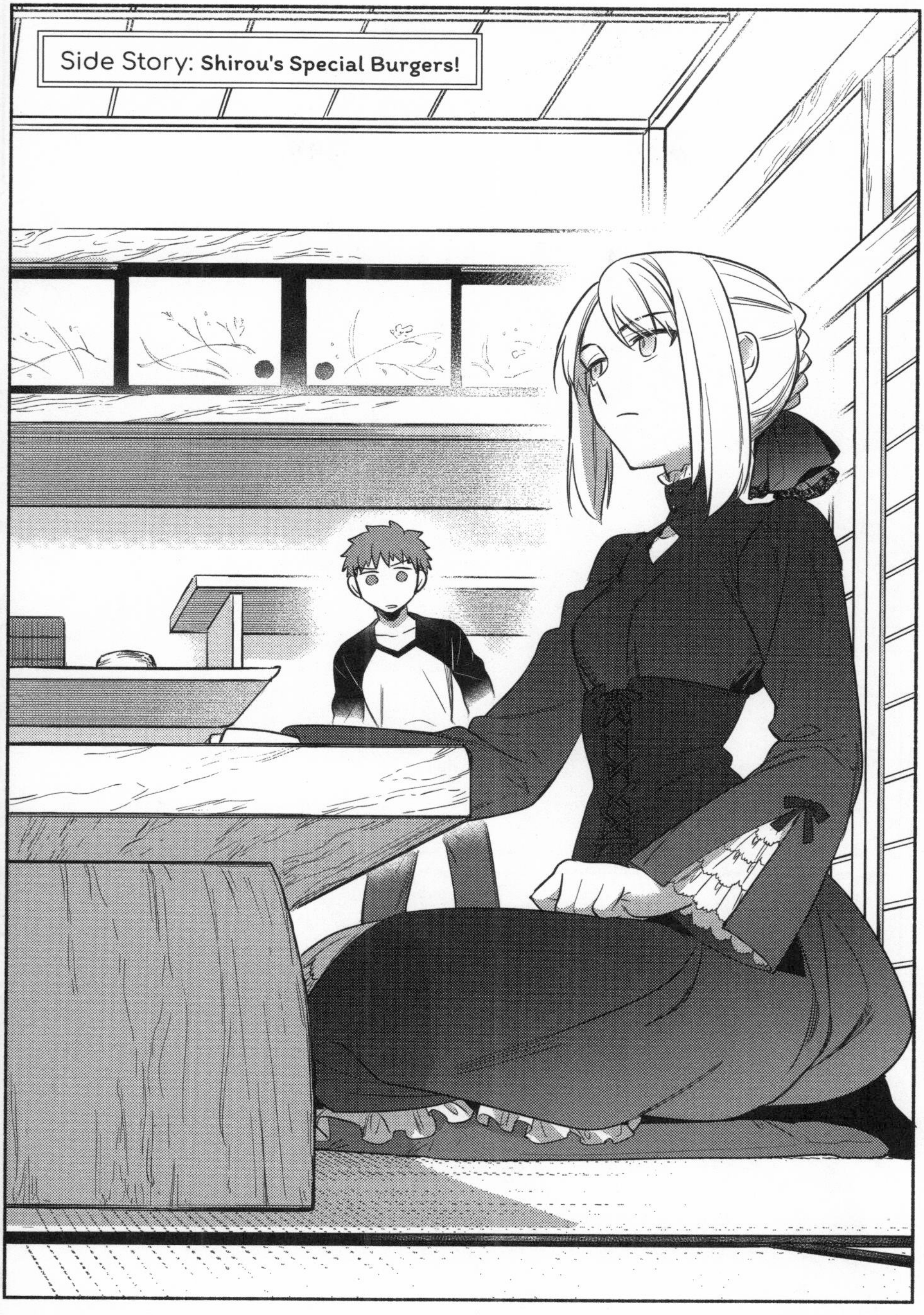
Side Story: Shirou's Special Burgers!

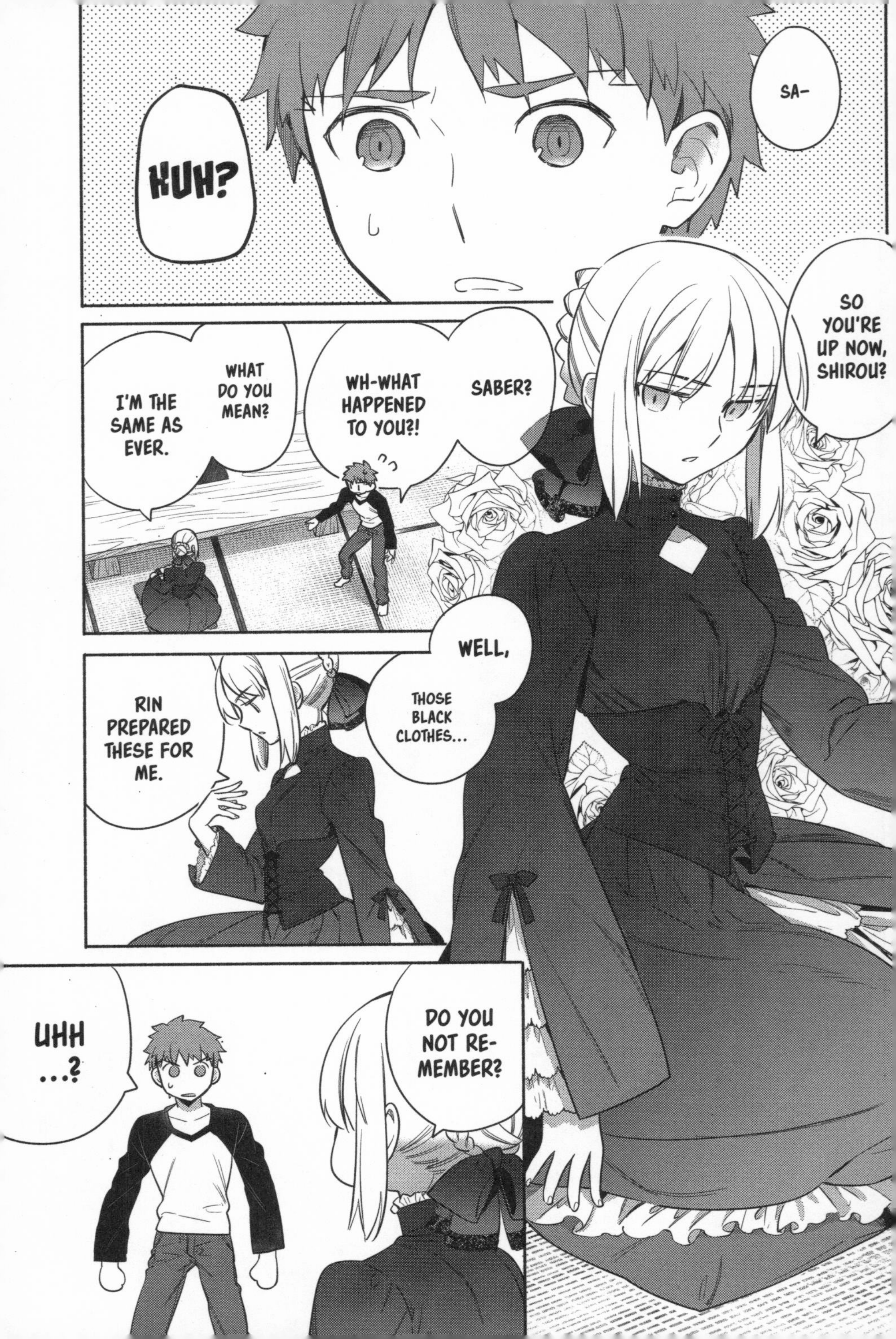
SA-
HUH?
SO YOU'RE UP NOW, SHIROU?
SABER?
WH-WHAT HAPPENED TO YOU?!
WHAT DO YOU MEAN?
I'M THE SAME AS EVER.
WELL,
THOSE BLACK CLOTHES...
RIN PREPARED THESE FOR ME.
DO YOU NOT RE- MEMBER?
UHH ...?

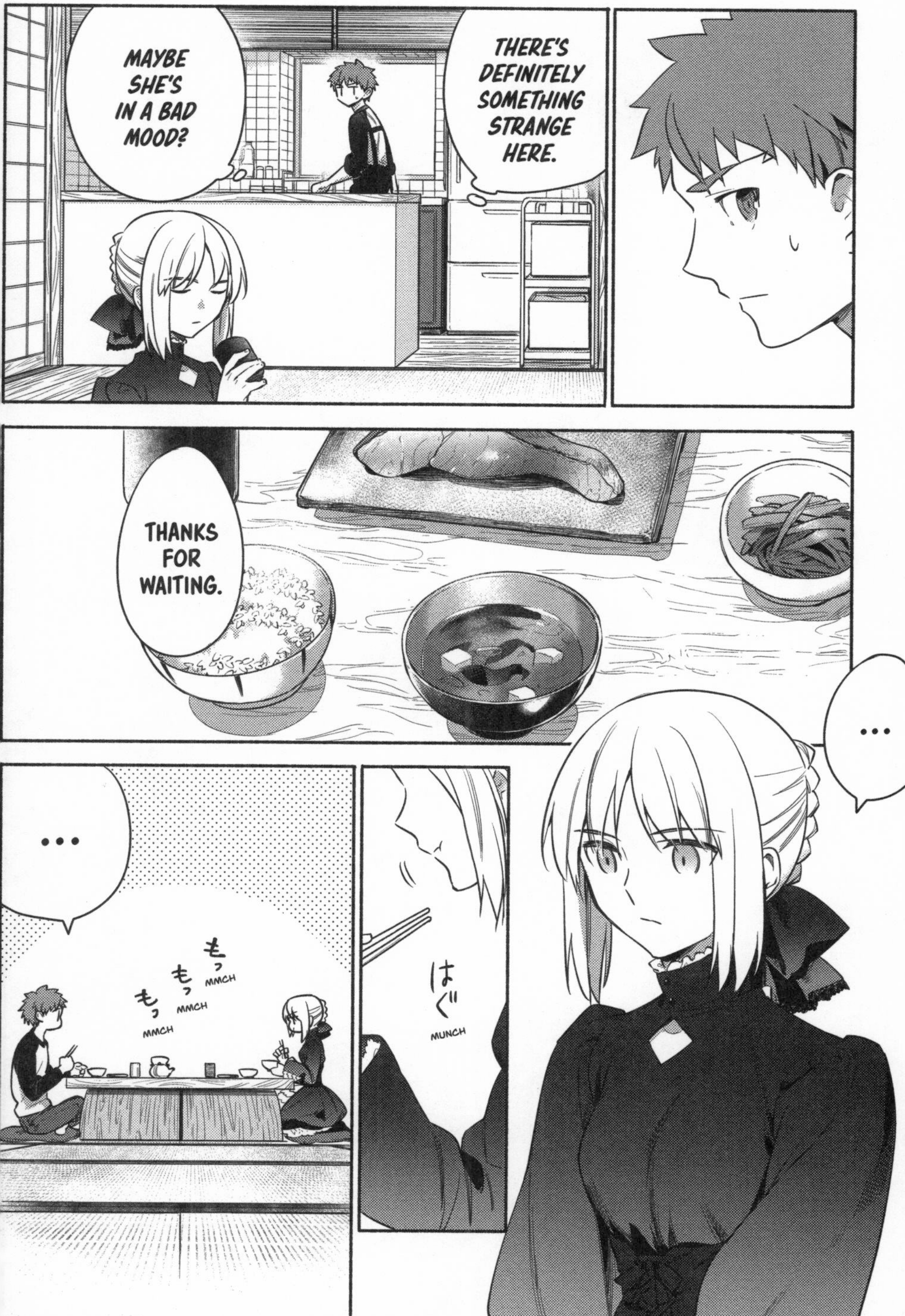
THERE'S DEFINITELY SOMETHING STRANGE HERE.
MAYBE SHE'S IN A BAD MOOD?
THANKS FOR WAITING.
...
はぐ
MUNCH
...
もっ
MMCH
もっ
MMCH
もっ
MMCH

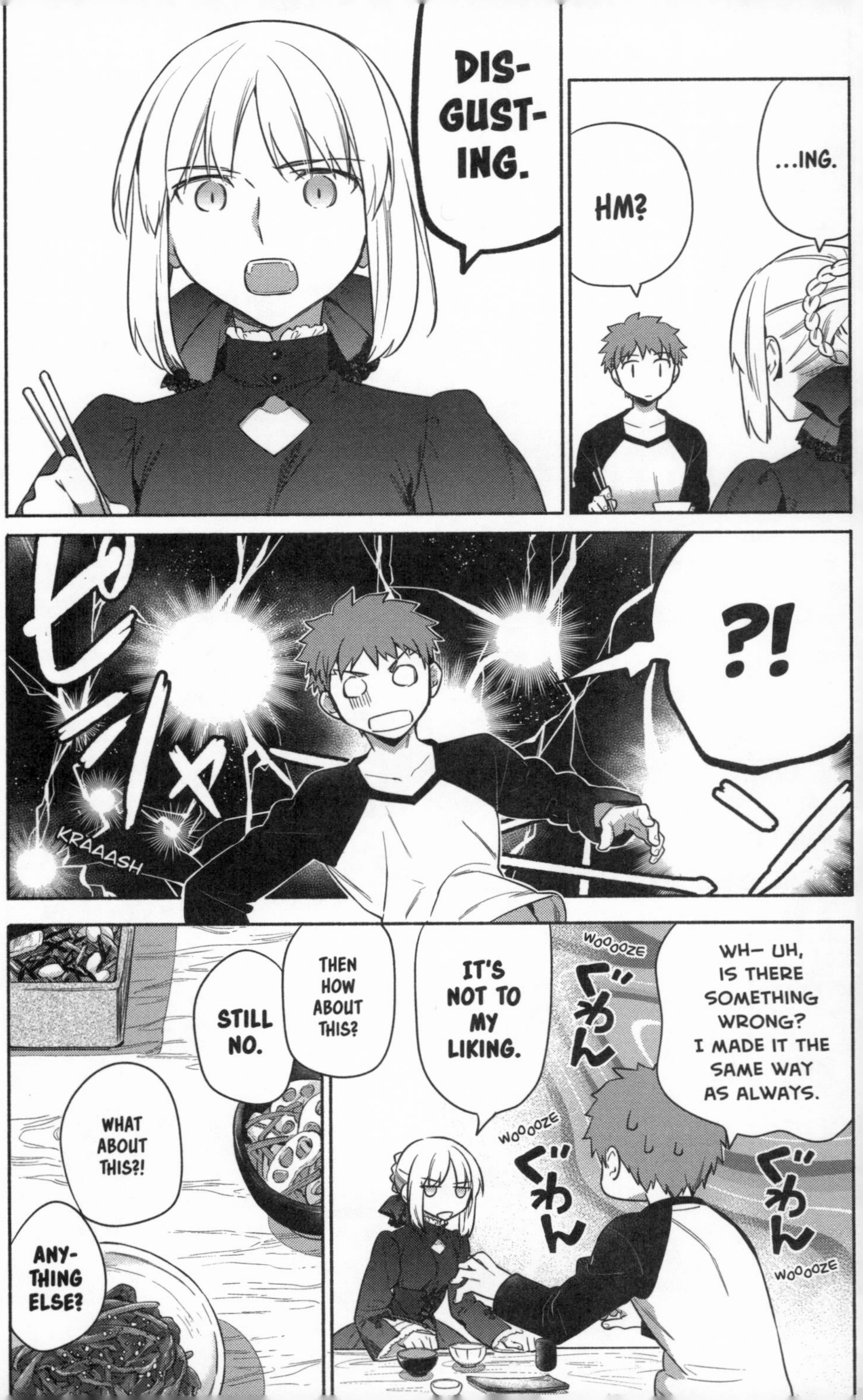
...ING.
HM?
DIS-GUST-ING.
?!
KRAAASH
WH— UH, IS THERE SOMETHING WRONG? I MADE IT THE SAME WAY AS ALWAYS.
WOOOOZE
ぐわん
IT'S NOT TO MY LIKING.
WOOOOZE
ぐわん
ぐわん
WOOOOZE
THEN HOW ABOUT THIS?
STILL NO.
WHAT ABOUT THIS?!
ANY-THING ELSE?

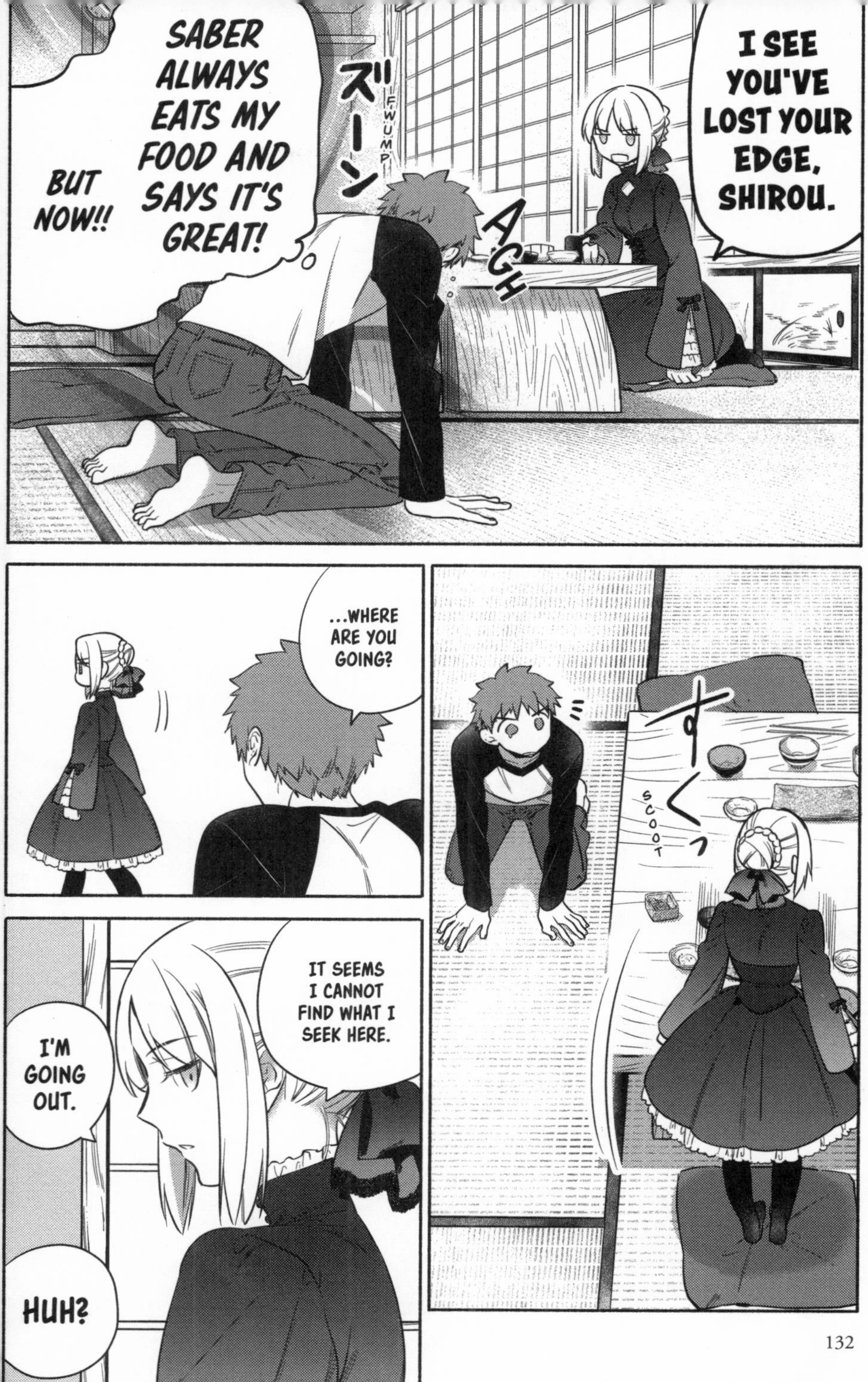
I SEE YOU'VE LOST YOUR EDGE, SHIROU.
ズーン
FWUMP
AGH
SABER ALWAYS EATS MY FOOD AND SAYS IT'S GREAT!
BUT NOW!!
すくっ
SCOOT
...WHERE ARE YOU GOING?
IT SEEMS I CANNOT FIND WHAT I SEEK HERE.
I'M GOING OUT.
HUH?

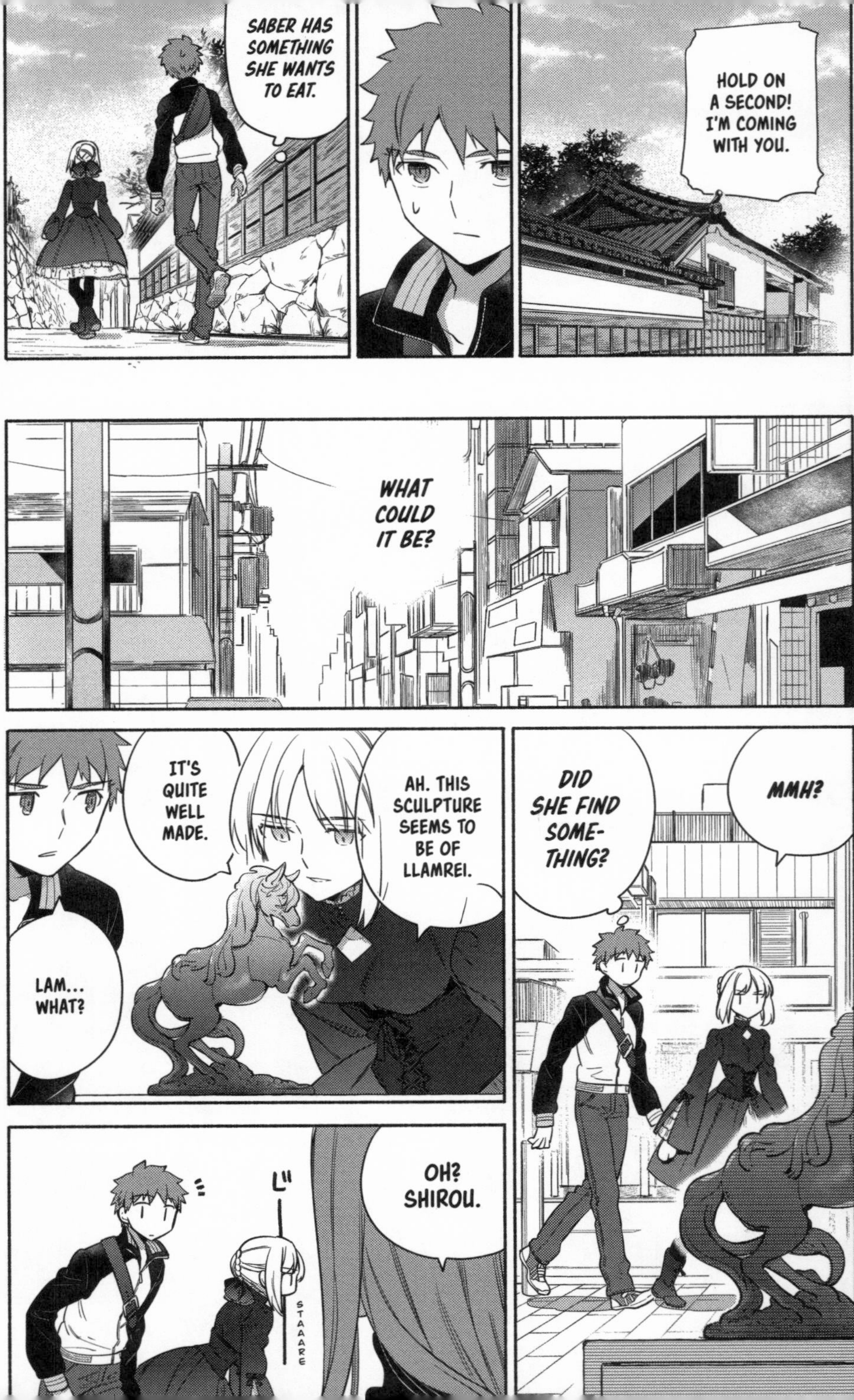
HOLD ON A SECOND! I'M COMING WITH YOU.
SABER HAS SOMETHING SHE WANTS TO EAT.
WHAT COULD IT BE?
MMH?
DID SHE FIND SOME-THING?
AH. THIS SCULPTURE SEEMS TO BE OF LLAMREI.
IT'S QUITE WELL MADE.
LAM... WHAT?
OH? SHIROU.
じ
STAAARE

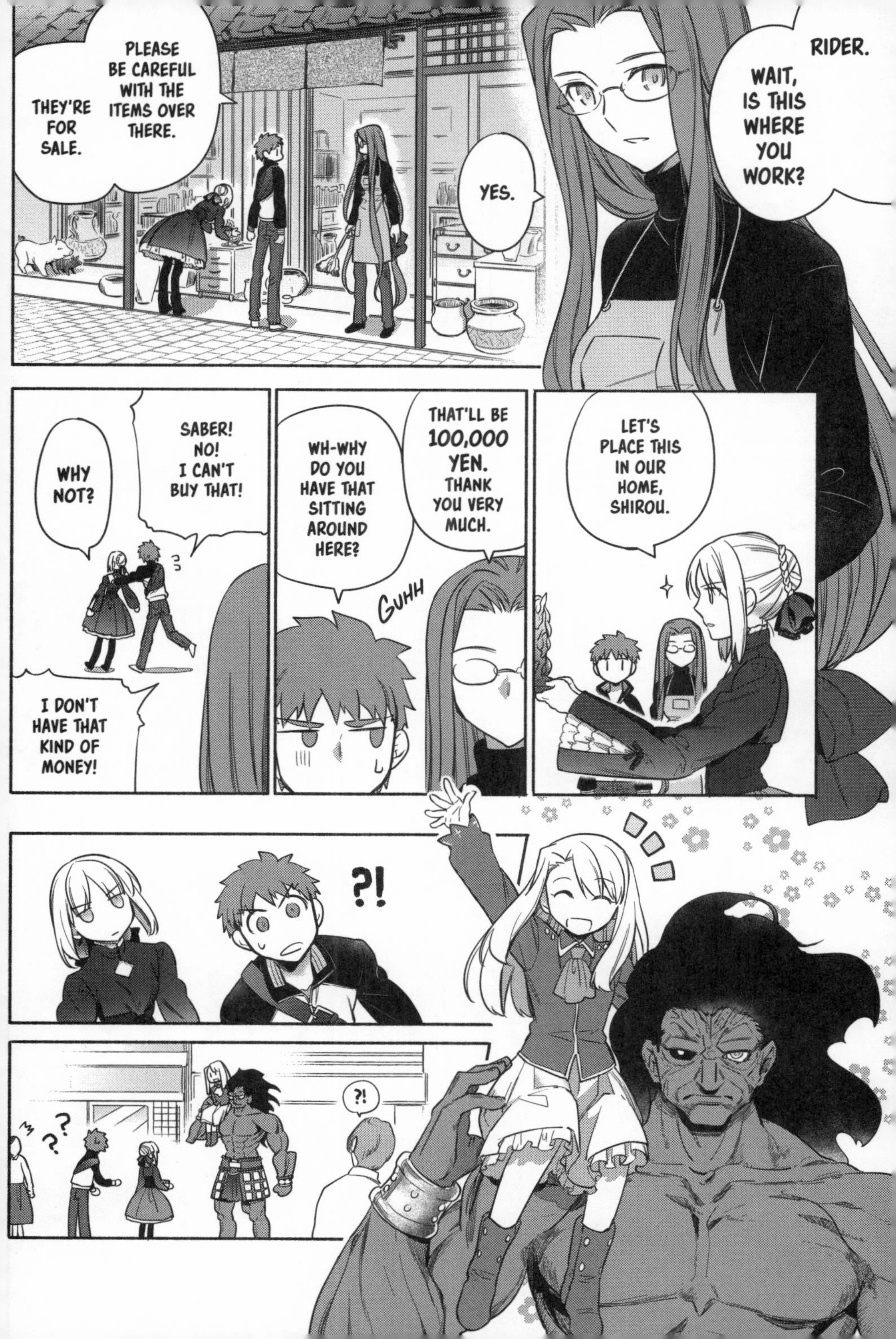
RIDER.
WAIT, IS THIS WHERE YOU WORK?
YES.
PLEASE BE CAREFUL WITH THE ITEMS OVER THERE.
THEY'RE FOR SALE.
LET'S PLACE THIS IN OUR HOME, SHIROU.
THAT'LL BE 100,000 YEN. THANK YOU VERY MUCH.
WH-WHY DO YOU HAVE THAT SITTING AROUND HERE?
GUHH
SABER! NO! I CAN'T BUY THAT!
WHY NOT?
I DON'T HAVE THAT KIND OF MONEY!
?!
?!

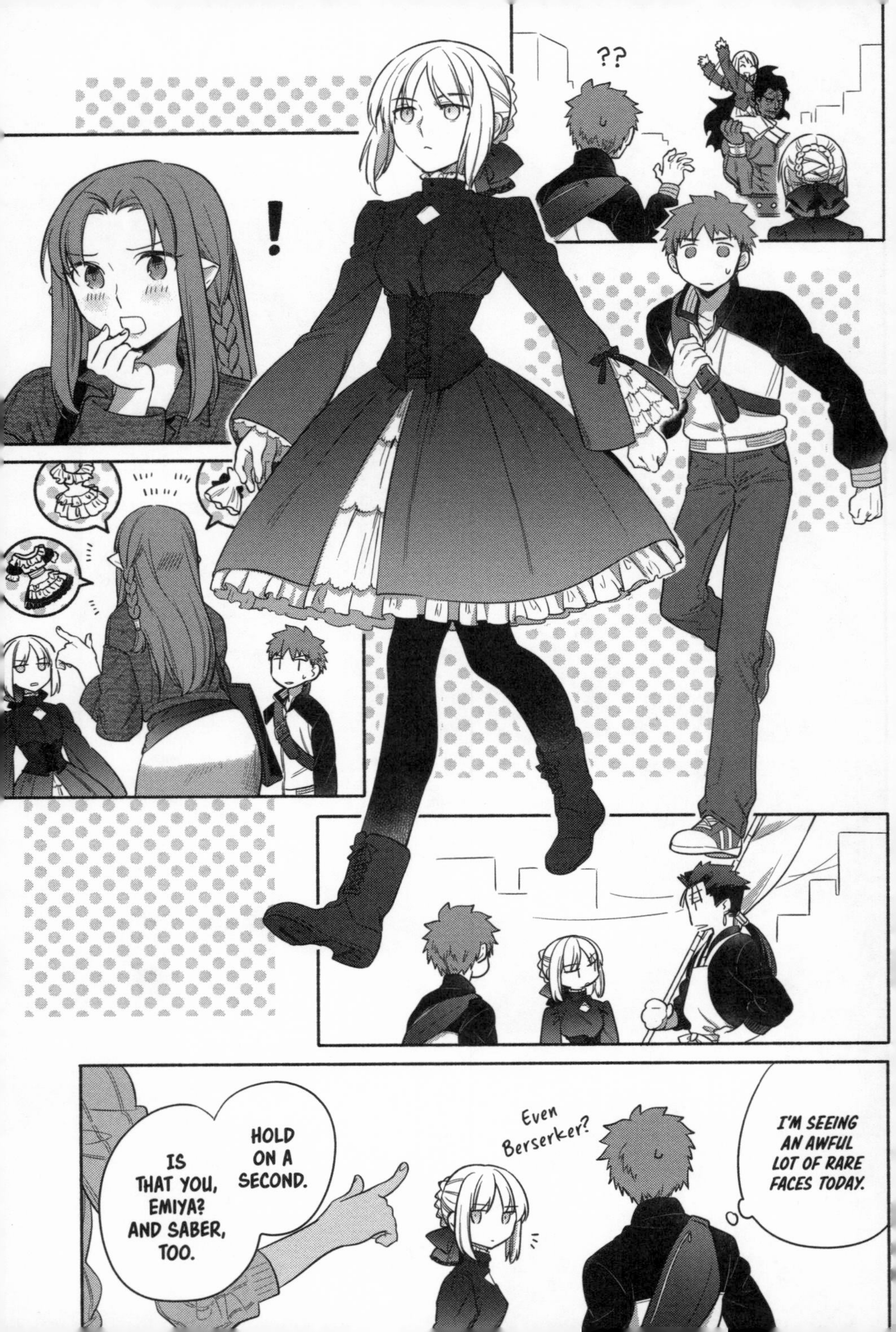
??
!
I'M SEEING AN AWFUL LOT OF RARE FACES TODAY.
Even Berserker?
HOLD ON A SECOND.
IS THAT YOU, EMIYA? AND SABER, TOO.

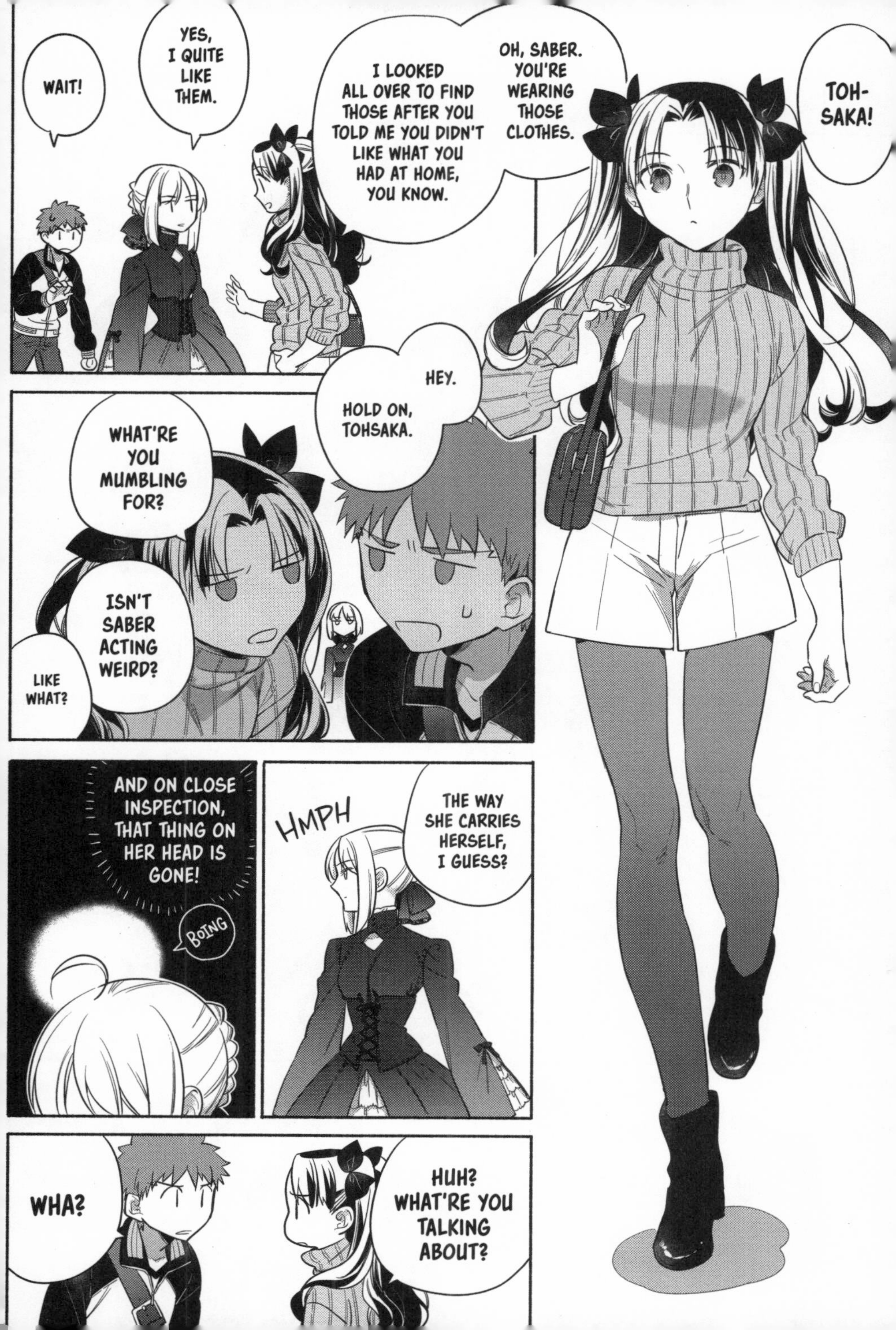
TOH-SAKA!
OH, SABER. YOU'RE WEARING THOSE CLOTHES.
I LOOKED ALL OVER TO FIND THOSE AFTER YOU TOLD ME YOU DIDN'T LIKE WHAT YOU HAD AT HOME, YOU KNOW.
YES, I QUITE LIKE THEM.
WAIT!
HEY.
HOLD ON, TOHSAKA.
WHAT'RE YOU MUMBLING FOR?
ISN'T SABER ACTING WEIRD?
LIKE WHAT?
THE WAY SHE CARRIES HERSELF, I GUESS?
HMPH
AND ON CLOSE INSPECTION, THAT THING ON HER HEAD IS GONE!
BOING
HUH? WHAT'RE YOU TALKING ABOUT?
WHA?

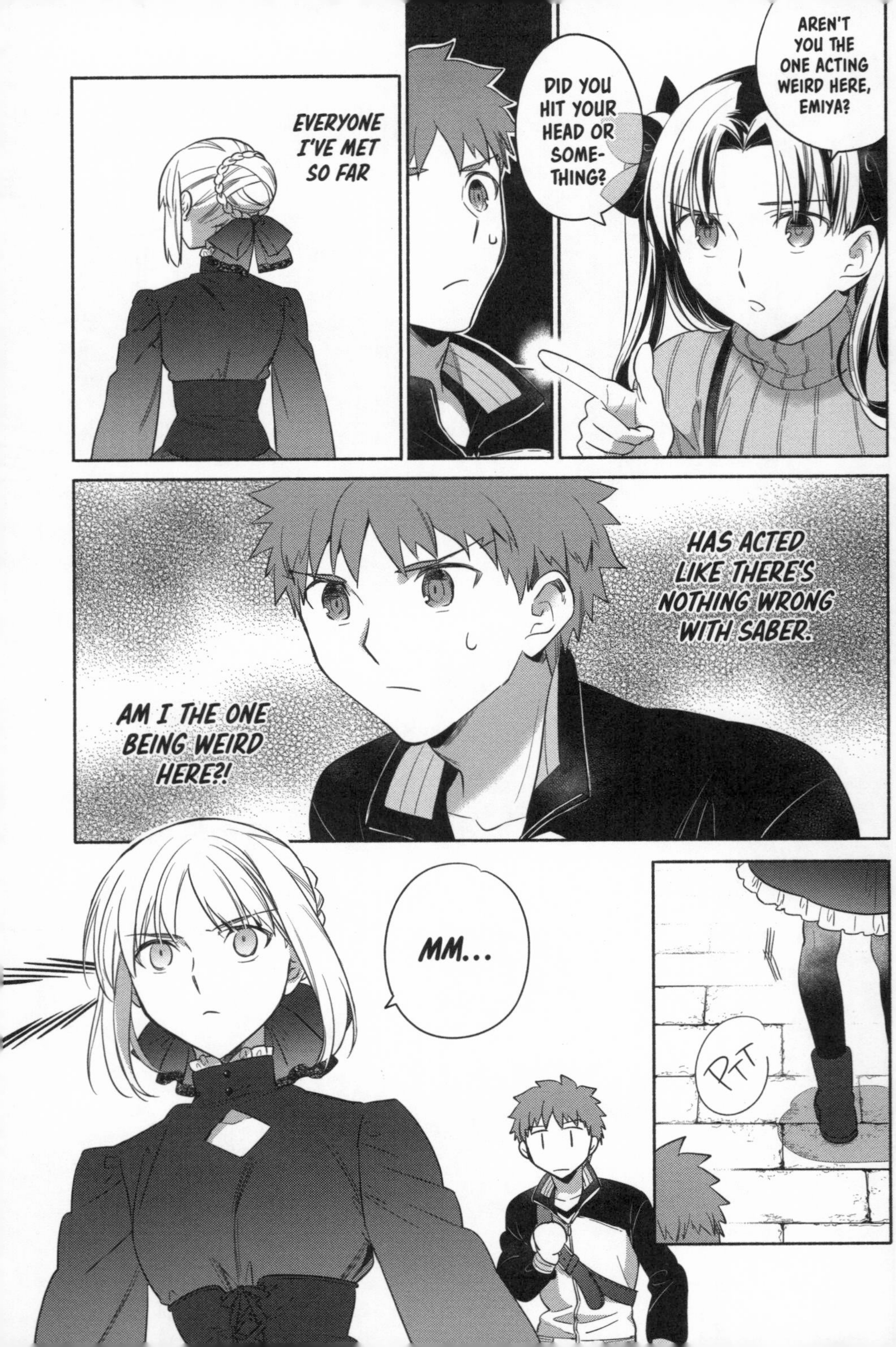
AREN'T YOU THE ONE ACTING WEIRD HERE, EMIYA?
DID YOU HIT YOUR HEAD OR SOME-THING?
EVERYONE I'VE MET SO FAR
HAS ACTED LIKE THERE'S NOTHING WRONG WITH SABER.
AM I THE ONE BEING WEIRD HERE?!
PTT
MM...

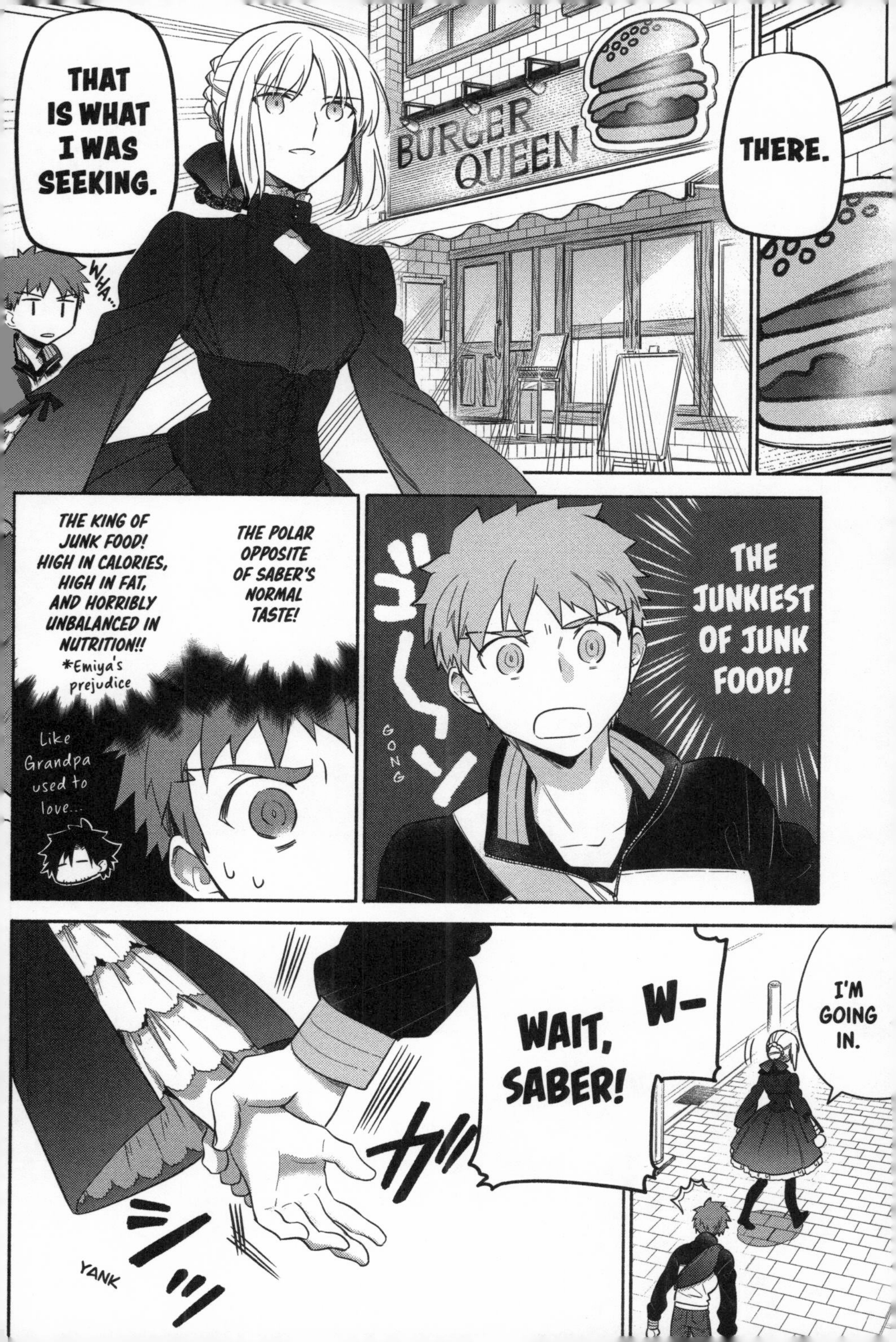

THERE.
THAT IS WHAT I WAS SEEKING.
WHA...
THE JUNKIEST OF JUNK FOOD!
GONG
THE POLAR OPPOSITE OF SABER'S NORMAL TASTE!
THE KING OF JUNK FOOD! HIGH IN CALORIES, HIGH IN FAT, AND HORRIBLY UNBALANCED IN NUTRITION!!
*Emiya's prejudice
Like Grandpa used to love...
I'M GOING IN.
W-
WAIT, SABER!
YANK

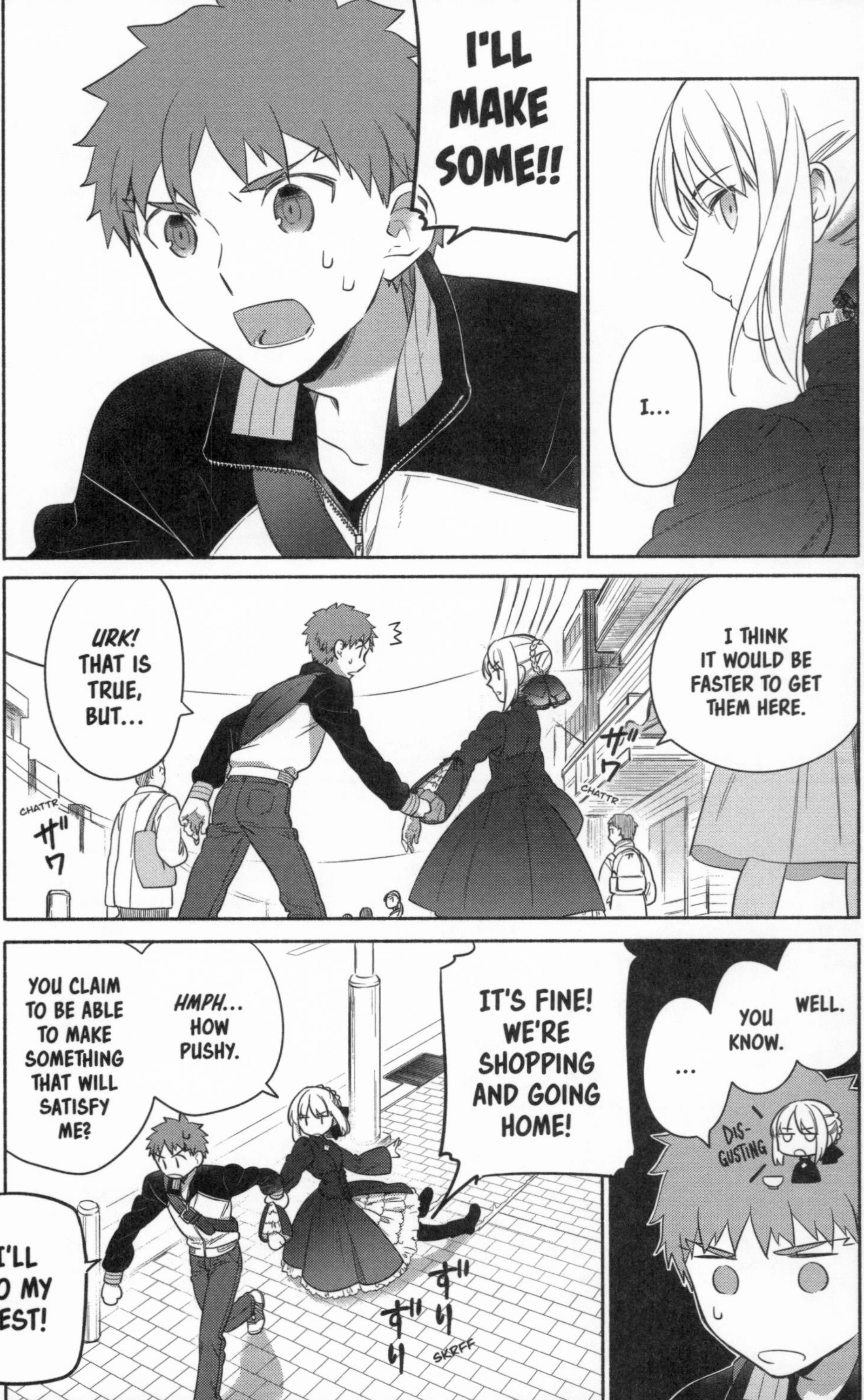
I...
I'LL MAKE SOME!!
I THINK IT WOULD BE FASTER TO GET THEM HERE.
ザワ
CHATTR
URK! THAT IS TRUE, BUT...
CHATTR
ザワ
WELL.
YOU KNOW.
...
DIS-GUSTING
IT'S FINE! WE'RE SHOPPING AND GOING HOME!
HMPH... HOW PUSHY.
YOU CLAIM TO BE ABLE TO MAKE SOMETHING THAT WILL SATISFY ME?
I'LL DO MY BEST!
ずり
ずり
SKRFF

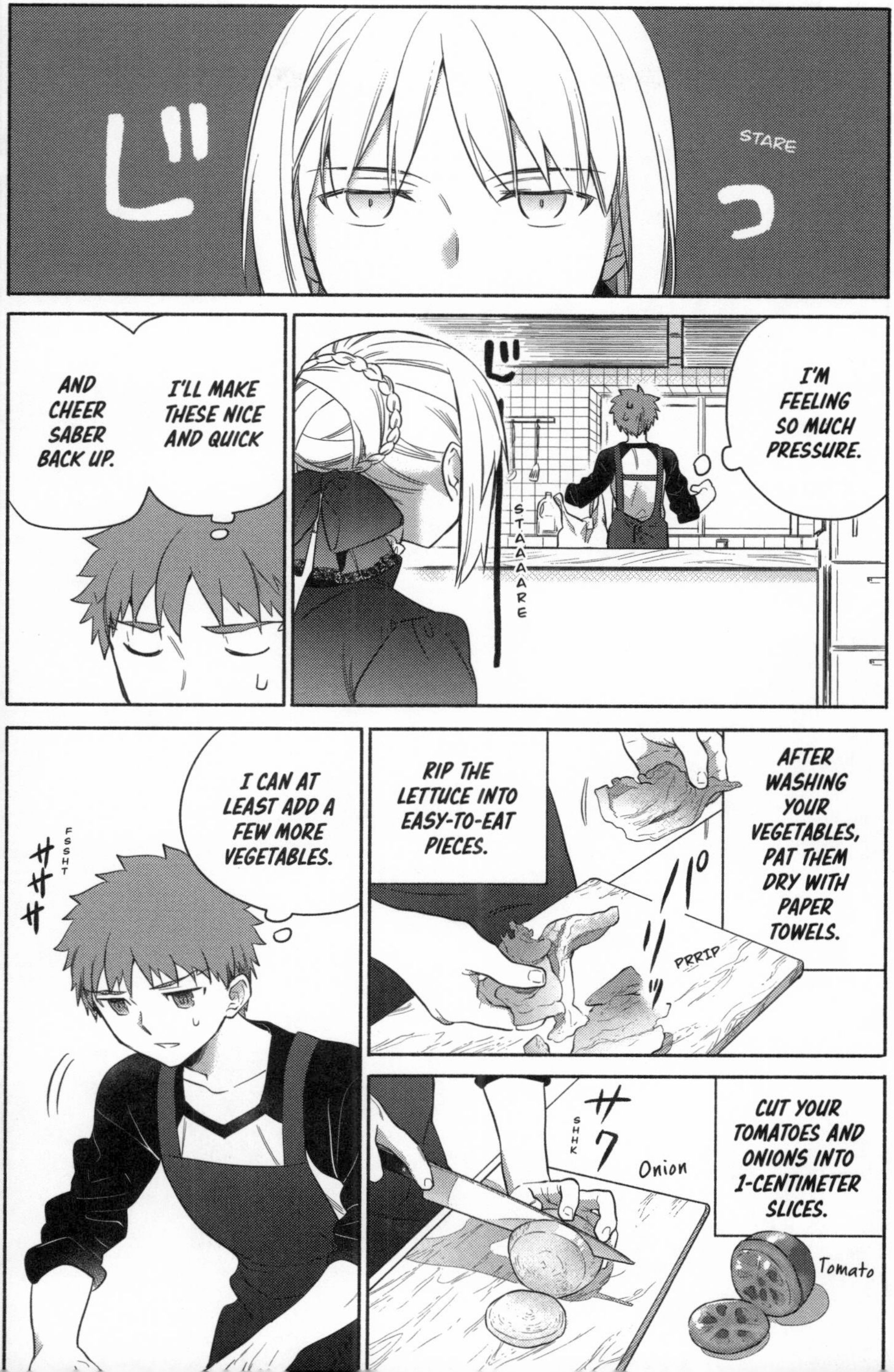
じっ
STARE
I'M FEELING SO MUCH PRESSURE.
じ
STAAAAARE
I'LL MAKE THESE NICE AND QUICK
AND CHEER SABER BACK UP.
AFTER WASHING YOUR VEGETABLES, PAT THEM DRY WITH PAPER TOWELS.
RIP THE LETTUCE INTO EASY-TO-EAT PIECES.
PRRIP
CUT YOUR TOMATOES AND ONIONS INTO 1-CENTIMETER SLICES.
SHHK
Onion
Tomato
I CAN AT LEAST ADD A FEW MORE VEGETABLES.
FSSHT

WITH YOUR GROUND MEAT IN A BOWL, ADD A PINCH OF SALT, THEN KNEAD UNTIL IT STARTS TO STICK TOGETHER.
FORM INTO PATTIES ABOUT A CENTIMETER THICK.
This is easier if you put a little oil on your hand.
SPLAT
THE MEAT WILL SHRINK A BIT WHEN COOKED, SO MAKE AN INDENTATION IN THE CENTER.
YOU SHOULD ALSO MAKE THE PATTIES A LITTLE BIGGER THAN THE BUNS BECAUSE OF THIS.
*Let sit for about an hour if you have time.
ADD OIL TO A PAN, THEN COOK YOUR ONIONS ON BOTH SIDES OVER MEDIUM HEAT. ADD A LITTLE SALT TO END.
Sticking a toothpick in like this will help them stay together.
SIZZ
NEXT, KEEP THE PAN ON MEDIUM HEAT AND COOK YOUR PATTIES.
AFTER ABOUT 2-3 MINUTES, THE EDGES WILL GROW WHITE. WHEN THEY DO, FLIP.
COOK FOR ANOTHER 2 OR SO MINUTES, THEN ADD SALT AND COARSE PEPPER TO FINISH.
ADD THE TOPPINGS BETWEEN THE BUNS IN THE FOLLOWING ORDER AND YOU'RE DONE!
Sauce
2 Tbsp ketchup
1 Tbsp tonkatsu sauce
Mustard to taste
Bun
Sauce
Tomato
Onion
Lettuce
Sliced cheese
Sauce
Meat
Bun
OKAY. THIS IS STARTING TO LOOK GOOD.
SNAP
KRAKL

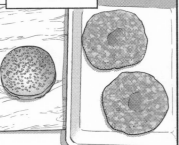

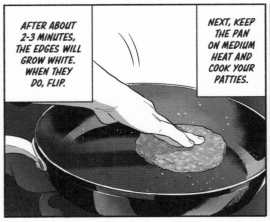

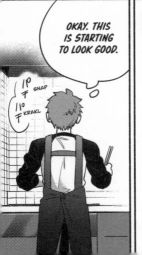

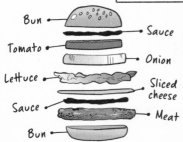

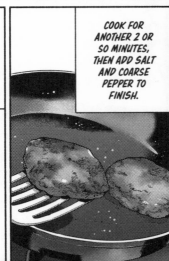

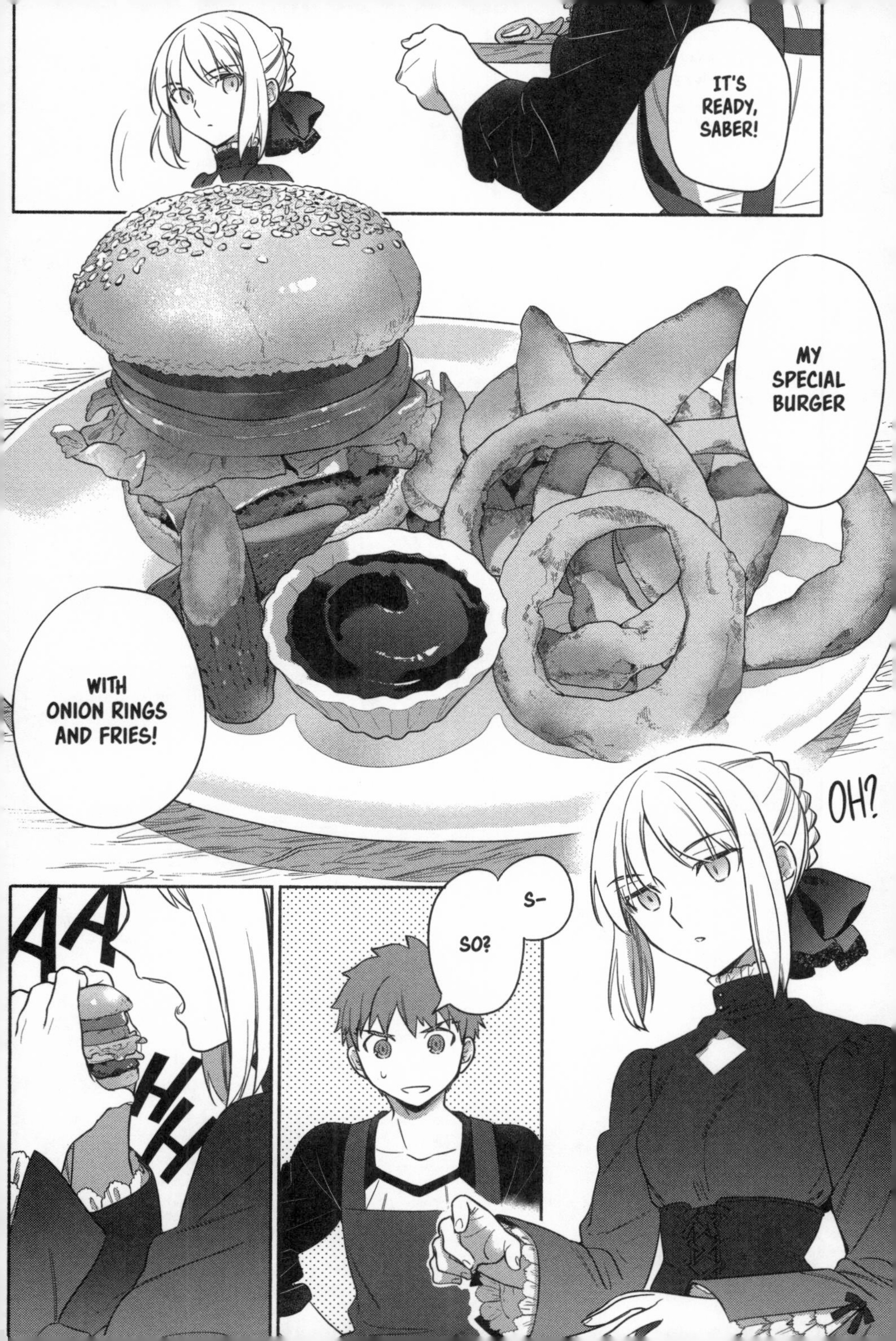
IT'S READY, SABER!
MY SPECIAL BURGER
WITH ONION RINGS AND FRIES!
OH?
S-
SO?
AAHHH

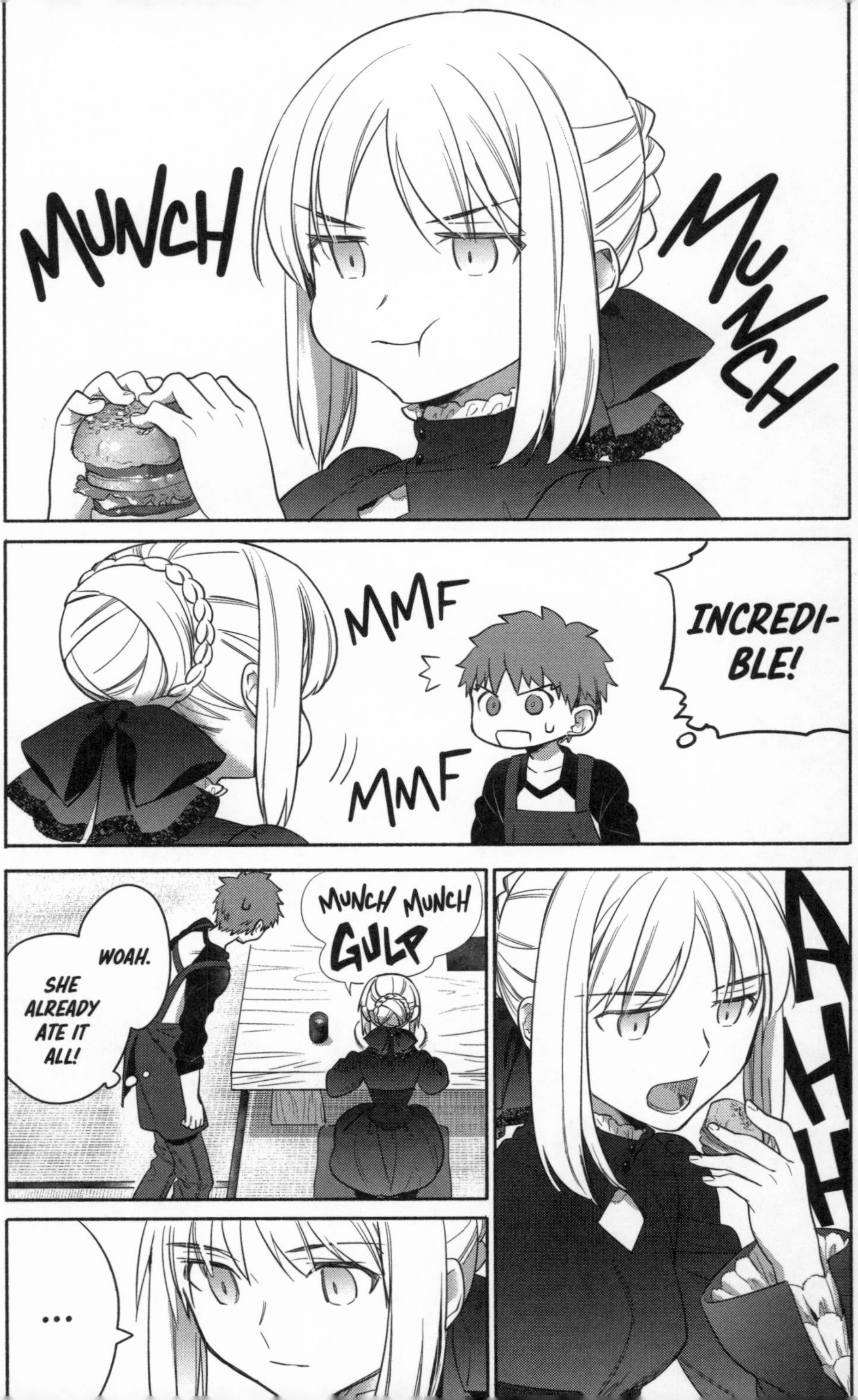
MUNCH
MUNCH
INCREDI-BLE!
MMF
MMF
AHH
MUNCH MUNCH GULP
WOAH. SHE ALREADY ATE IT ALL!
...

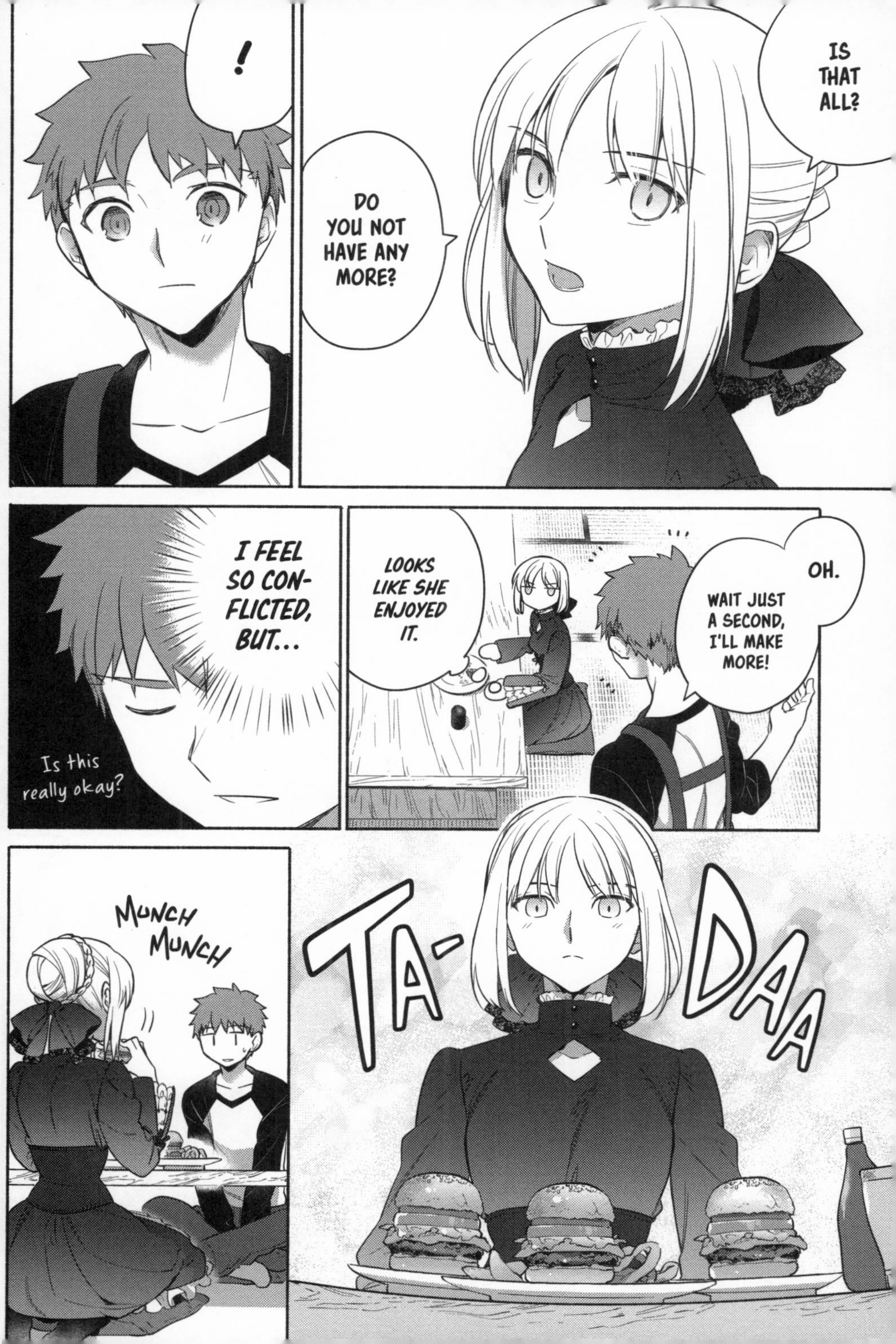
IS THAT ALL?
DO YOU NOT HAVE ANY MORE?
!
OH.
WAIT JUST A SECOND, I'LL MAKE MORE!
LOOKS LIKE SHE ENJOYED IT.
I FEEL SO CON-FLICTED, BUT...
Is this really okay?
TA-DAA
MUNCH MUNCH

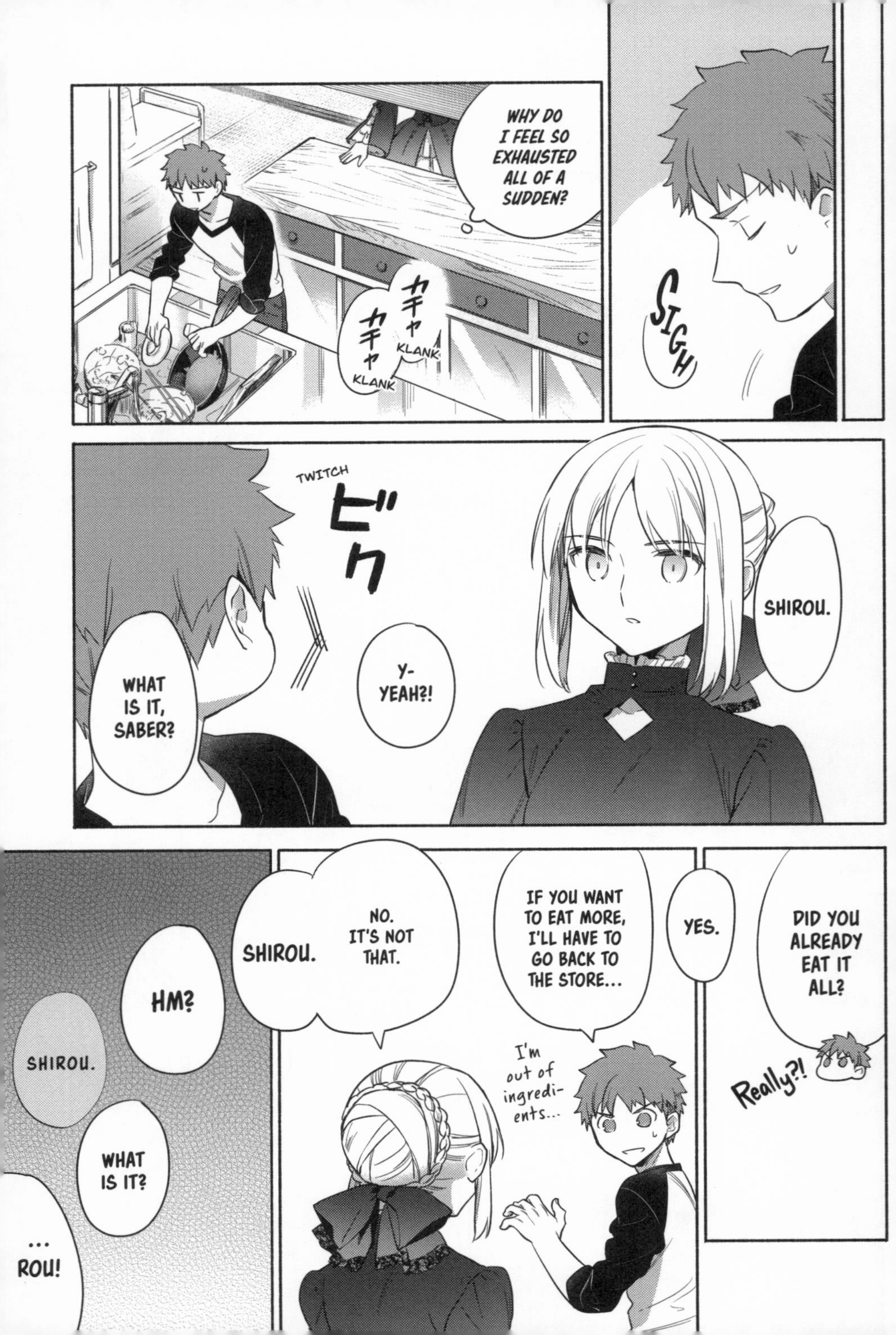
SIGH
WHY DO I FEEL SO EXHAUSTED ALL OF A SUDDEN?
カチャ KLANK
カチャ KLANK
SHIROU.
TWITCH ビク
Y-YEAH?!
WHAT IS IT, SABER?
DID YOU ALREADY EAT IT ALL?
Really?!
YES.
IF YOU WANT TO EAT MORE, I'LL HAVE TO GO BACK TO THE STORE...
I'm out of ingredi-ents...
NO. IT'S NOT THAT.
SHIROU.
HM?
SHIROU.
WHAT IS IT?
...ROU!

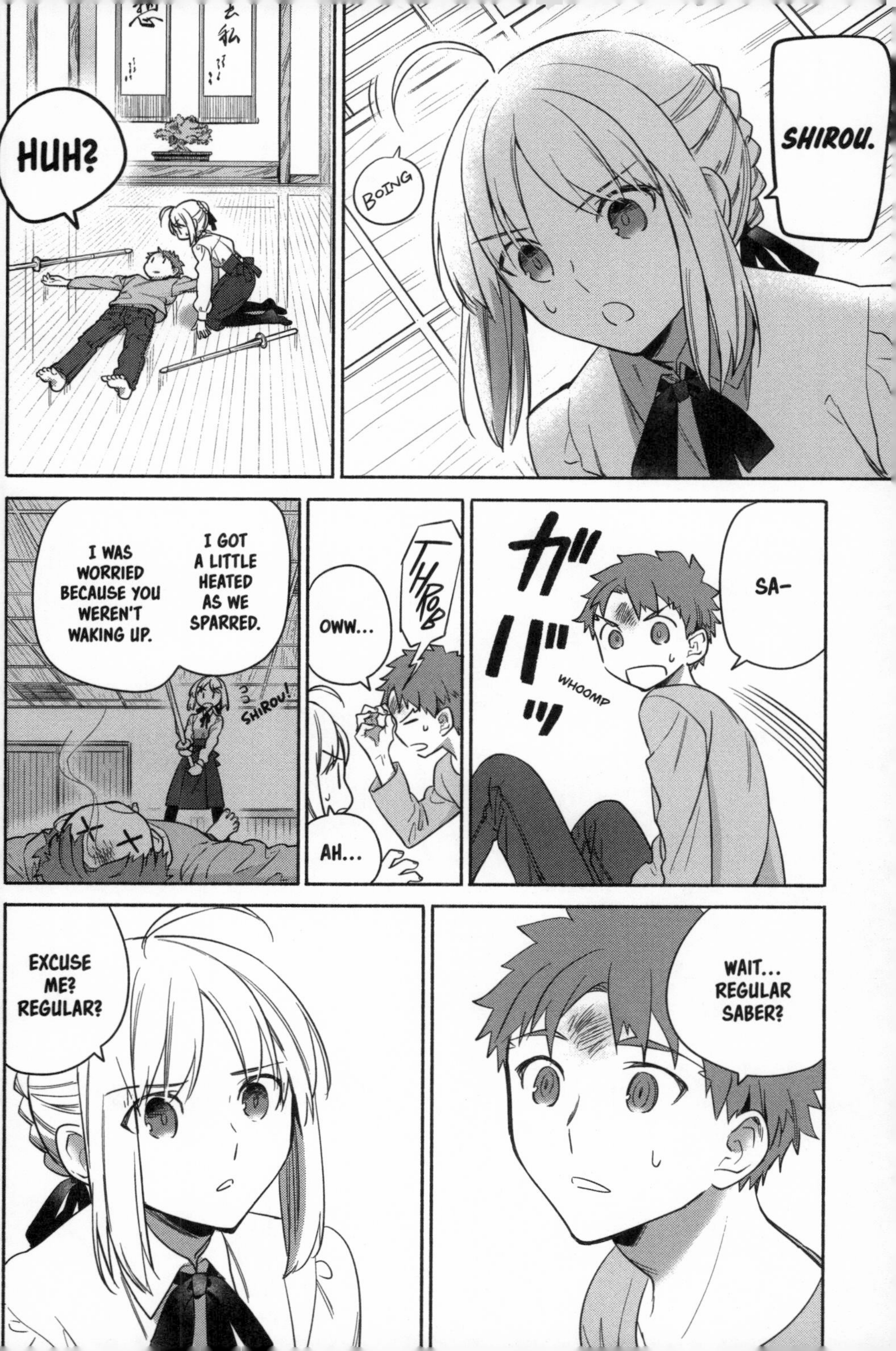
SHIROU.
BOING
HUH?
SA-
ガバッ
WHOOMP
THROB
OWW...
AH...
I GOT A LITTLE HEATED AS WE SPARRED.
I WAS WORRIED BECAUSE YOU WEREN'T WAKING UP.
SHIROU!
WAIT... REGULAR SABER?
EXCUSE ME? REGULAR?

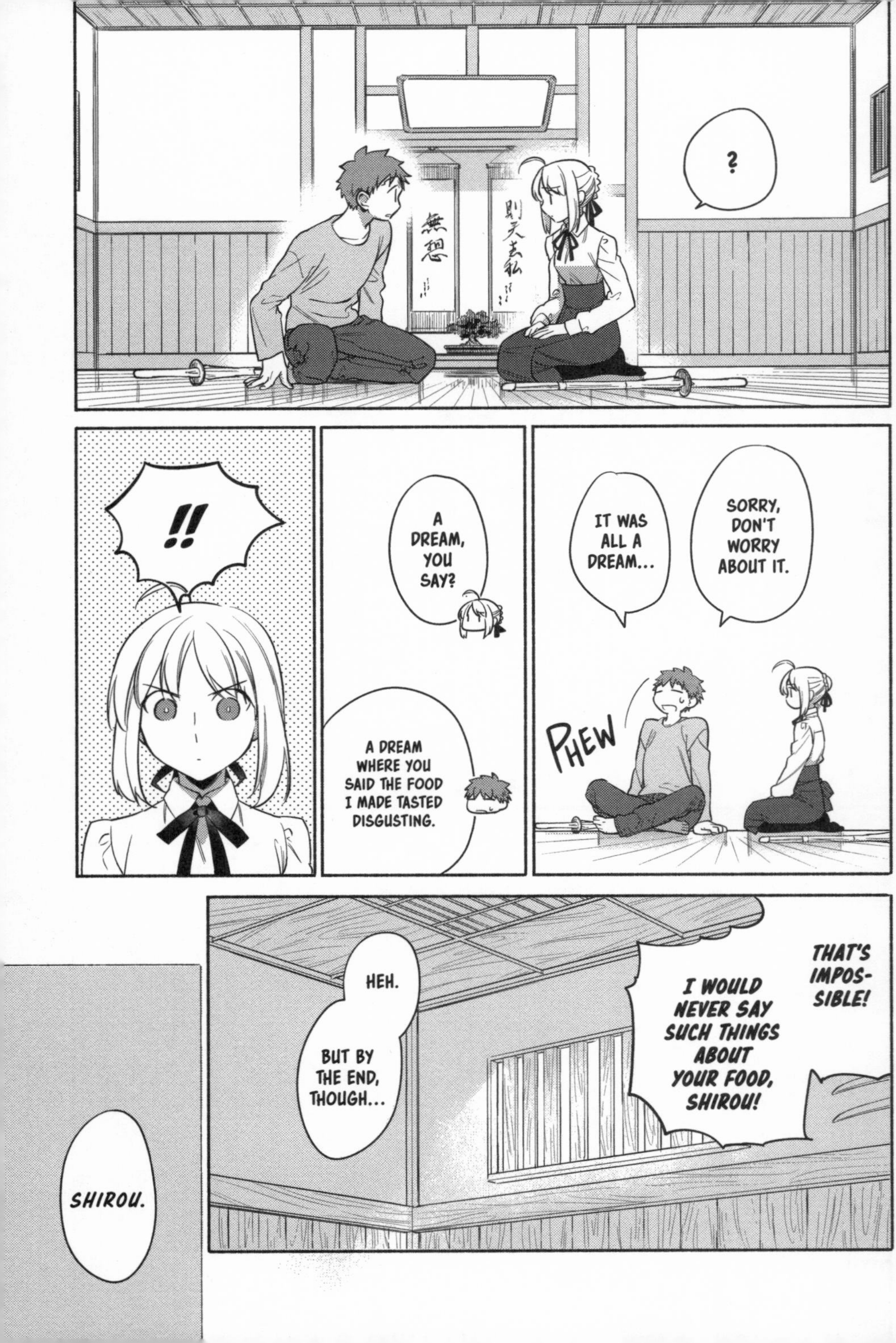

?
則天去私
無想
SORRY, DON'T WORRY ABOUT IT.
IT WAS ALL A DREAM...
PHEW
A DREAM, YOU SAY?
A DREAM WHERE YOU SAID THE FOOD I MADE TASTED DISGUSTING.
!!
THAT'S IMPOS-SIBLE!
I WOULD NEVER SAY SUCH THINGS ABOUT YOUR FOOD, SHIROU!
HEH.
BUT BY THE END, THOUGH...
SHIROU.

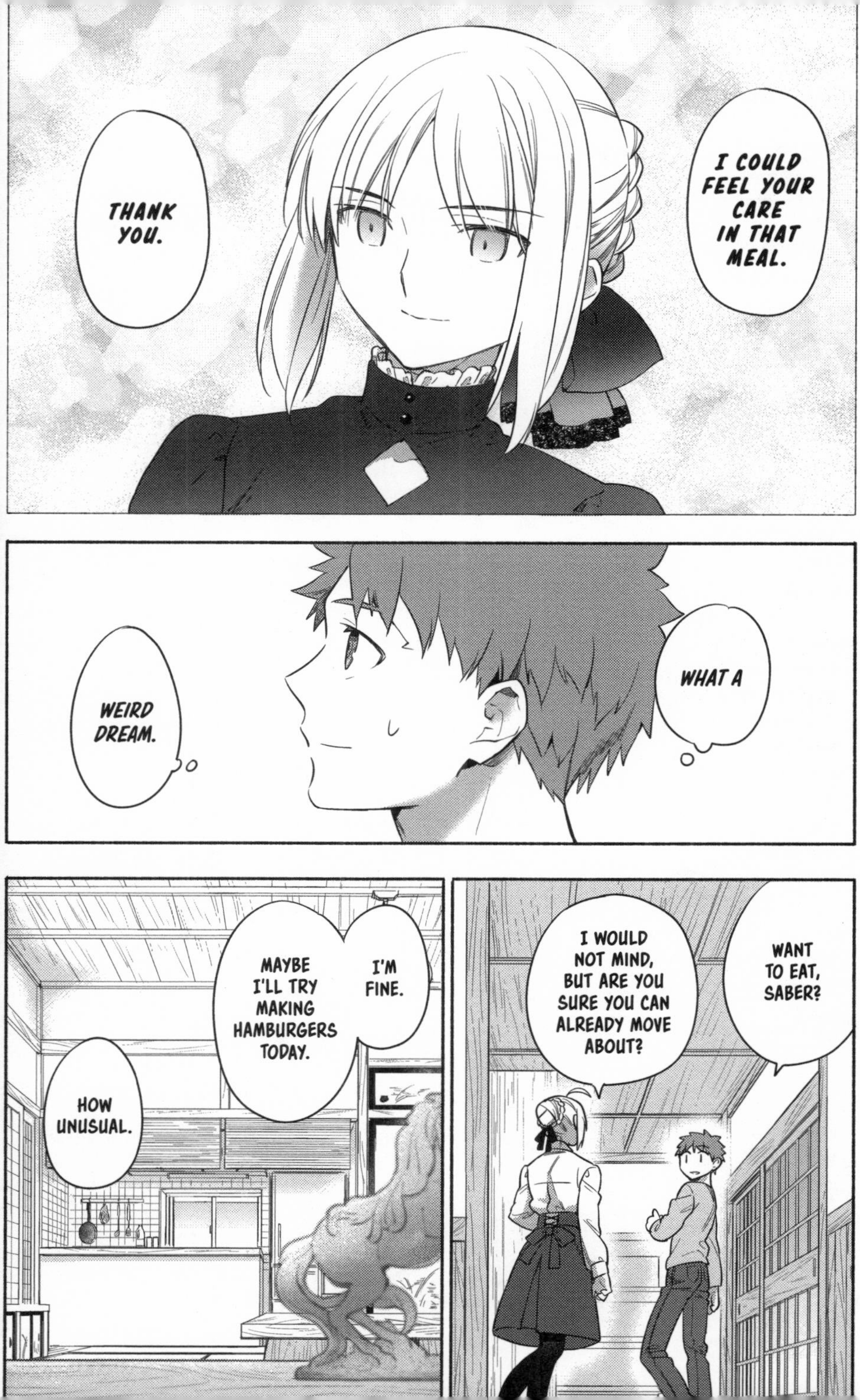
I COULD FEEL YOUR CARE IN THAT MEAL.
THANK YOU.
WHAT A
WEIRD DREAM.
WANT TO EAT, SABER?
I WOULD NOT MIND, BUT ARE YOU SURE YOU CAN ALREADY MOVE ABOUT?
I'M FINE.
MAYBE I'LL TRY MAKING HAMBURGERS TODAY.
HOW UNUSUAL.

Shirou's Special Burgers!

Ingredients – Serves 1

1 hamburger bun
120 g (4.2 oz) ground beef or
  pork-beef mixture
1 leaf lettuce
1/6 (30 g / 1.1 oz) tomato
1/4 (50 g / 1.8 oz) onion
1 piece sliced cheese
Salt and pepper to taste

Sauce

[A]
- 2 Tbsp ketchup
- 1 Tbsp tonkatsu sauce
- Mustard to taste

Sides

1–2 pickles
90 g (3.2 oz) frozen fries

Homemade onion rings

[B]
- 1/4 onion sliced
- 70 g (2.5 oz) flour
  + extra for dusting
- Pinch salt
- 3 Tbsp mayonnaise
- 1/2 bouillon cube
  (1 tsp vegetable bouillon)
- 90 ml (3 oz) water
- (Garlic powder if desired)

Frying oil
Ketchup to taste

Bonus: Hamburger sauce for 2

[C]
- 3 Tbsp ketchup
- 1.5 Tbsp tonkatsu sauce
- 1 Tbsp red wine
- 1/4 bouillon cube
- 10 g (.4 oz) grated onion
- 1 Tbsp water
- Pinch coarse pepper

1. Wash your vegetables, then pat them dry with paper towels. Tear the lettuce into easy-to-eat pieces. Cut your tomatoes and onions into 1-centimeter thick slices.
2. Add ground meat to your bowl. Add a pinch of salt, knead until it starts to stick together, then form into round patties about a centimeter thick. The meat will shrink a bit when cooked, so make them on the bigger side and create an indentation in the center. (Let sit for about an hour if you have time.)
3. Add oil to a pan, then cook your onions on both sides over medium heat. Add a little salt at the end.
4. Keep the pan on medium heat and cook the patties you made in step 2. After about 2–3 minutes, the edges will grow white. When they do, flip and cook for another 2 or so minutes, then add salt and coarse pepper at the end.
5. Mix [A] to create a sauce.
6. Add the toppings between the buns in the following order and you're done!

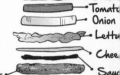

Bun
Sauce
Onion
Meat
Bun

Sides

1. If you have large pickles, cut them into easy-to-eat pieces.
2. If you have frozen fries, fry them in oil at around 170°C (338°F). Once they're a nice golden brown, fry at higher heat at 180°C (356°F) before putting on a cooling pan with a wire rack.

Homemade Onion Rings

1. Cut onions into 1-centimeter (.4 inch) wide rings, then separate.
2. Take the flour not used in [B] and dust the onions with it.
3. Dissolve the bouillon cube and mix all of [B] together.
4. Completely cover the cut onions in the mixture made in step 3.
5. Fry the onions prepared in step 4 in oil heated to 160°C (320°F). Once the sound of the frying onions turns into light snaps, turn to high heat and remove after finishing at 180°C (356°F).

Extra Hamburger Sauce

For a more luxurious sauce:

After removing the meat from your pan in step 4, remove any excess fat with a paper towel, add [C], heat over low to medium heat, and cut the heat once it begins to bubble!

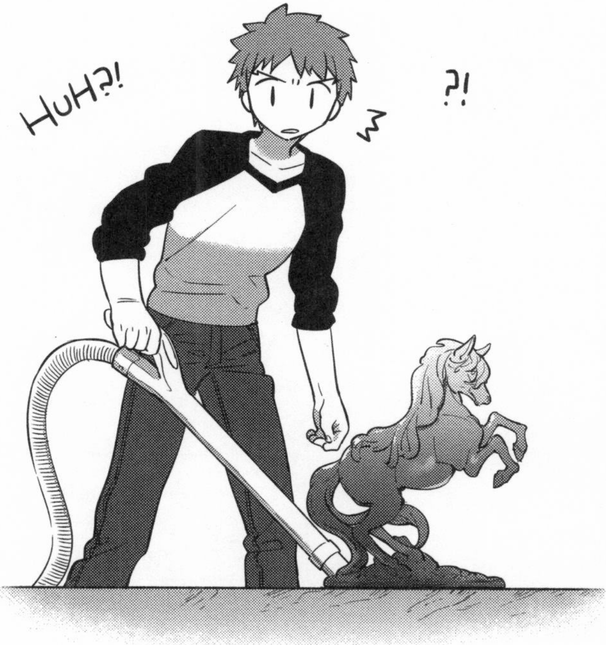
?!
HUH?!

Today's Menu for the Emiya Family

On *Today's Menu for the Emiya Family* Volume 4

Hello. This is Makoto Tadano, the food director for this title.

I'm so glad that we're already up to volume 4. Thank you all.

I get the chance to see your pictures and thoughts about the dishes in the series on social media and elsewhere. All of you are making such delicious-looking food that my stomach starts to grumble if I see your pictures while I'm hungry.

It makes me want to work harder too!

Alright, let's get to some notes and variations on some of the dishes.

Chapter 26: Ginger Pork

This recipe uses a coating of flour on the pork so that the dish stays stays delicious even when cold. Not using flour results in a lighter and more refreshing ginger taste, so feel free to try that as well. You can also use honey, grated apple, and more in place of mirin in the recipe to create a slightly different take on ginger pork. Give those a try!

Chapter 29: Comforting Hot Pot Udon

While this recipe uses lots of ingredients that are highly nutritious to help a sick Shirou's digestion, you can switch the chicken for pork, beef flank, and more to add more body. Adding red miso in the place of the soy sauce will let you enjoy a Nagoya-style miso udon. You can also enjoy this recipe in other ways by using a tomato hot pot broth or soy milk hot pot broth in place of the regular broth here.

Chapter 30: Chunky Pork Stew

Some of you may be wondering why we stir-fry the vegetables before the meat here. You'll want to cook the meat first if you want the meat to maintain its umami, but here we want the vegetables to soak it up as well, which is why we add the meat later. Stir-frying the vegetables first and softening them up will make it easier for them to absorb the umami from the meat added later. It also prevents the meat from sticking to the pot and crumbling, resulting the final dish having more tender pork.

Side Story: Shirou's Special Burgers!

The order of the burger toppings is important! Put the patty on the very bottom for a juicier burger, but it's better to put it in the middle or top if you want a lighter taste. This makes it easier to notice the flavor of the ingredients that hit your tongue first as you dig in. Also, putting the sauces and vegetables with umami at the top will allow them to drip down onto the other lower ingredients, which is why I think it's best to put them higher. Keeping this principle in mind should allow you to make lots of different kinds of original burgers, so please give it a try.

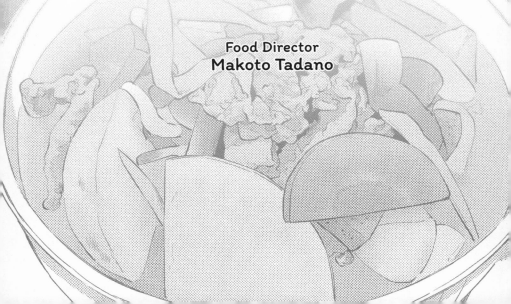

Emiya Family was shown as an anime from 2018 to 2019
at a one-episode-a-month pace.
Did you all enjoy volume 4 of the manga as well?
There are also "Understanding Today's Menu for the Emiya Family in 3 Minutes!"
videos posted on YouTube Japan after the anime's broadcast,
and I (just my hands) actually showed up in those myself!
I'm not used to being taped, so I caused a lot of trouble for the filming staff
because of how nervous I was, but I'm grateful for how well it all came out.
Fans can use the videos to understand the flow of how a dish is made,
while the incredible voice cast delights with their commentary on the dishes.
Once again, my sincere thanks to everyone involved in creating the
three-minute videos and more, as well as everyone who supported them!
I hope you all continue to enjoy the manga as well.

Food Director
Makoto Tadano

Today's Menu for the Emiya Family

AFTERWORD VOL. 4

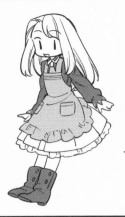

THIS IS VOLUME 4 OF *TODAY'S MENU FOR THE EMIYA FAMILY*. THANK YOU VERY MUCH FOR PICKING IT UP. THE THREE HEROINES OF THE GAME'S MAIN ROUTES APPEARED ON THE FIRST THREE COVERS, BUT THIS TIME IT FELT LIKE A NATURAL CHOICE TO PUT ILLYA ON THE COVER THIS VOLUME.

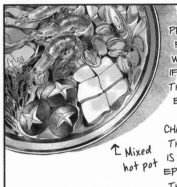

MAYBE YOU'VE NOTICED BY NOW, BUT I ALWAYS TRY TO MAKE SURE THAT THERE'S A CHAPTER FEATURING THE CHARACTER ON THE COVER.

I ALSO ASKED THIS IN VOLUME 3, BUT DID YOU GET A CHANCE TO WATCH THE *EMIYA FAMILY* ANIME? THEY BROADCAST ONE EPISODE A MONTH OVER THE COURSE OF A YEAR, AND THE FINAL EPISODE WAS SHOWN IN JANUARY OF 2019.

↰ Anime spoilers ahead

YOU'RE PROBABLY FAMILIAR WITH THIS IF YOU SAW THE ANIME, BUT THE FIRST CHAPTER OF THE MANGA IS THE LAST EPISODE OF THE ANIME.

↑ Mixed hot pot

THE PLAN WAS ACTUALLY TO HAVE EPISODE 1 BE OF CHAPTER 1 DURING MY FIRST MEETING ABOUT THE ANIME, BUT AT SOME POINT IT BECAME THE LAST EPISODE. WATCHING IT MADE IT FEEL LIKE A SUMMATION OF ALL THE EPISODES UNTIL NOW. I COULDN'T BELIEVE IT. WHAT AN AMAZING STRUCTURE THEY PUT TOGETHER! I WAS LOOKING FORWARD TO EACH NEW EPISODE EVERY MONTH, AND IT'S A LITTLE SAD TO KNOW THAT IT'S OVER NOW.

Time to marathon the Blu-rays!

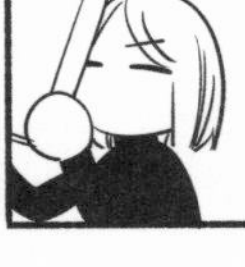

WE HAD ANOTHER MEETING A LITTLE WHILE AFTER THE FINAL EPISODE, AND THAT'S WHEN IT REALLY HIT ME JUST HOW MANY PEOPLE WERE INVOLVED IN CREATING THIS ONE ANIME. THANK YOU SO MUCH TO ALL THE ANIME'S STAFF, AS WELL AS EVERYONE ELSE INVOLVED IN MAKING IT!

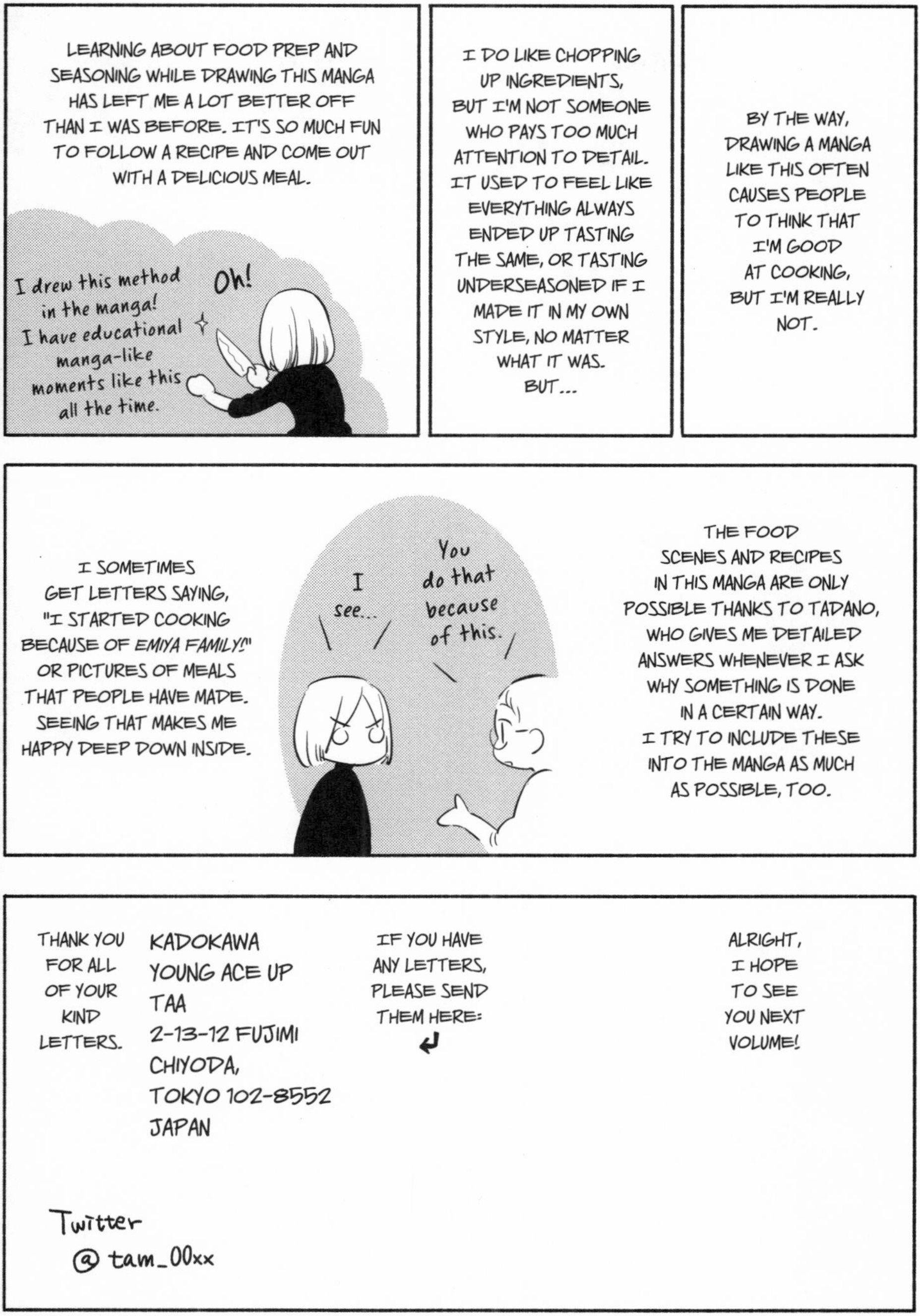
BY THE WAY, DRAWING A MANGA LIKE THIS OFTEN CAUSES PEOPLE TO THINK THAT I'M GOOD AT COOKING, BUT I'M REALLY NOT.
I DO LIKE CHOPPING UP INGREDIENTS, BUT I'M NOT SOMEONE WHO PAYS TOO MUCH ATTENTION TO DETAIL. IT USED TO FEEL LIKE EVERYTHING ALWAYS ENDED UP TASTING THE SAME, OR TASTING UNDERSEASONED IF I MADE IT IN MY OWN STYLE, NO MATTER WHAT IT WAS. BUT...
LEARNING ABOUT FOOD PREP AND SEASONING WHILE DRAWING THIS MANGA HAS LEFT ME A LOT BETTER OFF THAN I WAS BEFORE. IT'S SO MUCH FUN TO FOLLOW A RECIPE AND COME OUT WITH A DELICIOUS MEAL.
Oh!
I drew this method in the manga! I have educational manga-like moments like this all the time.
THE FOOD SCENES AND RECIPES IN THIS MANGA ARE ONLY POSSIBLE THANKS TO TADANO, WHO GIVES ME DETAILED ANSWERS WHENEVER I ASK WHY SOMETHING IS DONE IN A CERTAIN WAY. I TRY TO INCLUDE THESE INTO THE MANGA AS MUCH AS POSSIBLE, TOO.
You do that because of this.
I see...
I SOMETIMES GET LETTERS SAYING, "I STARTED COOKING BECAUSE OF *EMIYA FAMILY*!" OR PICTURES OF MEALS THAT PEOPLE HAVE MADE. SEEING THAT MAKES ME HAPPY DEEP DOWN INSIDE.
ALRIGHT, I HOPE TO SEE YOU NEXT VOLUME!
IF YOU HAVE ANY LETTERS, PLEASE SEND THEM HERE:
KADOKAWA
YOUNG ACE UP
TAA
2-13-12 FUJIMI
CHIYODA,
TOKYO 102-8552
JAPAN
THANK YOU FOR ALL OF YOUR KIND LETTERS.
Twitter
@ tam_00xx

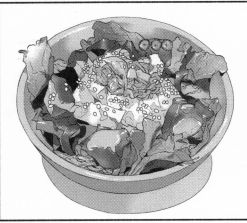

CHAPTER 25: SALAD BOWL

WE HAD A LOT OF CHAPTERS INVOLVING COMPLEX PREPARATION, SO WE GOT THIS CHAPTER BECAUSE I WANTED A DISH THAT WAS ABOUT AS SIMPLE AS THE FOIL-WRAPPED SALMON IN VOLUME 1. YOU'RE REALLY JUST PUTTING WHATEVER YOU LIKE ON TOP, SO WHY NOT GIVE SOMETHING LIKE THIS A TRY WHEN YOU'RE TIRED?

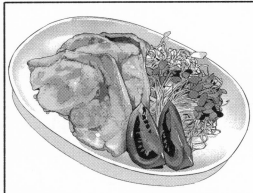

CHAPTER 26: GINGER PORK

THIS CHAPTER WAS ABOUT GINGER PORK BECAUSE I WANTED TO HAVE ONE ABOUT A STANDARD JAPANESE DISH THAT CAN BE ENJOYED REGARDLESS OF THE SEASON. MEDEA HAS EVEN STARTED TO BE CONSI-DERATE ABOUT NUTRITIONAL NEEDS!

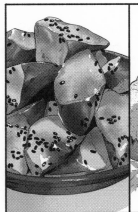
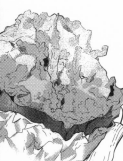

CHAPTER 27: SWEET POTATOES

THE INGREDIENT IN THIS CHAPTER IS PREPARED TWO WAYS. BOTH WAYS TASTE GOOD, DON'T THEY? I'M JUST HAPPY I GOT TO DRAW SABER AND ILLYA IN TRACKSUITS! THESE DAYS YOU NEED TO MAKE SURE WITH YOUR LOCAL AUTHORITIES ABOUT WHETHER IT'S OKAY TO MAKE A BONFIRE OR NOT.

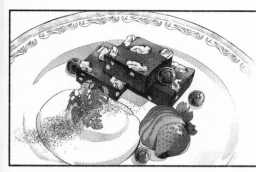

CHAPTER 28: BROWNIES

IN A RARE TURN, SELLA MAKES THE FOOD IN THIS CHAPTER. YOU UNDERSTAND WHY I WENT WITH BROWNIES AND NOT *GATEAU CHOCOLATE* OR CHOCOLATE FONDANT, RIGHT?!

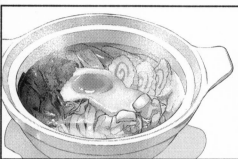

CHAPTER 29: POT-COOKED UDON

SHIROU IS CLEARLY IN BAD HEALTH BUT DOESN'T EVEN NOTICE IT... WHICH IS WHY I HAD THOSE AROUND HIM CARE FOR HIM. I REALLY LIKE THE BROTH IN THIS UDON.

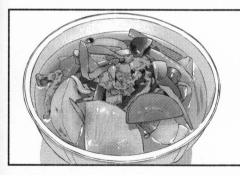

CHAPTER 30: PORK STEW

THE IDEA IN THIS SERIES IS TO MAKE DISHES FROM INGREDIENTS THAT CAN BE PURCHASED AT THE SUPERMARKET...WHICH IS WHY IN *EMIYA FAMILY* BOARS MIGHT SHOW UP, BUT THEY DON'T END UP EATING BOAR. I LIKE PORK STEW SO MUCH THAT I GOT HOOKED ON MAKING IT FOR A WHILE. I ACTUALLY GOT A CHANCE TO EAT BOAR HOT POT AT A LATER DATE. IT WAS DELICIOUS!

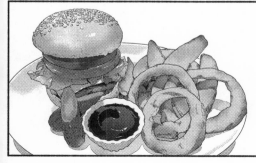

SIDE STORY: HAMBURGERS

YOU CAN TELL HOW MUCH SHIROU CARES BY THE FACT THESE BURGERS ARE A LITTLE VEGETABLE-HEAVY. I FELT SO BAD FOR HIM WHEN I DREW THE SCENE WHERE HIS FOOD IS CALLED DISGUSTING (LOL). WAS IT A DREAM? WHO CAN TELL...

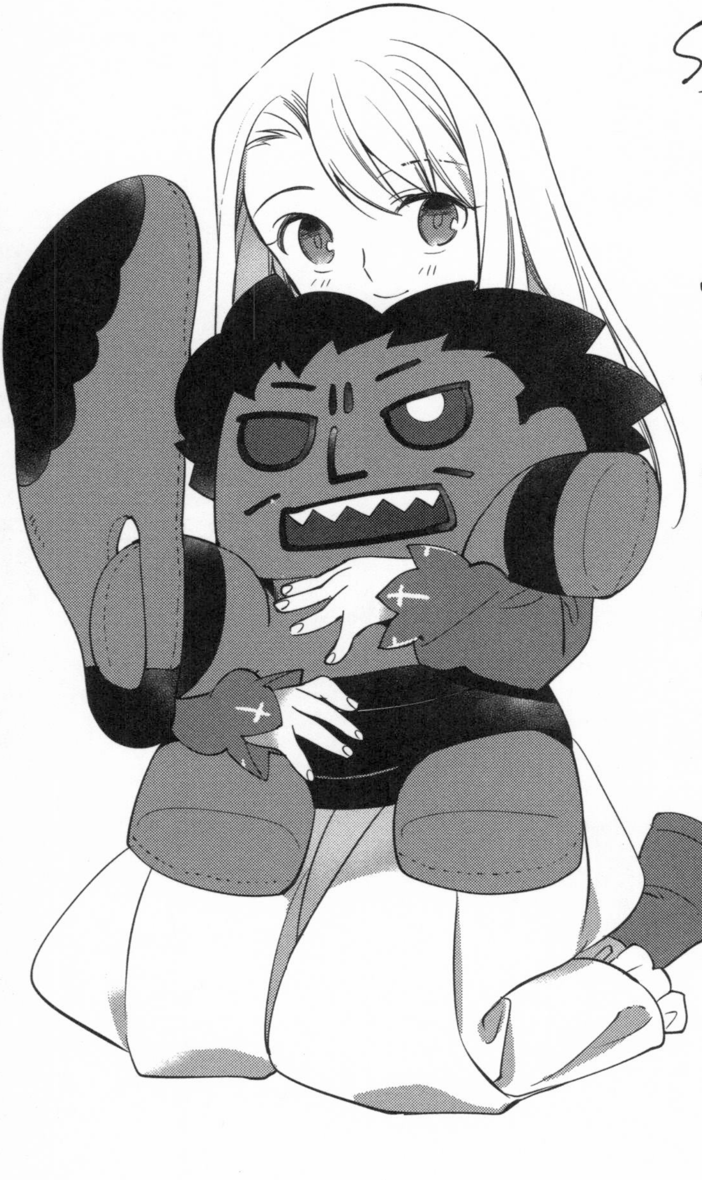

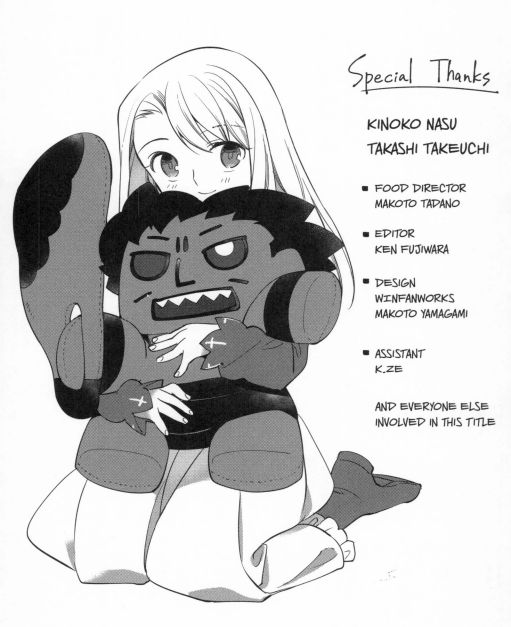

Special Thanks

KINOKO NASU

TAKASHI TAKEUCHI

- FOOD DIRECTOR
  MAKOTO TADANO

- EDITOR
  KEN FUJIWARA

- DESIGN
  WINFANWORKS
  MAKOTO YAMAGAMI

- ASSISTANT
  K.ZE

AND EVERYONE ELSE
INVOLVED IN THIS TITLE

Today's Menu for the Emiya Family

Volume 4

Translator: Ko Ransom

Production: Nicole Dochych
                      Laura Kovalcin

Proofreading: Seanna Hundt

EMIYASANCHI NO KYO NO GOHAN Volume 4
©TAa 2019 ©TYPE-MOON ©Makoto Tadano 2019
First Published in Japan in 2019 by KADOKAWA CORPORATION, Tokyo.
English translation rights arranged with KADOKAWA CORPORATION, Tokyo
through TUTTLE-MORI AGENCY, INC., Tokyo.
Published in English by Denpa, LLC., Portland, Oregon, 2022.

Originally published in Japanese as *Emiyasanchi no Kyou no Gohan* by
KADOKAWA CORPORATION, 2019.
Today's Menu for the Emiya Family serialized in *Young Ace UP* 2018-2019,
by KADOKAWA CORPORATION.

This is a work of fiction.

ISBN-13: 978-1-63442-954-2
Library of Congress Control Number: 2019931916
Printed in the USA

First Edition

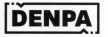

Denpa, LLC.
625 NW 17th Ave
Portland, OR 97209
www.denpa.pub

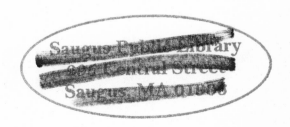